MAN, MYTH & MAGIC

AN ILLUSTRATED ENCYCLOPEDIA OF THE SUPERNATURAL

VOLUME 1

MAN, MYTH & MAGIC

AN ILLUSTRATED ENCYCLOPEDIA OF THE SUPERNATURAL

EDITOR
Richard Cavendish

**EDITORIAL
ADVISORY BOARD**

C.A. Burland
Glyn Daniel
E.R. Dodds
Mircea Eliade
William Sargant
John Symonds
R.J. Zwi Werblosky
R.C. Zaehner

Ex Líbris

BOB FARAH

MARSHALL CAVENDISH CORPORATION / NEW YORK

CONTENTS

1	Introduction
14	Aberdeen Witches
16	Abominable Snowman
16	Abracadabra
17	Achilles
19	Acupuncture
22	Africa
36	Agrippa
38	Ahriman
42	Aix-En-Provence Nuns
50	Alchemy
58	Alexander the Great
63	Algonquin Indians
67	All Hallows' Eve
69	Alphabet
78	Altar
80	Amazons
81	Amida
83	Anandamayi Ma
86	Angels
89	Animals
94	Animism
95	St Anthony
96	Antichrist
97	Aphrodite
106	Apollo
108	Apollonius
109	Apple
111	Aquarius
112	Aries
112	Armies
113	Arrow
114	Art
120	Arthur
134	Ash
134	Ashanti
137	Ashes
141	Asmodeus
142	Astarte
145	Astral Body
148	Astrology

SPECIAL FEATURES:

45	Life After Death
73	Black Magic and Witchcraft
101	Luck and Fate
129	Possession and Trance

© 1970 BPC Publishing Ltd.
Manufactured in Italy.
Library of Congress Catalog No. 70-141143

All of the material contained herein has previously been published
in separate parts under the title Man, Myth & Magic.

MAN MYTH & MAGIC

Purnell

Man Myth & Magic is an encyclopedia of the supernatural. Editor Richard Cavendish introduces this vast area of human speculation which is as full of contrast and colour, of darkness and light, as the mind of man himself

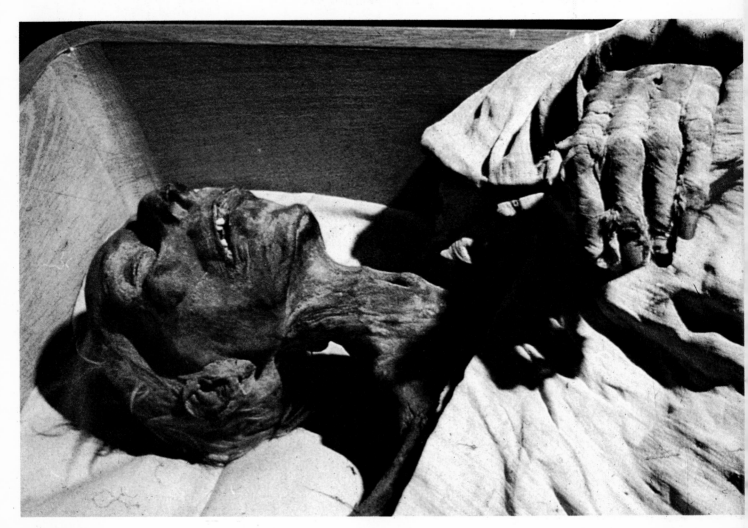

THE SUPERNATURAL is the night sky of our minds, the shadow side of our mental 'daylight' of reason and hard fact. Like the night, it contains mystery, beauty, enchantment and horror. It has a powerful attraction and almost all of us, one way or another, are involved in it.

We often talk about the modern age as a time of materialism, reason, technical and scientific advance, but the supernatural still plays a vitally important part in the world we live in. Many people, still, are religious. Many people still believe in astrology, palmistry and a variety of superstitions. It is scarcely possible to live for very long without acquiring an interest, however reluctant, in the question of life after death. And each of our minds has its shadow side, where old terrors mingle with old truths.

The supernatural surrounds us still, at many different levels: in churches, synagogues, mosques; in dreams; in the antiseptic corridors of parapsychology laboratories, where experimenters test the strange powers of the mind; in attempts to make contact with the dead; in children's games and nursery rhymes; in experiences induced by L.S.D. and other drugs; in newspaper stories of witchcraft, the black art and the desecration of churches; in reports of poltergeists and exorcisms; in faith healing; in the increasing interest in primitive religions and magic, and in oriental religions, yoga and meditation.

The last hundred years have been the most flourishing period in the history of magic and occultism in the West since the 17th century. They have also seen the rise of the modern study of comparative religion, the modern interpretation of mythology, the attempt to test objectively such phenomena as ghosts and telepathy, and the application of modern psychology to beliefs about the supernatural. These new lights in the darkness provide the basis of our approach in *Man, Myth and Magic*.

Across the Threshold

'Supernatural' is a convenient word for a huge area of human speculation about things believed to exist beyond the threshold of our ordinary day-to-day existence, our normal trudging journey from birth to death. John Wesley, the great preacher whose

Is There a Life After Death?

No one escapes death and yet from the beginning men have hoped and believed in a world beyond death. Mummification points to the belief in survival of death which goes back to the beginnings of human history and is suggested by Neanderthal burials more than 50,000 years ago. The rise of Spiritualism in the 19th century centred on the attempt to get in touch with the dead. The question haunts us still – is there life after death?

1 Mummified corpse of Rameses II, ruler of Egypt, who died in 1225 BC
2 Prehistoric ritual murder: the head of the hanged man of Tollund in Jutland. The bodies of sacrificed men were thrown after death into lakes, some of which dried up and became peat bogs, where the bodies were preserved
3 Aztec skull encrusted with turquoise mosaic, believed to represent Tezcatlipoca in his black aspect as lord of misfortune
4 Mexican skull made of marzipan. An offering to the dead of Mexico, who are believed to revisit the earth on 31 October each year, and are given food, sweets and cigarettes. Part of an exhibition of popular art in the Muséo Anahuacalli
5 'Behold, a pale horse, and its rider's name was Death, and Hades followed him : and they were given power over a fourth of the earth, to kill with sword and with famine and with pestilence and by wild beasts of the earth.' *Death on a Pale Horse*, the Fourth Horseman of the Apocalypse, by the mystic, poet and painter, William Blake

eloquence sent some of his hearers into ecstatic convulsions, believed that he showed his flock 'The Demonstrative Evidence of things unseen, the Supernatural Evidence of things invisible, not perceivable by the Eyes of Flesh, nor by any of our natural senses or faculties.'

The supernatural includes cases in which the normal order of Nature appears to have been momentarily upset: miracles, for instance; or the appearance of an otherworldly being in visible form; or levitation, the ability to rise from the ground and hover above it, unsupported — like the famous St Joseph of Copertino in the 17th century who was always shooting up into the air, to the embarrassment of himself and his ecclesiastical superiors.

But the supernatural also includes the operation of forces which are perfectly natural but whose workings are not generally admitted or understood. When men long ago saw lightning, they thought it supernatural and ascribed it to the gods. We know that they were wrong in thinking it non-natural but right in observing its existence.

Similarly, a hundred years ago, those who observed the existence of the strange powers of the human mind which we call extra-sensory perception or telepathy or clairvoyance, often thought that they had discovered something supernatural. There is some evidence now that these powers exist and if they do, they are natural powers and people in the past were wrong

to think them anything else. But they were right in observing their existence, and it may be that in the future other peculiar phenomena may be found to stem from real and, of course, natural capacities of the human mind.

On this subject and many others you will find a variety of views in this encyclopedia — though we have avoided the extremes of uncritical credulity on the one hand and a passionate scepticism, equally unconnected with the evidence, on the other.

We have not set out to convert you, to or from anything, but to explain the structures of ideas which men have built in the past, and which they continue to build now. You must decide for yourself where truth and value lie.

The Lady is For Burning

Witches are associated with demons, night, sensuality and evil. They still horrify and delight the imagination: and they still exist

1 Asmodeus was originally the Persian 'fiend of the wounding spear' a storm spirit and personification of rage. Later he developed into a supernatural force of lechery. He is represented as having three heads: those of a bull, a man, and a ram. In Paris in 1673 Madame de Montespan, mistress of Louis XIV, sacrificed children to Asmodeus, to secure her hold on the king's affections by black magic. From Collin de Plancy's *Dictionnaire Infernal,* 1863
2 St Anthony of Egypt was a 3rd century Christian ascetic who withdrew from the world and was plagued by bizarre and nightmare visions, which included multitudes of demons in frightening animal forms. *The Temptation of St Anthony,* an engraving by Martin Schongauer
3 The Young Sorceress, a painting by A. Wiertz in which the aspiring sorceress, blindfolded, bestrides a broomstick, surrounded by malevolent figures. It has been suggested that witches originally danced with broomsticks between their legs as a phallic rite. They were said to fly on hobby horses, forked sticks, eggshells, bunches of straw and shovels: long before the broomstick (sometimes smeared with flying ointment from the fat of an unbaptized child) was associated with them
4 Recent photograph of modern witches performing their rites

The Supernatural World

The world of the supernatural includes the great living religions alongside an astonishing variety of peculiar cults and groups, from the Holy Rollers and snake-handling sects of the United States to the new prophetic cults in Africa and the modern cargo cults of the Pacific. It ranges from some of the noblest expressions of the human mind in the lives and writings of mystics and the founders of religions to some of the ignoblest in the Black Mass or the smelling out of witches or the myths of race. It varies in importance from matters like survival after death and the existence of the soul to superstitions which – at least at first sight – are very trivial: from themes like fate, sin, sacrifice to tea-leaf reading, ouija boards and lucky numbers.

The supernatural even has room for humour, usually unintentional, as in this spell found in 1865 in the house of a magician called John Rhodes who had written it for one of his customers.

> I adjure and command you, ye strong, mighty and most powerful spirits who are rulers of this day and hour, that ye obey me in this my cause by placing my husband in his former situation under the Trent Brewery Company.

In this variety and contrast, the supernatural mirrors and illuminates the mind of man. *Man, Myth and Magic* runs in alphabetical order and you will find the psychology of *conversion,* a subject of fundamental human importance, followed immediately by the *Convulsionaries,* who threw hysterical fits in the 18th century. *Wagner* is cheek by jowl with *Voodoo*; Sergeant *Bertrand,* the French werewolf, is next door to Annie *Besant,* a leading Theosophist; and the old theme of the evilness of *woman* is followed by the lore of the *woodpecker.* You will find *dance* and the *Devil*; the *cross,* the *circle* and the *serpent; ghosts, masks, trees, witches* and a thousand other things which play a part in the supernatural world.

There is music in the world of the supernatural, from primitive drumming and dancing to the splendours of Masses and Requiems. There is art, from the cave paintings and the lumpy, obese 'Venuses' of prehistoric men through the works of a

At last it is possible to bring discussion of the supernatural out of the dark – a privilege denied even to our parents...

Blake, a Bosch, a Botticelli to the nightmare drawings of Austin Spare and the paintings of modern Surrealists. There is a treasure of symbolism, from the rich religious and magical ideas associated with numbers, letters, architecture, the moon and the sun, to the myths and folk beliefs connected with the horse or the dog or the cat, the wren or the raven, the salmon or the spider.

Shadows in the Mind

It has only recently begun to be recognized that myths, rituals, folklore and magic are not a tangled mass of trivial mumbo-jumbo but a vital part of the human experience and a vital sector of the study of man. What men have thought, all over the world and all through history, about the super-

natural is important not only for what it may tell us about the mysteries of life and death but for what it tells us about human beings.

Beyond the interest in the supernatural of which we are conscious, in ourselves or in others, there are all kinds of magical ideas which are deeply embedded in our minds, though we are not always aware of them.

One of the oldest and most important components of magic is the principle of mimicry. To injure an enemy, you make a doll of wax or clay or rags, which resembles the enemy as closely as you can manage. If it doesn't look much like him, you can christen it with his name, to make sure you hit the right target. You torture and destroy

the doll, you burn it or stick pins through it or wring its neck, in the belief that your enemy will suffer the same agonies in reality. By imitating an event, you hope to make it happen.

This notion may seem to be one which we sensible moderns have outgrown but if you keep a watchful eye on yourself, you may discover that you are not free of it. If you are being driven too fast in a car, you may find yourself pressing your foot hard down on an imaginary brake on the floor of the car. On the surface of your mind, you know perfectly well that doing this will not affect the driver, but deeper down is the old magical principle of mimicry. You are imitating what the driver ought to be doing, so as to make him do it.

Hirmer Verlag

The Hero Triumphs

The hero defeating monstrous evil powers is a favourite theme of mythology, ancient and modern.

1 Cerberus, the three-headed dog who guarded the entrance to the underworld in Greek mythology. He was tamed by Hercules, shown holding a club on this Greek vase of the 6th century BC
2 The myth of the hero continues to absorb men, as it always has: Superman
3 The Japanese hero Sakata-no-Kintoki killing the giant spider
4 A Christian hero-myth: *St George and the Dragon,* by Uccello

Or again, if you are watching a race and you want your favourite to win, do you find yourself tensing and straining every limb? You are imitating the effort you want your runner to make, in the magical hope of helping him on.

If you recognize this kind of behaviour in yourself – there are many varieties of it, the simplest perhaps being the reaction to danger of closing your eyes to make it go away – you will have a more sympathetic understanding of the unpleasing cure for warts once common in the Kentucky backwoods, which consisted of pricking the warts with a pin, smearing the blood on kernels of corn (as many kernels as there are warts), and feeding the corn to a red rooster, in the belief that the warts would be magically transferred to the rooster; or the old witch weapon of the string with nine knots, tied with concentrated hatred against an enemy and hidden close to him, which strangled him slowly to death unless it could be found and untied in time.

The Magic of Names

The magical use of names is rooted in many civilized people's minds today, as it was in ancient and primitive societies. In magic, the name of a thing *is* the thing. The name 'cat' is not merely a term of reference for a furry and charming creature with pointed ears, four legs, a tail and disquieting eyes; the name contains in itself the essence of the animal's being, the quality which makes it what it is and not something else. After all, a primitive magician might say, if it was not called 'cat' but 'dog', it would not be itself but something different.

The same principle applies to gods, spirits and human beings. In some primitive societies a man's real name is kept secret because if it becomes known to a hostile magician. he has power over the man and can destroy him. The man himself may not know his own real name, so secret is it, and he goes by another name, a cover name, a name which is not really him.

In the ancient world, to injure someone you hated, you could write down his name and a curse on a bit of lead or pottery and bury it. People did so with some frequency and the curses have been dug up by archaeologists – 'As the lead grows cold, so grow he

Victoria and Albert Museum/Michael Holford

Never before has the full range of this fascinating subject been assembled in a single work of reference-all the facets of man's experience of the supernatural seen together as a whole

cold' or 'I put quartan fever on Aristion to the death'.

This again seems a far cry from us but the principle survives among the many modern parents who take trouble over choosing a name for a child because they have at the back of their minds the feeling that the name chosen will affect the child's character. To name a boy Cedric, for instance, seems to many people at the moment to be running a serious risk of stamping a weak and weedy personality on the unfortunate infant. And if we call him James or Henry, won't he grow up to be like some nasty James or Henry that we know? It is a magical idea, deep in the mind, and a widespread one.

People who join occult (or religious) orders very often take new names, to show that they are starting a new life as new people. For instance the occult name of the black magician Aleister Crowley was Perdurabo, 'I will endure'.

The magic of names is also partly responsible for the feeling, still held by many, that someone who tries to get onto first name terms with you too quickly is invading your privacy: by using your own personal name he is trying to grasp the real you too soon.

Fate and the Future

Another set of supernatural notions survives in our attitudes to fate and the future. The powerful impulse not to 'tempt fate' comes up from some dark well in the mind below the level of reason. People constantly refrain from saying – or are horrified if they do say – that they have done well in some test, that the future looks bright, that all will go well; because they are frightened of an unseen power that will punish their presumption.

We sometimes mix this up with modesty but the desire not to seem conceited fails to explain the type of guilty horror that immediately afflicts many of us when fate is tempted. And even modesty implies the same principle at the root: not merely the wish to avoid offending other people but the idea of self-effacement in the sense of not attracting the attention of the gods, the fates, the unkind powers that rule men's destinies.

Every time you cross your fingers, say a prayer, or read your 'stars' in the paper, you express your surviving belief in the supernatural. This is a unique opportunity to make up your own mind on this vital area of human experience

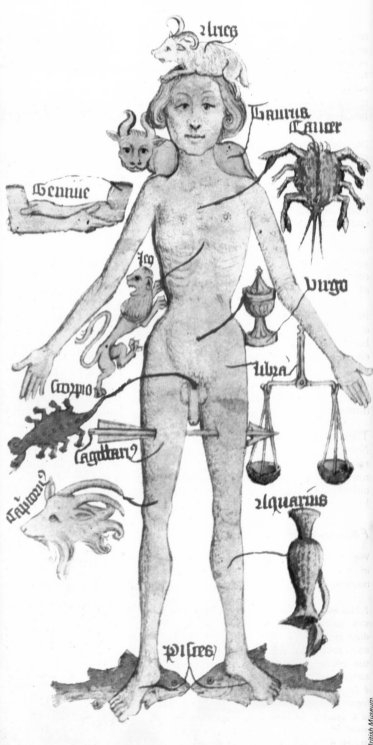

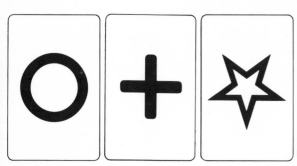

Don Last/Camera Press

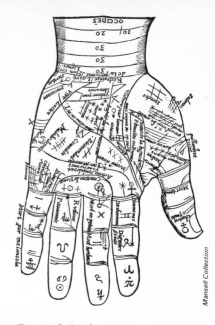

Mansell Collection

The idea of destiny, that the course of a man's life is marked out by forces which are beyond the threshold of the ordinary everyday world, comes out in the tendency to fatalism which a good many of us show, especially at moments of crisis – the feeling that 'It's out of my hands; I shall do my best but what will be, will be.'

Fatalism can be put down to an obvious psychological root, as a way of avoiding responsibility, escaping from the burden of a decision. But in many people it is not in fact used as an escape, and it seems to spring from something much deeper – from the old belief in a mysterious power controlling human life.

This belief seems to well up in people under stress who, at other times, are sceptical about the supernatural and see no convincing evidence for the existence of fate at all.

The same buried belief perhaps lies behind the intense interest which almost everyone takes in having his fortune told, however loudly he tells himself and everyone else that he knows it is all nonsense. People who do not think it nonsense visit astrologers and clairvoyants in droves, and the manufacture of lucky charms is a sizeable industry.

The Burning Galley

Not only do magical ideas survive in our minds but they seem to be needed. Quite a number of ceremonies and rituals have been either revived or invented in the last hundred years. A good example is the

spectacular fire-ceremony which involves most of the population of Lerwick, in the Shetlands, in late January each year.

About seven in the evening, in cold and pitch dark, five or six hundred guisers – dancers in grotesque and eerie costumes – light torches and parade through the town, singing and pulling along a replica of a Viking war-galley, with the head of a dragon at its high prow.

The long-ship is hauled in procession to an open space and the marchers surround it, several ranks deep. At a signal they hurl their blazing torches like a rain of shooting-stars into the air and down onto the galley, which catches fire and burns fiercely until the dragon's head bows to the ground and the timbers splinter and char away. Through the rest of the night the guisers go from place to place dancing, and a sizeable percentage of the town's population gets itself genially drunk.

The interesting thing about this ceremony is that its dramatic central feature is not a survival of an ancient pagan rite but a modern invention. The wearing of sinister costumes, the dancing and drinking, are genuinely old customs but the burning of the galley goes back only to the late 1880s. Down to 1889, the guisers carried blazing tar barrels round the town, a survival of a pagan fire-festival which celebrated the freeing of the sun from the chains of winter. Men made light and heat on earth to revive the sun and to make it give out increasing light and heat in the sky. In 1889 the tar barrels left the Shetlands stage and the

Viking galley made its first entry.

Other similarly youthful rituals could be cited, among them a curious American practice called the 'New Year's Shoot', found in some areas of North Carolina, originated less than 200 years ago by German-born settlers and carried on by their descendants. In it men gather at midnight on 31 December, carrying antique guns, and from then until about six a.m. they visit each house of the area, fire a volley, and greet the householders with a rhymed ceremonial speech delivered by the 'Speech Crier'. It begins:

> Good morning to you, sir,
> We wish you a happy New Year,
> Great health, long life,
> Which God may bestow
> So long as you stay here below. . .

For all its relative modernity, this rite has clear affinities with ancient noisy pagan ceremonies for driving away evil spirits and invoking fertility and prosperity. But like the Shetland fire ceremony, it has grown into a genuine folk institution: it effectively expresses a vague but powerful central idea in the minds of those who take part in it. In the case of the Shetland ceremony, perhaps whoever devised it saw the force of adding a ritual patterned on a ship-burial, which involved the liberation of the spirit from the body at death, with songs about the defeat of tyrants, to the relics of a ceremony which saluted the liberation of the sun from the tyrant grip of winter. The ship-burning reminds the Shetlanders of their Viking

Fate and the Future

We long to know the future, and search for it in the stars and the hand, in cards and numbers.

1 The Hanged Man, a card from the Tarot pack, still used in fortune-telling *2* Astrological diagram showing the parts of the body which each zodiac sign is supposed to affect *3* Testing the reality of extra-sensory perception, the subject tries to forecast the fall of these cards *4* The pattern of the future in the human hand, from Jean Belot's *Oeuvres,* 1649 *5* The wheel is a symbol of inevitable Fate, here an instrument of torture on which the proud are broken in hell *6* The same wheel in a different disguise – as a way of trying your luck

Bodleian Library Colour Filmstrip, MS Douce 134.83

Michael Busselle

At the roots of mythology and magic is a kind of thinking which is not random and which has its own curious logic...

ancestry and it is a declaration of the Shetland-Norse nationalist and separatist feeling which has grown steadily stronger all through this century.

Magic, Myth and Poetry

Why are magical ideas still rooted in our minds? We have thrown off many of the attitudes of the past, why not these? Because magical thinking is natural to the human mind: which is why rational thinking is generally agreed to be difficult and why there is a strong human sense that rational thinking is not enough.

Behind magic, and at the roots of mythology and religion, is a kind of thinking which is not random and which has its own curious logic, but it is not rationalist logic. It works through analogies, allegories, symbols — which means making connections between things which outwardly and rationally are not connected: the doll and the enemy, the tar barrels and the sun. It looks to man's deep inner wells of inspiration, imagination, insight, instinct as the supreme paths to truth. Magical thinking, in fact, is poetic thinking.

In this light, it is not surprising that myth and legend have been largely the creation of poets, and that the importance of myths and legends for us is their poetic appeal. The great classical myths, for instance, or the story of Adam and Eve in Eden are *true* stories to us, not because we think they ever happened but because, like poetry, they contain truth about human beings and human life, truth which cannot be fully translated into plain statement. This is the source of our contemporary fascination with the theme of the killing of the divine king, which lies behind some of the myths we have inherited and which has inspired several outstanding, and poetic, modern novels. It is the source of the great psychologist C. G. Jung's preoccupation with the symbolism of alchemy and mythology. And the myth of the hero continues to absorb men, as it always has.

The Secrets of Superstition

I suggested earlier that superstitions are trivial things 'at least at first sight'. If you try to explain them, you find yourself in areas which are the reverse of trivial. And

Michael Holford

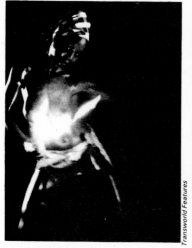

Transworld Features

J. B. Collins

The Shadow in the Mask

Pictures, symbols and ceremonies convey the intangible and bring the supernatural into the natural world.

1 Japanese Buddhist god named Jizo, who protects children and those who die young
2 Religious dancers, from a Cambodian temple
3 West Indian voodoo dancer
4 Snake-handling groups are among the oddest of modern American religious sects. The snake is touched to the face. Deaths are comparatively few
5 Mexican 'picture writing', which shows the New Fire ceremony, a temple and a palace
6 Early example of Christian religious drama: *The Martyrdom of St Apollinaire* by J. Fouquet

they can be explained, or many of them can, because idiotic as they may look, they are not random and senseless but the products of poetic logic.

For example, why is the number 3 supposed to be lucky? If you set out to find the answer, you will come across a host of odd but minor matters like the fact that in German folklore a werewolf must be stabbed three times in the brows to reveal the real person behind the hair and claws, or the custom in the Spanish royal family of calling a dead king three times by name before burying him. But before long you will come to the Christian Trinity, a doctrine of the highest significance for multitudes of human beings.

You must then consider, why a trinity, why three divine Persons instead of some other number of Persons? Why did the number 3, which the Pythagoreans considered the perfect number because it had all the necessary equipment – a beginning, a middle and an end – become in Christian theory a number which is perfect because it does not have a beginning or an end?

You will be led on to trinities in other religions, to the first discovery of the musical intervals, to the fact that some ancient peoples used 'three' to mean any number greater than two, to the erotic symbolism of 3 as the number of the male genitals, which is the reason for its frequent appearance in love-charms. All these things have contributed to the symbolic meaning of 3, through a chain of ideas

running roughly from 'all things' to 'the godhead', 'the best' and ultimately 'the most fortunate'.

The interest of this type of inquiry is not limited to the fascination – though it is a powerful one – of delving into the odd and mysterious, of conjecturing what song the Sirens sang or what name Achilles assumed when he hid himself among the women. Even from so unpromising a starting point as a minor superstition, the enquiry takes you deep into the wellsprings of the human mind, now as in the past. That is what a study of man and the supernatural is about, and that is why it matters.

Parts of this article first appeared in the Observer Magazine, *24 November, 1968.*

British Museum

Giraudon

Produced in consultation with the world's foremost authorities: more than 200 expert authors from all over the world

EDITORIAL BOARD

C. A. BURLAND, formerly of the Department of Ethnography at the British Museum, joined its staff in 1925 and retired in 1965. A specialist in the arts and religions of primitive peoples, he has conveyed his enthusiasm for these subjects to a wide audience in many excellent popular books – which include *The Magical Arts*; *The Ancient Maya*; *The Aztecs*; *Man and Art*; and *The Arts of the Alchemists*. His latest book has the intriguing title of *The Exotic White Man*.

GLYN DANIEL, a Welshman and one of Britain's foremost archaeologists, is editor of *Antiquity,* editor of the Thames and Hudson 'Ancient Peoples and Places' series, and a writer of detective stories. He has also appeared frequently on television. He is an expert on megalithic tombs and monuments, prehistoric art and the history of archaeology. His numerous books include *The Idea of Prehistory*; *The Megalith Builders of Western Europe*; and *The Origins and Growth of Archaeology*. He has been a Fellow of St John's College, Cambridge, since 1938.

E. R. DODDS was Regius Professor of Greek at Oxford from 1936 to 1960. An exceptionally distinguished classical scholar, educated at Campbell College, Belfast, and University College, Oxford, he is probably best known for his brilliant books, *The Greeks and the Irrational* and *Pagan and Christian in an Age of Anxiety*. Professor Dodds lists psychical research as his recreation in *Who's Who* and is a past President of the Society for Psychical Research, the Classical Association and the Hellenic Society.

MIRCEA ELIADE, Professor of the History of Religions at the University of Chicago, is widely regarded as the world's greatest authority on comparative mythology and religion. A Rumanian, educated at Bucharest University, he taught at the Sorbonne from 1945 and moved to Chicago in 1956. His numerous books include *The Myth of the Eternal Return*; *Myths, Dreams and Mysteries*; *Yoga, Immortality and Freedom*; and *Shamanism*.

CONTRIBUTORS INCLUDE:

Joan Aiken *Conan Doyle*
Violet Alford *hobby horse*
A. H. Armstrong Professor of Greek, Liverpool *Neoplatonism*
Rev E. A. Armstrong *birds*
Geoffrey Ashe *St Brendan; Camelot; Glastonbury; Lost Tribes of Israel*
P. W. Avery Fellow of King's Cambridge *Rumi*
Edward Bacon *Atlantis*
R. H. Bainton formerly Titus Street Professor of Ecclesiastical History, Yale *Christianity*
Robert Baldick Fellow of Pembroke, Oxford *battle of bewitchment*

Roger Bannister *Olympic games*
R. W. Barber *phoenix*
J. C. Baroja *Basque witchcraft*
Raymond de Becker *dreams*
C. D. Broad former Professor of Moral Philosophy, Cambridge *F. W. H. Myers*
Ivor Brown *drama; mystery plays*
F. F. Bruce Professor of Biblical Criticism and Exegesis, Manchester *Dead Sea Scrolls*
Sir Cyril Burt former Professor of Psychology, London *Jung; psychology*
Rev H. Chadwick Regius Professor of Divinity, Oxford *dying god*
Norman Cohn Director of the Centre for Research in Collective Psychopathology, Sussex *Camisards*
J. R. Conrad Professor of Anthropology, Southwestern, Memphis *bull*

Rev T. Corbishley S.J. *St John of the Cross; St Teresa of Avila*
Rev J. H. Crehan S.J. *exorcism*
H. R. Ellis Davidson *German and Scandinavian mythology*
Richard Deacon *John Dee*
Mary Douglas Dept. of Anthropology, University College, London *taboo*
Tom Driberg M.P. *food and drink Druses; Peculiar People; Theosophy*
A. P. Elkin former Professor of Anthropology, Sydney *Australia*
E. E. Evans-Pritchard Professor of Social Anthropology, Oxford *Nuer*
C. von Fürer-Haimendorf Professor of Asian Anthropology, London *head-hunting; Nagas; Sikhs*
Alan Gauld Lecturer in Psychology, Nottingham *psychical research*

O. Gigon Professor of Classical Philology, Berne *Hermetica*
Max Gluckman Professor of Social Anthropology, Manchester *finding of witches; ritual; Zulu*
Mrs K. M. Goldney Vice-President, Society for Psychical Research *Sir W. Crookes; Eusapia Palladino*
J. R. Goody Fellow of St John's, Cambridge *ancestor worship; burial*
R. M. Grant Professor of Divinity, Chicago *Montanists; Simon Magus*
Robert Graves *mushrooms*
John Gray Professor of Hebrew and Semitic Languages, Aberdeen *Baal; prostitution; Syria and Palestine*
Celia Green Director, Institute of Psychophysical Research, Oxford *out-of-the-body experiences*

EDITOR

RICHARD CAVENDISH is a leading authority on magic and witchcraft. His book *The Black Arts*, a study of black magic in Europe published by Routledge and Kegan Paul, has been acclaimed for its combination of clarity and insight by critics on both sides of the Atlantic, and he has lectured and appeared on television and radio as an expert on these subjects. Educated at Christ's Hospital and Brasenose College, Oxford, Mr Cavendish has travelled widely in the Far East and the United States, and is the author of three novels.

SPECIAL CONSULTANTS

Rev S. G. F. BRANDON is Professor of Comparative Religion and Dean of the Faculty of Theology at Manchester University. A Chaplain to the Forces during the war, he is the author of numerous books and the editor of a forthcoming *Dictionary of Comparative Religion*.

KATHARINE BRIGGS, President of the British Folk-Lore Society, has written several novels as well as books on folklore and fairies. She has recently completed her monumental *Dictionary of British Folk Tales*.

WILLIAM GAUNT, painter, art historian and critic, is special correspondent to the *Times* on art subjects. His books include *The Pre-Raphaelite Tragedy*; *The Aesthetic Adventure*; *The March of the Moderns*; *Arrows of Desire*.

DOUGLAS HILL is a Canadian writer and editor. Co-author of *The Supernatural*, author of *Magic and Superstition* and of a forthcoming book on ghosts, vampires and other beings believed to have returned from the dead, he has also published *The Opening of the Canadian West* and *Regency London*.

FRANCIS HUXLEY is Ford Foundation Fellow in Social Anthropology at St Catherine's College, Oxford, and one of the most brilliant of British anthropologists. He is well-known for his book *The Invisibles*, a study of Voodoo.

WILLIAM SARGANT, a formidable and controversial figure in the field of psychiatry, has been Physician in Charge of the Department of Psychological Medicine at St Thomas's Hospital, London, since 1948. He is well known as a pioneer of physical methods of treatment in psychiatry, stemming from his work during the war on the treatment of battle neurosis. His book *Battle for the Mind* is the leading work on brainwashing and conversion. Dr Sargant is preparing a new book on possession and trance states, and has discussed his experiences in this field in his autobiography, *The Unquiet Mind*.

JOHN SYMONDS is the author of a masterly biography of Aleister Crowley, *The Great Beast*. He is Crowley's literary executor and edited Crowley's autobiography for Jonathan Cape. His other books include *Madame Blavatsky: Medium and Magician* and a book on the Shakers. He also writes children's books and novels, one of which — *Light Over Water* — treats a theme of yoga and alchemy. But the only yoga he himself practises is running round Hampstead Heath twice a week.

R. J. ZWI WERBLOWSKY, the youngest member of our Editorial Board, is Professor of Comparative Religion and Dean of the Faculty of Humanities at the Hebrew University of Jerusalem. He studied in Switzerland and taught at Leeds University and at the Institute of Jewish Studies in Manchester before going to the Hebrew University of Jerusalem in 1956. He is the author of numerous books and articles on comparative religion, the Cabala and Jewish mysticism.

R. C. ZAEHNER, Spalding Professor of Eastern Religions and Ethics at Oxford, is a prodigiously distinguished scholar, linguist and wit. Himself a Roman Catholic, he is an authority on Oriental religions and mysticism. Educated at Tonbridge, Christ Church, Oxford, and King's College, Cambridge, his books include *Mysticism Sacred and Profane*; *The Dawn and Twilight of Zoroastrianism*; *Hinduism*; *The Catholic Church and World Religions*; and he edited *The Concise Encyclopedia of Living Faiths*. He is a Fellow of All Souls.

Tom Harrisson *Borneo*
Jacquetta Hawkes *Crete; Ikhnaton*
Hamish Henderson *tinkers*
Rosalind Heywood *mediums (mental)*
Christina Hole *haunted houses; Robin Hood; springs and wells*
Anthony Huxley editor of 'Amateur Gardening' *herbs; plants; trees*
Christopher Isherwood *Vedanta*
Barbara Jones *burial (modern)*
Douglas Kennedy Vice-President, English Folk Dance and Song Society *folkplays; Morris dances*
Francis King *Japanese Buddhism*
G. W. Lambert Vice-President, Society for Psychical Research *Versailles*
Marghanita Laski *conversion*
James Laver *costume; head-dress*

Godfrey Lienhardt Institute of Social Anthropology, Oxford *king (primitive)*
Sir Max Mallowan *Gilgamesh; Ishtar; Marduk*
Eric Maple *demons; love magic*
M. G. Marwick Professor of Sociology, Stirling *witchcraft*
R. G. Medhurst Council, Society for Psychical Research *mediums*
Reinhold Merkelbach Professor of Classics, Cologne *Isis; Mithras; mystery religions*
Venetia Newall Hon. Secretary of the British Folk-Lore Society *egg*
J. H. K. Nketia Director, Institute of African Studies, Ghana *Ashanti*
Seán Ó Súilleabháin *poets*
A. R. G. Owen Fellow of Trinity, Cambridge *miracles; poltergeists*

H. W. Parke Professor of Ancient History, Trinity, Dublin *oracles*
E. D. Phillips Reader in Greek, Queen's, Belfast *Cybele; Hecate*
Stuart Piggott Professor of Archaeology, Edinburgh *Druids*
Kathleen Raine *William Blake; Golden Dawn; W. B. Yeats*
B. I. Rakoczi *cards; divination*
B. R. Rees Professor of Greek, Univ. College of S. Wales *magical papyri*
J. B. Rhine *E.S.P.; psychokinesis*
Louisa Rhine *spontaneous psi experiences*
H. T. F. Rhodes *Black Mass*
Helmer Ringgren Professor of Exegesis, Uppsala *king*
R. H. Robinson Professor of Indian Studies, Wisconsin *Buddhism*

Elliot Rose *European witch persecutions; Salem*
Anne Ross *Celtic mythology*
S. F. Sanderson *gypsies*
H. H. Scullard Professor of Ancient History, London *Etruscans*
David Snelgrove Reader in Tibetan, London *Tibet*
W. H. C. Tenhaeff Professor of Parapsychology, Utrecht *object reading*
Gillian Tindall *familiars; Isabel Gowdie*
Alexander Walker *films*
James Wellard *Africa; Congo*
M. L. West Fellow of University, Oxford *Athene; Orpheus and Orphism*
Sir Mortimer Wheeler *India*
Bryan Wilson Fellow of All Souls, Oxford *enthusiasm; Messianic movements; speaking in tongues*

Abbots Bromley

Town in Staffordshire, England, scene of the annual Horn Dance in September; no one knows how old the dance is but its closest parallels are the ritual dances of primitive societies, reaching back to the Stone Age.
See HORNS.

After the executions of the Aberdeen witches in 1597, it was said that the black reek and stench of the burnings hung over the town for weeks. The victims were strangled to death before their bodies were burned. Many innocent people were undoubtedly accused but there is some evidence for the existence of a real witch organization in north-east Scotland

ABERDEEN WITCHES

IN THE ARCHIVES of the city of Aberdeen is a remarkable collection of documents (*Records of the Dean of Guild, 1596–1597*) which give details of the proceedings against many persons accused of 'the detestable practice of witchcraft and sorcery'. Marginal notes indicate that the documents were those used in court, most of them consisting of 'dittays', or charges against the accused.

The collection of evidence against those suspected of witchcraft and sorcery was made by the ministers and elders of the Reformed Church in the various parishes. Unhappily, suspects could be named by anyone – a feature that afforded full scope to the malicious – and many harmless old people were named. Suspects were summoned before the Kirk Sessions for examination and those considered guilty were remanded to Aberdeen Assizes. Even when allowance is made for the ignorance and superstition of the time, it is difficult to excuse the ministers of the Gospel, educated men, whose evidence was the means of sending many innocent people to a horrible end.

However, some of the evidence suggests that there existed a definite organization practising the black art in north-east Scotland; the group known to history as the Aberdeen witches.

Two main points can be established concerning the group. First, the practice of witchcraft was a confidential cult, almost a family concern, its secrets handed down from generation to generation. Secondly, it was well organized, and although each of its members operated individually in their own localities each was required to attend general meetings, to take part in the ceremonies and for instruction in 'working woe' (doing harm).

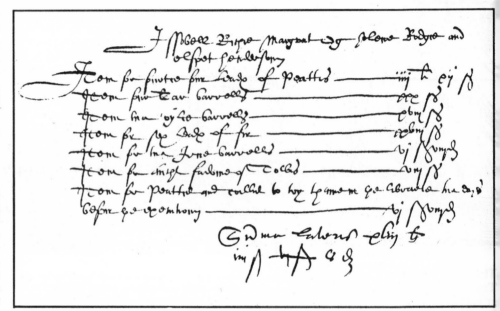

Above Part of the accounts of money spent on the execution of four witches. These include items for coal, peat, tar barrels, the stake, rope, and the fee of the executioner

Below Witches were frequently accused of paying bestial and revolting homage to the Devil by kissing his backside: from Guazzo's *Compendium Maleficarum*, 17th century

Mansell Collection

The Devil and the Queen of Elphen

The witches were organized in covens — groups of 13. At the general meetings the Devil himself presided, usually 'in the likeness of a great grey stag, boar or dog'. Presumably he was a man dressed as an animal. The meetings were said to involve dancing and sexual relations with the Devil — who went under the name of Christsonday — and with a woman called the Queen of Elphen (queen of the elves) who, 'is said to be very pleasant, and she can seem old or young when she pleases, and she makes whoever she likes king, and lies with whoever she likes'. They were accused of saluting the Devil and the Queen by kissing them on the buttocks. There seems to have been no age limit on entrance and many of the accused testified to having been introduced as young children.

Each member of a coven specialized in some particular form of sorcery and these covered a wide range. Isobel Cockie bewitched mills and livestock, while Margaret Ogg devoted her attentions to butcher-meat with dire results; Helen Rogie brought illness and death by modelling figures of her victims in lead or wax, and Isobel Strachan was notorious as a fascinator of nice young men; Isobel Ritchie made a special line in confectionery for expectant mothers, while Isobel Ogg's forte was the raising of storms. It would seem that the witches had one faculty which was common to all, that of causing 'the sudden sickness' whereby their victims lay 'one half of the day roasting as if in an oven, with an unquenchable thirst, the other half of the day melting away with an extraordinary cold sweat'.

Perhaps the most dramatic moment in the Aberdeen Assizes came when Andrew Man turned king's evidence against his colleagues. A witch from boyhood and the father of several children by the Queen of Elphen, he convinced the Court that, with his long and extensive experience, he was in the unique position of being able to identify any witch or warlock brought before him. Accordingly, he was appointed official witch-finder to the Assizes and with a three-inch needle pricked the suspects' bodies for the 'Devil's Mark' — a spot insensible to pain and believed to be inflicted by the Devil.

Strangled by the Executioner

While awaiting trial, the suspects were confined either in the cells of the Tolbooth or in Our Lady's Pity-vault, for the Reformation had brought degradation to this place of worship. A number of the accused took their own lives in prison and their bodies were thrown outside to be dragged through the streets until their battered, shapeless carcasses were unrecognizable.

When the Assizes closed in April 1597, 24 people — 23 women and one man — had been found guilty of witchcraft. All were condemned to death — 'to be taken out between the hills, bound to a stake, strangled by the executioner, and their bodies burnt to ashes'. The few whose guilt was 'not proven' were ordered to be branded on the cheek and banished. The final tragic scene took place 'between the hills', in the grassy hollow

The European obsession with witchcraft raged for about 300 years. In Germany, as in Scotland and France, it was the custom to strangle or hang the witches before burning them to ashes. Burning three witches at Derneburg, Germany, in 1555

lying between Aberdeen's Castle-hill and the neighbouring Heading-hill — the depression now covered by Commerce Street — and the 'black reek and stench from the burnings hung over the burgh for many weeks'.

At one stage in the Assizes, it appeared that the number of executions would increase and the Dean of Guild, fearing rising costs might prejudice the burnings, took it upon himself to lay in a supply of coal to the value of £26 4s. His foresight paid dividends as shown by the final entry in the records dated 21 September 1597, which states that the provost, baillies and council 'considering the faithfulness shown by William Dun, the Dean of Guild, in the discharge of his duty, and, besides this, his extraordinary taking pains on the great number of witches burnt this year and to encourage others to work as diligently in the discharge of their office, grant and assign to him the sum of £47 3s 4d'.

Before the end of the year and while the subject of witchcraft and sorcery was still in people's minds, King James VI of Scotland (later James I of England) published his book *Demonologie* in defence of witch hunting. It proved to be a best seller.

FENTON WYNESS

ABOMINABLE SNOWMAN

THE ABOMINABLE SNOWMAN of the Himalayas is supposed to be a creature half-human and half-animal, hairy and about the size of a child of 12 or 14, which walks erect on two legs, swinging its arms. Its hair is described as reddish or light brown, and not very thick. European travellers called the snowman 'abominable' because of the horror with which the Sherpas, a Himalayan people, regard the creatures which they call *yeti*.

Expeditions have searched without success for the yeti. Mountaineers have found what were thought to be its footprints in the snow, but research has revealed that these tracks were made by other animals. Anthropologists have shown that the Sherpas' stories are questionable, and the view that the snowman is a legend is now widely accepted. Legends of hairy mountain-men have also been reported from the Gobi desert, Mongolia and the North American Rocky Mountains.

According to Sherpa folklore a monkey king was converted to Buddhism and lived as a hermit in the mountains. An ogress fell in love with him and he abandoned his solitary life to marry her. The children she bore him were covered in hair and had tails, and they were the first yeti.

A Tibetan holding a cap allegedly made from the scalp of a yeti. It has been shown that these caps are really made of deer-hide

ABRACADABRA

THE WORD ABRACADABRA has been so widely used in magic that it has passed into the patter of the stage conjuror and appears in dictionaries as a term for magical nonsense-words in general. Daniel Defoe, in his *Journal of the Plague Year,* published in 1722, says that many people who were terrified of the plague acted as if it was an evil spirit which threatened to take possession of their bodies. They tried to ward it off with 'certain words or figures, as particularly the word Abracadabra formed in a triangle or pyramid.'

In the Middle Ages the word was believed to cure fevers. The earliest instructions for using it come from a poem on medicine by Quintus Serenus Sammonicus, a doctor who accompanied the Roman Emperor Severus on his expedition to Britain in 208 AD. It has to be written down, dropping a letter in each line. The usual way of writing it is:

```
A B R A C A D A B R A
A B R A C A D A B R
A B R A C A D A B
A B R A C A D A
A B R A C A D
A B R A C A
A B R A C
A B R A
A B R
A B
A
```

'Abracax', a demon with snakes for feet, associated with abracadabra. From Collin de Plancy's *Dictionnaire Infernal*, 1863

The paper on which the word is written must be tied round the patient's neck with flax, worn for nine days, and then thrown backwards over the shoulder into a stream which runs eastwards.

The idea is evidently that as the word shrinks away to nothing, so will the fever. Several other shrinking charms of this kind are known, including a Jewish spell against a demon named Shabriri, thought to cause diseases of the eye. To get rid of him, you say Shabriri Briri Riri Iri Ri, whittling him away to nothing.

Abracadabra resembles, and may be descended from, a Jewish cure for fever:

Ab Abr Abra Abrak Abraka
Abrakal Abrakala Abrakal
Abraka Abrak Abra Abr Ab

And the people called unto Moses and Moses prayed to God and the fire abated. May healing come from heaven from all kinds of fever and consumption – heat to N son of N.

Amen Amen Amen. Selah Selah Selah.

This must also be hung round the patient's neck, and he must not look at it for the next 24 hours. It apparently builds the heat of the fever up to breaking-point and then makes it dwindle away, as 'the fire' abates.

Another possibility is that Abracadabra is connected with Abraxas, a god who appears on magical charms, gems and rings used to ward off evil from the 2nd century AD onwards. Abraxas originated with the followers of an eccentric Christian thinker named Basilides, who taught at Alexandria from about 120 to 140. One of his theories was that Jesus had not really been crucified.

The followers of Basilides seem to have constructed the name Abraxas for the god who ruled each year and its 365 days. The letters of the Greek alphabet also stood for numbers, and the Greek letters of Abraxas add to 365. Below this god were 365 orders of spirits, occupying 365 heavens, the lowest of which was the domain of the spirits who rule the Earth. The seven letters of Abraxas may stand for the seven planets known in antiquity, believed in astrology to control the workings of fate.

The central character of Homer's Iliad *was honoured as a semi-divine being, and his effect on Western ideas of 'the hero' has lasted to the present day*

ACHILLES

THE PLOT OF THE *Iliad*, one of the most blood-drenched stories ever told, turns on the pride and the ungovernable temper of Achilles (Achilleus in Greek), the most formidable of the Greek champions who laid siege to Troy. 'The Wrath of Achilles is my theme', Homer begins, 'that fatal wrath which . . . sent the gallant souls of many noblemen to Hades, leaving their bodies as carrion for the dogs and passing birds.'

The *Iliad* is usually dated to the 8th century BC. It is quite possible that Achilles was originally a real man, however legendary the exploits with which Homer and later authors credited him. Homer calls him 'the great runner' for his skill as an athlete and 'the city-sacker' for his prowess as a fighter. In Hesiod, who wrote some years after Homer, he is 'lion-hearted Achilles, the destroyer of men'. Later still, as a result of the fame which the *Iliad* brought him, he was honoured in many parts of the Greek world as a hero, a being halfway between a god and a man.

At the village of Achilleum near Troy there was a temple sacred to Achilles and a statue of the hero wearing, oddly enough, a woman's earring. At Elis on the Greek mainland he had a monument and on a certain day, towards sunset, the women of Elis honoured him by lamenting his death. He had a temple and a statue on Leuce, the White Island in the Black Sea opposite the mouths of the Danube, where offerings were made to him and games were held in his honour. It was said that passing sailors heard his voice across the water, reciting Homer to the accompaniment of the clash of battle and the thunder of horses' hooves.

The Wrath of Achilles

The story of the *Iliad* begins, in the tenth year of the siege of Troy, when the Greek supreme commander, Agamemnon, seized a beautiful slave-girl who had been allotted to Achilles as a prize of battle. Insulted, Achilles refused to fight any more and his absence gravely weakened the Greek resistance to fierce Trojan attacks. Agamemnon tried to make the quarrel up, offering to return the girl to Achilles with many splendid gifts. But Achilles was still nursing his fury and refused to be reconciled.

Lacking Achilles, the situation of the Greeks now became so dangerous that Patroclus, the dearly loved friend of Achilles, went out to fight the Trojans. Patroclus was killed by the best of the Trojan warriors, Hector. When this news was brought to him, Achilles became berserk with grief and rage, and readied himself for battle — in spite of the warning from his mother, the sea-nymph Thetis, that he was doomed to die after Hector's death.

Next day, bearing new arms given to him by the gods, Achilles 'chased his victims with the fury of a fiend, and the

British Museum

earth was dark with blood'. His horses trampled over dead men and fallen shields as he raged on in search of glory, until he found Hector and killed him in single combat, gloating over the Trojan's death agony.

Achilles maltreated Hector's corpse, dragging it in the dust behind his chariot, and he intended to throw it to the dogs to gnaw. But Hector's father persuaded him to return the body to the Trojans so that it could be decently buried.

The *Iliad* ends with the funeral rites for Hector but it is clear that Achilles has not long to live and that he will be killed by Hector's brother Paris and the archer-god Apollo. The *Odyssey* describes his death in battle, with the flower of the Greek and Trojan warriors falling round him in the struggle over his corpse. The sea-nymphs came from the ocean to weep salt tears for him and the nine Muses sang his dirge. His bones were mingled with those of his friend Patroclus and buried outside Troy.

Something Superhuman

Achilles has all the virtues of the Homeric hero. He is brave, passionate, ferocious in battle, beautiful to look at, intensely proud, fated to an early death. His failing is his uncontrollable anger. His treatment of Hector's corpse is so savage that Homer calls it 'shameful outrage' and condemns as 'an evil thing' his slaughter of a dozen Trojan prisoners at the funeral of Patroclus. When Hector's father comes to beg for his son's body, Achilles tries to console him and mercifully gives him the corpse. But even

The greatest of the Homeric heroes and the central character of the *Iliad*, Achilles was later worshipped as a semi-divine being. Famed for his savagery in battle, he is here shown slaying Penthesilea, the queen of the Amazons. From an Attic amphora

then he is sufficiently aware of his weakness to be afraid that he may suddenly fly into a rage and kill the old man.

Achilles' Heel

Many of the best-known stories about Achilles appear in later writers, including some which have parallels in folk tales all over the world, like the story that his mother tried to make him immortal by dipping him into a fire, but her husband thought she was trying to kill the child and stopped her. A famous variant of this is that she dipped him in the Styx, the river of the underworld, which made all of him deathproof except the heel by which she held him. It was in this heel that he received his mortal wound, from an arrow fired by Paris or Apollo.

His mother, Thetis, was so beautiful that both Zeus and the sea-god Poseidon desired her. But she was fated to bear a son who would be mightier than his father, and when the two gods heard this their ardour cooled, and they gave her in marriage to a mortal named Peleus. It was at the wedding of Thetis and Peleus that the apple marked 'for the fairest' was thrown among the gods, the apple of discord that caused the Trojan War in which Achilles met his death.

Achilles was only a boy when the Greek

armies gathered for the siege of Troy. His mother hid him on the island of Scyros, where he was dressed as a girl and brought up with the king's daughters. But the crafty Odysseus came to Scyros bringing presents of cloth for dressmaking and also a spear and a shield. Achilles revealed himself by ignoring the cloth and seizing the weapons. What name Achilles bore when hidden among the women is an old problem. One suggestion is that he was called Pyrrha, 'red-head', for the colour of his hair.

At Troy, after the death of Hector, Achilles is said to have defeated various other notable fighters, including Penthesilea, Queen of the Amazons, a tribe of warrior women, who had come to fight on the Trojan side. When he had killed her with a

Achilles, on the left, gaming with another Greek leader, Ajax. Games and contests of all kinds were dear to the hearts of the warrior-aristocrats who were Homer's heroes. Achilles seems to have won, as beside him is written the Greek for 'four', while beside Ajax is 'three'. From an amphora, c 530 BC

spear-thrust, he was so smitten by her beauty that he made love to her dead body.

Some said that Achilles and Patroclus were homosexual lovers. There is no such suggestion in Homer but the accusation was made against many famous figures.

Most of these later stories, to a modern eye at least, tend to lessen the stature of the hero, as compared with the picture of him in Homer. But there is a suitably grim tale in

the *Hecuba* of Euripides. After the fall of Troy, the ghost of Achilles rose in the sheen of golden armour and stood high on the crest of his tomb, demanding its share of the spoil, in the shape of Polyxena, daughter of the king of Troy. The Greeks slaughtered the girl on Achilles' grave-mound, so that she could accompany her new master to the after-world, and the blood welled from her neck over her golden robes.

FURTHER READING: Homer's *Iliad* and *Odyssey*, both translated by E. V. Rieu (Penguin, 1950 and 1946); M. Grant, *Myths of the Greeks and Romans* (New American Library, 1964); R. Graves, *The Greek Myths* (Braziller, 1959); and see also M. I. Finley, *The World of Odysseus* (Viking Press, 1964).

ACORN

AS THE FRUIT of the oak tree, which is sacred to so many cultures, the acorn has found a place in a good deal of magical lore. It has been a fertility symbol, along with most other seeds, nuts and fruits — though acorns always imply a special kind of long-term, high-potency fertility. It has been widely used as a good-luck charm: even today replicas of acorns are found with other talismans on key rings or charm bracelets.

In an old European form of marriage divination, an anxious young girl might take two acorns. She would name one of them for herself and the other for her lover, and

drop them into a basin of water. If they floated together, the lovers would marry happily. Otherwise, the omen was bad.

A traditional British belief states that acorns should be carried as a means of preserving youthfulness. In the southern USA, the acorn entered into folk medicine, as a cure for rheumatism.

The ancient Celtic Druids, who venerated the oak, ate acorns as part of their ritual preparation for foretelling the future. In Scandinavian myth, the oak was sacred to the thunder god Thor, and so acorns would be placed in windows to appease the god and protect the house against lightning. Some of this latter practice has lasted into quite recent times: the roller window blinds which

were widely popular a few years ago often had tassels on them shaped like acorns.

The acorn fills a central role in the religion of many Californian Indian tribes. For them, acorns were the main staple food (aside from fish), as vital to their well-being as maize was to tribes east of the mountains. So tales about acorns abound in the mythology of tribes such as the Luiseño. Other tribes, like the Hupa or Yuki, held a great annual Acorn Feast as the central feature of their harvest celebrations. In that ritual, acorns were ceremonially cooked and eaten while prayers were made to the god of vegetation, to protect the stored crop and to ensure future harvests.

(See also OAK.)

This Chinese medical technique of jabbing the patient with needles seems to concentrate entirely on physical treatment of disease but in fact it is based on beliefs about supernatural forces at work in the body

ACUPUNCTURE

ACUPUNCTURE is a system of healing which is centuries old in China, is still used there and taught in medical schools, and has been practised fairly extensively in the West since the 1930s. Needles are inserted into the skin, to a depth of about a tenth of an inch. They are left for a few minutes and then removed. 'To the casual observer', says Felix Mann, a leading Western authority on the subject, 'it could appear that what had been done was negligible and yet, in the right kind of case (whether severe or mild), the result can be such as to give the impression that the cure was effected by magic.'

The impression of magic comes partly from the fact that the needles are often inserted at points which have no apparent connection with the ailment that is being treated. A needle stuck into the little toe can cure headache, for biliousness a needle may be inserted into the patient's shoulder, and acupuncturists usually attack hay fever by treating the liver. There is no doubt that acupuncture is sometimes effective but no satisfactory scientific explanation of it has yet been produced.

Philosophically, acupuncture is based on theories about forces which are believed to govern everything in the universe, including human health. Medically, it is based on the fact that points on the body's surface become tender as a result of illness. If you have a headache, for instance, you may develop tender spots at the junction of the neck and the back of the head. When these spots are pressed, the pain is relieved.

The Chinese discovered about a thousand points on the skin where stimulation relieves or cures disease. These points are divided into 12 systems. All the points belonging to any one system are connected by an invisible line called a meridian, and each meridian is linked with one of the major organs of the body, including the heart, lungs, liver, kidneys and bladder.

The meridian of the liver runs from near the liver to the inside of the leg and down to the big toe. The heart meridian runs from the heart down the inside of the arm to the little finger, which is roughly the track along which you feel pain if you have a heart attack.

Each of the points has its own name. The point on the spleen meridian called Tian Xi, Heavenly Ravine, is connected with bronchitis, rebellious cough, throat noises, peptic ulcer and other conditions. The point Yung Men, Cloud Gate, on the lung meridian may be treated to relieve shortness of breath, asthma, rheumatism and swelling of the neck, tonsillitis or acne.

Some of the points correspond to the vital spots which are attacked in judo and karate. The two points on the neck at the base of the skull, which can be treated to cure headache and nosebleed, can also be struck to produce unconsciousness. Some points are related to those used in yoga. To promote efficient breathing on long walks, yogis may stimulate the point in the armpit which is on the lung meridian of acupuncture.

The Twelve Pulses

Acupuncture is concerned not only with healing but also with preventing disease. The Chinese attitude to medicine leans heavily towards keeping people in good health to begin with, rather than waiting for them to be ill and then trying to cure them: so much so that they produced a system which is the reverse of our own: Chinese patients paid the doctor as long as they stayed healthy and stopped paying him when they fell ill. When a disease first develops, before it takes hold and shows itself, there is a stage when the body's mechanism is slightly disturbed, but not enough for the patient to notice his symptoms. It is this type of condition which the acupuncturist tries to diagnose and halt.

Diagnosis is made by taking the pulse. The pulses at the left and right wrists are each divided into six sections, giving 12 pulses in all, corresponding to the 12 meridians. Each pulse may have any of 27 qualities, on which the doctor's diagnosis depends. The sensitivity required in taking the pulse is so fine that not only is the patient's present condition accurately determined but past illnesses described and future ones predicted.

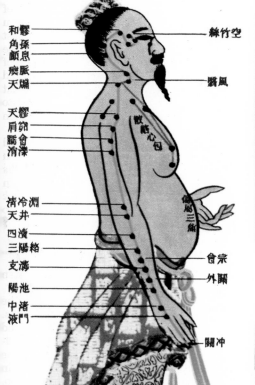

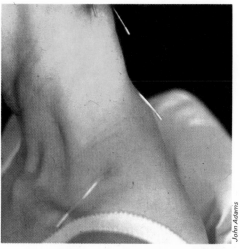

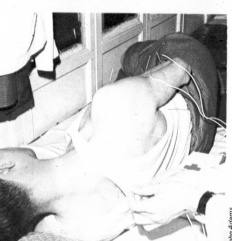

John Adams

In acupuncture needles are inserted into one or more of a thousand points on the skin, to relieve pain or cure disease. The points are divided into 12 systems and all the points in a system are connected by a line called a meridian *1* This chart shows some of the points and meridians. *2* and *3* Acupuncture has become popular in the West since the 1930s. A patient undergoing treatment, with needles placed in the neck and shoulders. *4* This box contains needles used by a modern Western acupuncturist

John Adams

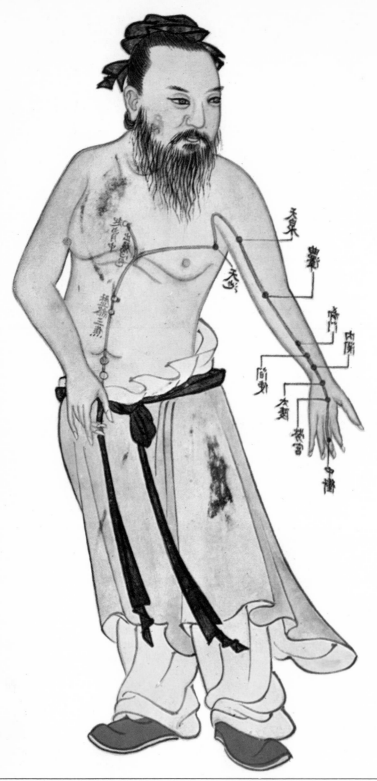

The Flow of Qi

Acupuncture is extremely ancient and the oldest book on the subject, the *Nei Jing* or Book of the Yellow Emperor, dates from c 200 BC but contains material which is much older. It has been suggested that the system developed when people noticed that a warrior slightly wounded in battle by a blow from a stone or a sharp weapon, might be cured of some ailment by the wound.

Acupuncture depends on belief that in the healthy human body there is a continuous circulation of vital energy or 'life force'. This energy is called Qi (or Ch'I), which basically means 'air' or 'breath'. The identification of the life force with air, based on the simple observation that you cannot live without breathing, is found all over the world (see BREATH).

Qi circulates through the 12 meridians, starting from the lungs which draw breath, once every 24 hours. If it fails to flow properly, the organs of the body will suffer from a deficiency of energy or, where it is blocked, from a surplus of it. Acupuncture tries to bring the flow of life force back to normal by 'sedating' a meridian which has too much Qi or 'tonifying' a meridian which has too little.

If a meridian is 'empty', deficient in Qi, the previous meridian is tonified. Qi flows from the lungs through the large intestine, the stomach, the spleen and the heart to the liver. If the spleen is 'empty', the stomach meridian is tonified and the energy then flows on from it to the spleen. A secondary result is that because the stomach is now full of energy, the flow from the large intestine meridian is dammed back, so that there is an increase of energy in the large intestine.

Although taking the pulse is the main method of diagnosis in acupuncture, there are other signals which give the acupuncturist a clue to your physical condition. If you have a soft voice with a clear tone, this suggests that you have a satisfactory flow of Qi. A strong, rough voice suggests that you have too much flow of Qi, an excess of vital energy. A weak voice, lacking in resonance, suggests a weak and unstable flow of Qi. Similarly, a pure and umblemished skin with a rosy tint points to a healthy flow of Qi, a congested and reddish skin to too much Qi, a thick, fatty skin, greyish in colour, to too little.

Interplay of Yang and Yin

Qi is the product of two great forces, or principles or polarities, called Yang and Yin. These forces run through the whole universe and everything which exists depends on the interplay between them. 'Life', as Felix Mann puts it, 'exists as the result of tension between two extremes', and their different forms of combination with each other produce the five basic elements of which everything is made, the elements of wood, fire, earth, metal and water. If they are thought of in terms of electricity, Yang is the positive charge and Yin the negative: if in terms of sex, Yang is male and Yin is female. The sun, light, strength, the right side, fire, dryness and many other qualities belong to Yang. Their opposites, the moon, darkness, weakness, the left side, water and wetness belong to Yin.

Western Views

Western interest in acupuncture first sprang up in France and Germany, where today acupuncturists are numbered in many hundreds, even thousands. In Britain, too, the practice has grown rapidly — so that the British Acupuncture Association now runs a training course of up to four years, admitting only qualified medical men. The Association owns Britain's only in-patient clinic, but there are many out-patient treatment clinics all over the country, including some 30 owned by the Berkeley Acupuncture group.

Modern practitioners generally follow the ancient Chinese precepts, but with one or two modern refinements. The Chinese found the 'meridians' on the skin by a highly skilled sense of touch; but clinics today often use an electric machine, developed in Germany many years ago, that registers meridians on a dial.

Acupuncture has not yet made much headway in the USA. In 1964 there was only one practitioner in New York; today there are only a few dozen in the whole country. Perhaps too many American doctors share the opinion of a writer in the *World Medical Journal* who described acupuncture as 'an ancient but arbitrary myth which has no foundation in logic or in anatomy'.

The organs and meridians of the body are classified in terms of Yang and Yin. The heart, lungs, spleen, kidneys and liver belong to Yin, and a patient who has a weak heart will be said to be suffering from a deficiency of Yin. The intestines, stomach, bladder and gall bladder belong to Yang. Health and a satisfactory flow of Qi depend on a perfect balance between Yang and Yin in the body.

When the Yang and Yin energies in a man's body are reasonably in balance, he is healthy. If one becomes too strong or too weak, he is ill. If the Yang and Yin energies become separated altogether, he is dead. The acupuncturist stimulates the appropriate points on the skin with needles, either to restore the flow of the weakened energy or to restrict the flow of the stronger energy, and so bring the two energies back into balance. (For a similar idea in the West, see MAGNETISM.)

It is said that seasonal changes affect the flow of energy. The Yang is more active than the Yin in spring and summer: the reverse is the case in autumn and winter. The Yin energy is stronger than the Yang at the time of the new moon.

Opposites and Balance

The theory of Yang and Yin was systematized by a philosopher named Tsou Yen in the 4th century BC. But the belief that all things are made of opposites is not by any means confined to China.

Early Greek thinkers saw that the universe can be described in terms of opposites. Day gives way to night, summer to winter, heat to cold, youth to age. They also developed the theory that everything is made of four basic materials or elements, each combining two of the primary qualities, which are two pairs of opposites: hot and cold, dry and wet. The theory of the four elements and qualities was scarcely challenged until the 17th century. The idea that the world is made of opposites, with the consequent necessity for balancing and reconciling them harmoniously with each other, like Yang and Yin in the healthy body, was a basic doctrine of alchemy, also appears in astrology, and has remained one of the fundamental theories of occultism in the West (see OPPOSITES).

FURTHER READING: There are selections from the *Nei Jing* in I. Veith, *The Yellow Emperor's Classic of Internal Medicine* (University of California Press, 1966). See also Felix Mann's excellent books, published by Heinemann, London, *Acupuncture: The Ancient Chinese Art of Healing* (1962, and Random House, 1963), *The Meridians of Acupuncture* (1964) and *The Treatment of Disease by Acupuncture* (2nd edn, 1964), and J. Lavier, *Points of Chinese Acupuncture* (Weiser).

Far left **This figure shows the points believed to control diseases of the heart and the sexual organs**
Right **Japanese chart, drawn in the 19th century, showing some of the points on the skin where acupuncturists insert needles to cure disease**

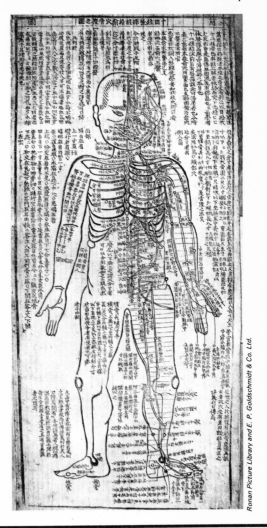

Ronan Picture Library and E. P. Goldschmidt & Co. Ltd.

Mansell Collection

Adam

According to the book of Genesis, the first human being, created 'in the image' of God: the belief that man is a miniature copy of God has powerfully influenced European magic: Adam's disobedience in Eden was the 'original sin' and the belief that Christ was 'the second Adam', who came to free mankind from the consequences of Adam's crime, has been a major doctrine of Christianity.
See FIRST MAN.

Mansell Collection

Adonis

In Greek mythology, a handsome youth, the lover of the goddess Aphrodite; he spent part of the year with her and part underground with the goddess of the underworld; associated with fertility and vegetation.
See APHRODITE; TAMMUZ.

Radio Times/Hulton

Aesculapius

Roman name of the Greek god Asclepios, whose province was healing; patients came to sleep at his shrines and were cured by healing dreams.
See HEALING GODS.

Aetherius Society

Aetherius Society

Modern group which believes itself to be in touch with spiritually advanced beings who live on Venus, Mars and Neptune; the society has 'charged' 19 mountains all over the world with spiritual force.
See FLYING SAUCERS.

AFRICA

'You are useless, you gods!'

Africa is a continent of many gods – pagan, Mohammedan and Christian – of spirits, magic, witchcraft, and prophecy. This article gives the background for later entries dealing with individual tribes and customs

THE CONTINENT OF AFRICA contains some 6,000 different tribes. So complex are African languages, races, cultures and religions that anthropologists cannot yet agree about many of the facts that are available to them.

It follows that where there are so many sorts of men, there are many gods, or concepts of God, and many religious sects with their peculiar rites, magical practices and traditional myths. Some idea of the enormous diversity involved can be seen by comparing the Egyptian Copt, a tall, fair-skinned Christian, with the Bushman of southern Africa, a stunted, black-skinned pagan. Both are Africans, and both are typical in their way of African racial types, cultural groups and religious beliefs.

But there are certain basic concepts which underly all African religions; and these concepts, far from being the mumbo-jumbo popularly associated with medicine-men, witch-doctors, black magic, fetishes, ju-jus and the rest of it, are still a powerful spiritual and social force.

Paganism: Gods of Nature

To most Africans, God in one of his many manifestations, or called by one of his many names (there are over 200 principal epithets ranging from 'the Everlasting One of the Forest' to 'He who roars so loud that the nations are struck with terror') is an ever-present being; and his priests (medicine-men and witch-doctors) are recognized leaders of the tribal community.

Estimates give the number of non-Christians and non-Moslems in Africa as

Left Christian cross-bearer in procession, during the Queen's visit to the Sudan in 1965. There are over 68 million Christians in Africa
Right Cicatrization, cutting the skin with a sharp implement to produce raised scars, is practised by various African peoples, partly for beauty and partly for religious and magical purposes connected with initiation, pregnancy or love. This Nuba woman from the southern Sudan was first scarred when she was seven or eight

Stephanie Dinkins/Camera Press

157,031,000, or over half of the total population. In earlier times, before the true character of African traditional beliefs was understood, these people were called simply 'heathens'. They were poor benighted savages who 'bowed down to wood and stone'. The more accurate term used today is 'pagans', from the Latin *paganus*, a word which originally meant a peasant or countryman.

The African pagan (like the pagan everywhere for that matter) believes in a polytheistic system in which a chief god presides over lesser deities, rather as a king ruled over his domain in ancient times. Nearly all African cults had their Supreme Being, called by a hundred different names which vary from tribe to tribe. But no matter what the chief god is called, he is invariably conceived of as the Maker of the World, the Master of Human Destiny, an omnipotent and omnipresent 'king of kings' and 'lord of lords'. And under the rule of the Supreme Being are all the lesser godlings, each with his special function.

The question that has puzzled observers since white men first arrived in Africa is whether this Supreme Being, whatever his name, is an abstract idea – a sort of creative energy which animates and pervades the universe, but has no direct relationship with man; or whether this god is a personal being, like the Jehovah of the Hebrews, or the 'Our Father' of the Christians. It is, perhaps, typical of the difficulties inherent in a study of African religion that no native has come forward to clarify the question; and that white men can only make

their observations from the outside, with no help at all from written scriptures, texts or recorded ecclesiastical history.

Yet all observers who have managed to make contact with pagan Africans agree that the idea of a Supreme Being, though vague, is universal, even among the most primitive of peoples, like the Bushmen of the Kalahari Desert. It is also clear that the worship of this Supreme Being is, on the whole, a lackadaisical affair. The Creator of the Universe is, after all, bound to be somewhat indifferent to a mere human and his problems.

On the other hand, the lesser gods – the spirits of the earth and the ghosts of departed heroes – are thought to be much more sympathetic.

They can be flattered, wheedled and even threatened. A not unusual African prayer will go as follows: 'You are useless, you gods! You give us only trouble! You are a bunch of so-and-so's! What do we get from you? Nothing!'

It is evident that this 'personalized' relationship with the deity is not confined to African pagans. Christians, in particular Roman Catholics, often approach God through such intermediaries as the Virgin, the Apostles, local saints, martyrs, and others. And in the Moslem religion, Mohammed and his fellow prophets (including Jesus Christ) are the buffers, as it were, between humble man and Almighty God.

The African, surrounded from birth by all the wonders and terrors of nature,

logically pays more heed to sun, rain, storms, rivers and animals than we do, as these objects are his immediate friends or enemies. From the dawn of time primitive man discovered objects of reverence and fear all around him. The former had to be thanked; the latter placated. This was the origin of all religious activity and remains the cardinal principle of African paganism. And if we remember that, in the beginning, men noticed that their enemies – crocodiles, snakes, lions and the like – were quiescent once they had caught and devoured their prey, we can begin to understand the origin of human sacrifice. Such sacrifices were common throughout the continent of Africa until quite recently, and nobody knows the extent to which they are still practised today.

Nature worship, then, is perhaps the most significant aspect of African paganism, and it is found in a hundred different forms throughout the continent. We are familiar with it in the animal gods of ancient Egypt; and among those gods, the crocodile and serpent were accorded special veneration. They still are in parts of Africa. It is difficult for Western man, with his inbuilt horror of snakes, to understand the African's attitude; yet our obsessions about reptiles are perhaps more illogical and less 'scientific' than primitive man's regard for these lowly creatures. After all, there are more beneficent serpents than maleficent, and we often kill our friends in our ignorance.

The African is more cautious in his approach; and instead of indiscriminately

The Magician Must Surely Die

Fundikira, the chief of Unyamwezi . . . fell ill in the autumn of 1858, and, as usual, his relations were suspected of compassing his end by Uchawi, or black magic. In these regions the death of one man causes many. The Mganga (witch doctor) was summoned to apply the usual ordeal. After administering a mystic drug, he broke the neck of a fowl, and splitting it into two lengths inspected the interior. If blackness or blemish appear about the wings, it denotes the treachery of children, relations and kinsmen; the backbone convicts the mother and grandmother; the tail shows that the criminal is the wife, the thighs the concubines, and

the injured shanks or feet, the other slaves. Having fixed upon the class of the criminals, they are collected together by the Mganga, who, after similarly dosing a second hen, throws her up into the air above the heads of the crowd and singles out the person upon whom she alights. Confession is extorted by tying the thumb backwards till it touches the wrist or by some equally barbarous mode of question. The consequence of condemnation is certain and immediate death; the mode is chosen by the Mganga. Some are speared, others are beheaded or 'ammazati' – clubbed: – a common way is to bind the cranium between two

stiff pieces of wood which are gradually tightened by cords until the brain bursts out from the sutures. For women they practise a peculiarly horrible kind of impalement. These atrocities continue until the chief recovers or dies: at the commencement of his attack, in one household eighteen souls, male and female, had been destroyed; should his illness be protracted, scores will precede him to the grave, for the Mchawi or magician must surely die.

Sir Richard Burton
The Lake Regions of Central Africa

Surrounded from birth by all the wonders and terrors of Nature, primitive man discovered objects of reverence and fear all around him

Leni Riefenstahl

Above left **These figures stand outside a shrine of the god of thunder in western Nigeria**
Above **Typically arid landscape in the Sudan. The African's reliance on Nature for water, food and all the necessities of life is the basis of Nature worship, the most significant aspect of African paganism, found in many different forms all over the continent**

killing all snakes, whether poisonous or not, he tries to placate the 'snake spirit' itself. Python worship, for instance, is characteristic of several West and East African tribes.

Less than a hundred years ago, travellers described the python 'temples' where these snakes were fed, watered, venerated and even danced to. The python god was given

many wives who brought food and water to him and made him comfortable with grass mats and a decorated house. In return, his spirit watched over the tribe and, in the person of the priest, forewarned the community of dangers, accidents and the like. The penalty for killing a python was death by burning, and in 1864 the explorer Sir Richard Burton saw a python-killer burnt alive in his hut, from which he escaped only to be clubbed to death by priests.

Another fundamental fact of African paganism is the firm belief in life after death. No one dies from natural causes in any case. He ceases to live because he has been 'interfered' with — perhaps by human enemies, perhaps by evil spirits. Hence, when he 'passes over', this does not mean

that he has gone for good but, to the contrary, he continues to take part in the communal life, now in his spirit form.

Africans, however, do not 'worship' these spirits so much as consult them or ask them for favours, or even argue with them. The ghosts themselves are present in some peculiarly personal belonging or frequented place — their hut, or the log they sat on at council meetings, or the tree they rested beneath. The well-known 'stool huts' of the Ghanaian kings are explained in these terms. The stools symbolize the 'soul' or personality of the departed kings and are preserved for many generations. Moreover, whereas our ideas of personal life after death are often comparatively vague, the African has a firm belief in reincarnation,

Black men were puzzled by assurances that they were children of God on the one hand -and slaves of white men on the other

a belief no doubt founded on the physical resemblance of a child to his parents and grandparents. Eventually one of the ancestors returns from the spirit world to enter the body of a newly-born child.

Summarizing the main tenets of African paganism, we can conclude that there is an underlying concept of a Supreme Being who made the world and presides over the destiny of mankind; that this world is full of spirits enshrined in natural phenomena and dead ancestors; and that there is no final 'death', but an active after-life together with an eventual return to earth in a reincarnated body.

Islam: Religion of the Desert

Moslems make up the second largest religious group in Africa, estimated at 97,934,000, the majority in North Africa which is almost wholly Mohammedan.

The Arabs began their conquest of Africa in the 7th century and had wiped out almost all traces of Christianity within a hundred years. Only the Coptic Church of Egypt and Ethiopia survived — small communities of Christians who were to be cut off from their brethren in the outside world for almost ten centuries.

There is no denying the immense appeal of Islam to the nomadic people who inhabit the lonely wastelands of the Sahara — 3,000,000 square miles of mountain ranges and sand seas. Islam originated in the desert among desert people, and its prophet Mohammed conceived its spiritual and moral code in terms of desert needs. It is an eminently practical religion, well-suited to the actual conditions obtaining in Africa, where polygamy, for instance, is recognized by all unprejudiced observers as a necessary institution. By way of contrast, Christianity, with its emphasis on original sin and sexual inhibitions, is comparatively unsuited to the African temperament and life.

Once North Africa had been conquered by their armies, Arab traders and merchants began their penetration of regions

Nuba wrestlers cover themselves with ashes, partly to reduce slipperiness but also because they believe that the ashes give them extra vigour. The belief that ashes, like fire which created them, carry new life and strength is widespread all over the world

which even the Carthaginians and Romans had not explored. These traders were primarily after loot in the form of ivory, gold and, above all, slaves. And wherever they went, the Arab traders took with them the new religion, an absolutely uncompromising faith and fervour which left subject peoples no alternative: one was either a believer or an infidel. And this often meant, in practical terms, a choice of life or death.

Millions of pagan Africans all over the continent chose to 'co-operate' with the fierce and well-armed invaders, as they were to 'co-operate' with the Portuguese Christians during the 17th and 18th centuries. At the same time, the Moslem concept of the One God was, as we have seen, not alien to African thinking.

Moreover, Koranic law (as opposed to Christian morality) did not basically conflict with tribal custom. It recognized the institution of slavery, for instance — an institution which was actually an economic necessity in non-industrial, non-mechanized societies. But Islam controlled and to some extent softened the cruel system by introducing laws regulating the treatment of slaves, concubinage, the status of the resulting children, and the rights of slaves as human beings, particularly if they chose to be converts to the true religion.

The bulk of the Negro population who suffered from the cruelty of kings and chieftains must have welcomed the new laws. Before the arrival of the Arabs, the best that a Negro captured by a rival tribe could expect was a lifetime of intolerable serfdom or, if he was a young man, castration. The more likely fate was to have a leg chopped off and to be left to die. A number of European travellers in central Africa scarcely a hundred years ago give eyewitness accounts of this treatment of prisoners taken in tribal wars. The Arab traders, with an eye to the Mediterranean markets, considered this practice a waste of manpower; and wherever they converted people to their faith, they introduced a more humane relationship between master and slave.

In addition, the Arabs being themselves a non-industrialized people did not upset the simple economy of Negro life by introducing the machines and paraphernalia of western civilization. But they did bring many needed arts and crafts which enabled

the primitive tribes slowly to improve their standard of living.

The results are obvious throughout Moslem Africa. Islam is a living force with strong political overtones. Once converted to the Mohammedan faith, the African can seldom be converted to Christianity, and most missionaries now openly admit that it is a waste of time to try to proselytize in Islamic countries like Morocco, Algeria, Libya and Mauretania. Wherever Islam has had a few centuries to take root, it gives the impression of being wholly integrated into the spiritual, social and political life of its African converts.

White Faith in a Dark World

From about AD 100 to AD 600 the Christian Church in Africa was one of the great bulwarks of the faith, a church with millions of adherents, hundreds of bishops, and an imposing list of martyrs and leaders. This powerful organization covered the whole of northern Africa from the mountains of Ethiopia to the shores of the Atlantic. Yet it was wiped out almost overnight (except for the Copts) by the conquest of the Arabs from the 7th century onwards. Christianity was unable to obtain a new foothold on the African continent for the next thousand years.

Today, the Christian Church claims a total of 68,208,509 members, of whom 29,100,000 are Roman Catholics, 17,500,000 belong to the Coptic and Eastern Churches, and 21,608,509 are Protestants. The handbooks that provide these statistics warn that they should be accepted with caution, since it is almost impossible to take an exact census in many parts of Africa.

None the less, the figure of over 68,000,000 adherents is an imposing one, as Christian missionaries have only been at work in Africa since about the end of the 15th century, when the Portuguese began their explorations and conquests of the Dark Continent.

One of the objectives of these conquistadores was, in their own words, 'the exaltation of the Catholic faith', and priests invariably accompanied the armies and navies of the invaders. They had considerable success in terms of numbers, for we hear that one Jesuit priest on a short tour through the Congo in 1531 baptized 1,500

Gianni Roghi/Camera Press

Prediction and magic both depend on the belief that things do not happen by accident. The pattern of the crab's movements in the bowl provides an omen of the future

Negroes, using a hose for the purpose. A number of native kings were also persuaded to divorce all their hundreds of wives save one, no doubt with disastrous results to the tribal organization.

But unfortunately for the success of the missionaries, the European slave-traders were simultaneously busy exporting millions of Africans overseas to the New World — an estimated 100,000,000 having been shipped out as slaves between 1441, when the trade began with the arrival of the Portuguese, until 1888 when it officially ended. The black men were not unnaturally puzzled by the assurances on the part of the missionaries that they were children of God on the one hand and slaves of white men on the other. The problem was summed up by a Jesuit priest who worked in the Congo from 1881 to 1887. 'The Negro saw, and compared with his rude intelligence, the teaching and the works', he writes. 'They did not coincide. While the Christian missionary proclaimed the lofty dignity of the child of God by grace, the Christian trader merely counted one more "piece" for his gang.'

However, brave and truly Christian men like Livingstone continued with their work, and they have been followed by thousands of evangelists who have penetrated into every corner of Africa within the last hundred years. Today, through churches, chapels, mission schools and hospitals, the African is in daily contact with Christianity in its more practical form.

Spiritually, Africans tend to adapt Christian doctrine and ritual to their own temperament and way of life. The same process is noticeable in other parts of the world where Negroes meet in Christian worship. Services are more lively, and to some critics smack of far more ancient rites than the Christian ones. Song, dance and religious ecstasy remind us of pagan Africa, showing how deep-seated is the old traditional religion of the forest.

It is not surprising, therefore, that a considerable number of African Christians have broken away from the orthodox European sects to establish churches of their own. At the latest count there are an estimated 4,594 separate sects with a membership of 7,000,000 scattered over 33 states. Perhaps nothing could show more forcefully how deep-rooted the ancient

tribal beliefs are than these breakaway churches, for we see in their organization and ritual definite pagan elements — like 'prophets' and 'prophetesses' (medicine-men and witch-doctors), 'healings' (white magic), dreams and visions (divination) and so on.

Further, these African churches are strongly asserting their 'Africanism' as against the European missionaries' 'white' view of the world. The names of some of these new sects clearly indicate their independence from the Western churches.

Thus we have 'the Church of Jesus Christ on Earth and its leader the Prophet Simon Kimbangu' in the Congo; the 'Church of the Cherubim and Seraphim' and the 'Church of the Lord Aladura' in Nigeria; and the 'Christian Marching Church of Central Africa' which is centred in Rhodesia.

Judging from the ritual of these breakaway sects, Christianity in central and southern Africa will soon have little resemblance to established religion as we know it in the West.

Medicine-Men and Witch-Doctors

These religious officials, who are found throughout pagan Africa, have always been popularly presented in the West as bogymen dressed up in absurd masks, feathers and animal skins, who leap about to the accompaniment of drums. They are alleged to deal in pure mumbo-jumbo in order to hoodwink the superstitious savages who are under their spell.

The facts are that these priests fulfil a useful function in all primitive communities. It is true that their skills, methods, medicines and cures do not conform with modern science. But this is not the fault of the medicine-men. Until European doctors arrived on the scene, the Africans had no alternative but to put their trust in those members of their tribe who had some understanding and some control of the physical and mental ills that afflicted the community. In other words, where malign spirits seemed to play so great a part in men's lives, specialists were needed to study cause and effect; and over the centuries there emerged a class of men who appeared to have some skill and some success in the prevention and cure of sickness. This was the origin and the role of the medicine-man.

In some cases, the medicine-man has developed effective cures based on his knowledge of drugs derived from plants. From centuries of experiment and observation, he has developed a pharmacopoeia for such day-to-day needs as inducing vomiting in the case of poison; purgatives for ridding children of worms; sedatives for quietening hysterics; and potions for chest colds, headaches, whooping-cough, dysentery, snake bite, swellings and stings. If his remedies were all totally ineffective, the medicine-man would quickly lose his standing in the community, as a doctor would in ours.

It must be admitted, however, that the medicine-man also relies for his cures on his special brand of hocus-pocus, as an examination of his 'little black bag' would reveal — a fantastic collection of trivia — bits of bone, wooden figures, lumps of old iron, shells, beads, feathers. A great deal of the medicine-man's treatment is psychological and belongs to the sphere of faith healing. Some Western observers of his methods, particularly in the case of neurotics, go so far as to say that he has as much success as our psychiatrists, if not more.

All European observers agree that the African's obsession with witches is the most evil aspect of paganism. Yet the witch-doctor, like the medicine-man, is not at all the ogre of popular imagination. He flourishes in primitive societies because of the belief that both the spirit and the human world are peopled by two opposing forces — the good and the evil. The witch-doctor is on the side of the good, and his chief job is to protect the community from evil spirits and wicked men.

He must always be ready to cope with mysterious events and diseases, like the death of a chieftain, sudden fevers, barrenness in women, sterility in men, mental disturbances and all other calamities believed to be caused by witches. In such cases his standard practice is to 'smell out' the evil-doer by the ancient and barbarous method of 'trial by ordeal'. This usually consists of administering poison either to the suspects or to their animals, the degree of the resultant sickness being considered infallible evidence of guilt. To make sure there is no mistake, a confession is extorted from the accused by torture. The punishment for witches is death.

Medicine-men and witch-doctors are not the bogymen and ogres of popular imagination

Less barbarous is the witch-doctor's method of predicting the future. For this purpose he has a basket crammed with odds and ends which he shakes about, selecting the topmost object and interpreting the omens from it. A white bone means happiness and laughter in the village. A piece of iron means death. A wooden figure with a black tuft on its head means the appearance of a European who will cause misfortune. For this ju-ju, the witch-doctor speaks in a falsetto voice in mimicry of a European.

The Rain-Maker

Another important function of the witch-doctor is rain-making, which is a wholly religious activity with the Africans as it is a wholly scientific process with us. Agriculture, the harvest, and hence life itself depend upon rainfall. If the rain does not come, the god must be placated by every means in the witch-doctor's power, and elaborate ceremonies are common throughout central Africa for this purpose. They usually follow a general pattern of singing, dancing and praying with the rain-maker working himself into a state of ecstasy in order to invoke the god. If his efforts are successful, he will become a great hero. If they are not, he may be accused of being a witch masquerading as a witch-doctor, for here again, to the primitive African, calamities like drought are always ascribed to black magic. It can easily be seen that the career of rain-maker is a dangerous one; but it is undertaken by the witch-doctor as a *religious* duty, even when he knows that all he can really do to end a drought is to beg the god to send the rain. African rain-making ceremonies, insofar as they depend upon mystical rites, are not radically different from those found in drought-stricken Christian countries. The liquefaction of the blood of St Januarius at Naples, supposed to be an omen of good rains and a bountiful harvest, is an example.

We see, then, that the witch-doctor, cruel or ridiculous though his methods may

In Africa, as in many other parts of the world, the craft of the smith, the controller of fire, is associated with religion and magic. Other members of the tribe are not allowed to see the tools of this smith in Cameroon, West Africa, who is also a priest

Gianni Roghi/Camera Press

Rhythmic drumming and dancing is used to induce states of trance in which spirits take possession of the performers, making a channel of communication between the normal and supernatural worlds
Left African drummer in trance
Right Two Bushman women at a dance to cast out evil spirits
Far right Samburu women in Kenya, dancing to induce trance

Death, Guilt and Sex

The Zulu in the 19th century:

One superstition had a decided effect on military activity. A warrior who killed an opponent stood to develop a serious ailment, culminating in madness, unless he took immediate preventive action. The first step in the cleansing process was to rip open the fallen foe's abdomen with a single slash of the assegai, in order to allow his spirit to escape. The victorious warrior then had to eat and sleep apart from the other men until his cleansing was completed. This involved travel to his home kraal, but before resuming relations with his wives he had to have intercourse with a woman not of his own kraal; this transferred the disease to her in latent form, and she in turn would pass it on to the next man to have intercourse with her. If no woman was available, the warrior could resort to sodomy. The superstition led to short campaigns, since after every battle most of the victorious army at once decamped for home.

Donald R. Morris *The Washing of the Spears*

Jurgen Schadeberg

seem to us, is attempting in his way to serve the community by upholding the good and by waging war on evil.

Rites: Temples, Altars, Sacrifices

Primitive Africans, not knowing how to build in stone, seldom erect formal temples to their gods. As worshippers of nature, they prefer natural shrines, and the 'sacred grove' is universally venerated as the abode of spirits. A typical sacred grove may contain a pool, serpents, a phallic-shaped stone, or a hut which houses clay figures representing tribal gods and ancestors. To these shrines the worshippers bring their offerings of eggs, cowrie shells, little scraps of cloth and even empty bottles. The idea of the sacred grove is, of course, one of the most ancient and fundamental elements of all primitive religion.

There are many curious customs connected with pregnancy and childbirth among the African tribes, since primitive peoples have never understood the physiological processes involved. The phenomenon of birth is, therefore, a mystical event, surrounded by special rites and taboos.

For instance, we find in central Africa the taboo about seeing a pregnant woman up a tree. In such a case, a man is expected to shoot the unfortunate woman. Elsewhere it is taboo for a pregnant woman to sit on a rock, since this will prolong her labour.

Many women bear their children while working in the fields. Difficult deliveries are abnormal, though European doctors report that Negro women bleed worse the nearer their diet comes to that of the white man. On the occasion of their delivery, African women have no desire for the presence of their husband, since 'the child will be ashamed to be born' if a man is present.

When a girl baby is born, the umbilical cord is cut by a hoe to ensure that the female will be a good field worker. The cord of a boy is cut with an arrow to make him a good hunter.

Marriage is a social contract, without any particular religious associations. Prospective husbands are usually more interested in a woman's fertility than in her virginity, since the African's attitudes towards sex are relatively simple and he has few of the

At the death of an Ashanti queen in 1816 more than 3,500 slaves were murdered in her honour...

obsessions or inhibitions of civilized men in this respect.

The African does not make the sharp distinction between life and death that we do. Death is merely another change in status. The deceased is not 'dead' in our sense. He remains a very real presence in the community, continuing to benefit the living by his wisdom and advice.

His soul returns to that reservoir of power which we have called the Supreme Being. His body passes as a ghost to that 'other world' which is common to all African pagan religions. He must, therefore, be provided for in death as in life. Hence he is buried with solemn rites and interred with the necessities of existence — food, clothes, cooking pots and, in the case of the kings and chiefs in olden days, with wives and slaves who were sacrificed for the occasion.

It is reliably recorded that at the death of an Ashanti queen in 1816 more than 3,500 slaves were murdered in her honour. Cases of human sacrifice on the occasion of a king's death are no longer known in Africa today.

Initiation Ceremonies

The purpose of initiation customs, most of which are extremely severe, is to promote unity, co-operation and conformity to the life and law of the tribe. The most typical of them, and one that is almost universal throughout Africa, is circumcision. Nearly all African boys and large numbers of the girls undergo this mutilation, which is regarded as more of a religious ordeal than a surgical operation. The incidence of death as a result of clumsy methods, dirty knives and post-operative severity is considered as evidence of the religious nature of the rite.

The initiation is directed by the village elders and administered by the medicine-man. The boys, aged between 10 and 17, are sent away from the village into a special camp, which they are not allowed to leave for as long as six months. During that time they are considered to be on probation. In fact, they are treated much as young criminals were treated in the bad old days in European prisons, half-starved, whipped for the most trifling offences, crowded into pens, and not allowed to wash until the long

Sudden death from sheer terror is not unknown...where a man discovers an evil fetish in his house

Left Animals have been important in the African approach to the supernatural since the animal gods of ancient Egypt. An ant-eater and an elephant appear on these ceremonial staffs held by the orators or spokesmen of native chiefs in Ghana

Right Young masked girls in Basutoland taking part in pagan initiation ceremonies. These ordeals are sometimes so severe that they cause serious injury or death

ordeal is terminated. These boys, once circumcised, swear blood brotherhood with each other. Those who survive the initiation emerge as full adult members of the tribe, with all the rights and privileges of the elders, including the right to marry.

A number of tribes also practise a similar rite on girls, who are taken to a 'camp' where they undergo clitoridectomy as proof, if they survive, that they are adults and entitled to begin new lives as wives and mothers.

Secret Societies

For the African, membership in a secret society begins at the very outset of his initiation into the tribe with the long circumcision ordeal shared with his companions. From the moment he returns from the camp to his village, the young Negro is involved in secret activities of one kind or another for the remainder of his life.

The principal secret societies seem to be directly related to pagan beliefs in spirits, witchcraft and cannibalism. Typical are the West African Leopard Societies whose members are supposed to transform themselves into the most feared animal of the forest. And like the leopard, they claw their victims to death and devour parts of them. European administrators made many attempts to root out 'leopard men', usually unsuccessfully.

Probably the most widespread and socially accepted secret organizations are those of self-appointed vigilantes engaged in the perpetual war against witches. Nigeria is the home of a secret witch-hunting society which has a curious resemblance to the Ku-Klux-Klan of the United States. The witch-hunters wear tall conical head-cloths to mask their human features and descend on villages at night to root out suspected witches.

Governments in Africa do not approve of secret societies but are powerless to suppress them. They are, on the one hand, an integral part of social life; and on the other, a powerful political force. The importance of such secret societies throughout Africa is typified in the Mau Mau organization of the Kikuyu in Kenya.

White and Black Magic

The distinction between white (good) and black (evil) magic is clear throughout Africa. The former is helpful and protective and falls within the sphere of the medicine-man, who prepares healing potions and of the witch-doctor who wages war on witches; the latter is the monopoly of wizards and sorcerers.

White magic tackles the problems of disease, both physical and mental, of accidents and misfortunes, and of natural disasters like drought. It works in the open, in the light of day, and nearly always entails a public ceremony. Black magic is black because the practitioner, man or woman, works in the dark.

Africans have not the slightest doubt that the evil charms, spells and methods of these wicked people are effective and even lethal.

Sudden death from sheer terror is not unknown in cases where a man discovers an evil fetish like a cracked bone secreted by a wizard in his house; or sees a trail of powder laid around his hut; or finds a clay image of himself pinned down with pegs and pierced with thorns in the head and heart. The psychological effect of such methods is not hard to assess. For where such evil objects are being used against a man, obviously the intention is evil and he is therefore in grave danger.

Whatever else has changed on the continent of Africa, the deep-rooted belief in magic, both white and black, has not. And no one can say how many innocent men and women have been terrified, tortured and even murdered as a result of the African's obsession with witchcraft.

Witches: The Continuing Fear

Africans base their fear of witches on the argument that somebody — some person or spirit — has to be responsible for the inexplicable. Why, for instance, should one man be struck down by lightning and another spared — especially if the dead man is a good hunter, a loving husband, a kind father? We call such a happening 'coincidence'. The African calls it witchcraft. For witches, although they are mortal, have supernatural powers which they invariably use to harm, never to benefit, their neighbours. A few of them are men — wizards or warlocks; but the majority are women, though not necessarily the poor old crones of Western tradition. An African witch can be young, because her evil powers and activities have nothing to do with her age or appearance.

In fact, there is not much she can do about her inherent wickedness, though if she is lucky her supernatural powers will be quiescent, and she will be able to live a normal life as a member of her community. But if she is an active witch, she will be bound to use her evil powers until she is caught by the witch-doctor.

A witch invariably practises her activities at night, at which time she leaves her body and flies off, sometimes as a ball of fire, sometimes as a night bird, to the tops of trees or a secret grove, where witches convene for their nocturnal orgies. These orgies take the form of cannibalism, for witches feed on human flesh and are especially partial to the meat of babies and young

---

Magic, Lightning and Failure

In most cases magic does not attempt the impossible; rain-magicians do not make rain in the dry season, and magic against thieves is made against unknown persons, not named persons. Hence there will be many successes, which are remembered. The failures can be interpreted within the system by invoking other beliefs. Every year before the Trade Winds bring their rains, Zulus call in special magicians to treat their villages against lightning. Most villages are not struck, but if a man's village *is* struck, he will say the magician was bad, his medicines were poor, a taboo was broken, a witch wielded the lightning, or Heaven itself was powerfully determined to strike the village. We reason similarly. If your house, which you have protected with lightning conductors, is nevertheless struck, you may say that the workman was bad, the wires poor, a rule of craft in installation was broken, the charge was too strong. You do not rush to the Royal Society to deny the validity of scientific theory. The total system of beliefs thus allows for a good deal of failure.

Max Gluckman
Custom and Conflict in Africa

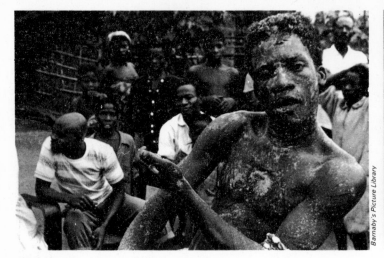

Barnaby's Picture Library

children. The flesh-eating, however, seems to be regarded by many Africans as a mystical rite, a devouring of the 'soul' of the victim, whence the slow withering away of his actual body. The witch-doctor must, therefore, hasten to identify the witch responsible, before she figuratively consumes a vital organ like the heart, lungs or liver. Consequently, if he catches the witch and proves her guilt by the various magical tests employed (trial by ordeal), a quick confession is extorted from her by torture. She is then summarily disposed of.

These ideas of witches and witchcraft are so deeply implanted in the African mind that not even the impact of urbanization, education and technological changes has affected the basic convictions. All Christian missionaries admit that these beliefs constitute the greatest obstacle to genuine conversion. But before witchcraft can be eradicated from Africa, somebody has to explain to the unsophisticated native why some innocent person should be singled out for misfortune. Neither God nor the good spirits would do such a cruel and unjust thing. Therefore, the act must have been the work of an evil power in the person of a witch or a sorcerer.

Medicines, Charms, Fetishes

African medicines are of two kinds: straightforward potions distilled from plants and roots, prescribed in much the same spirit as Western medicines and drugs are prescribed for simple ailments; and magical potions or powders concocted from weird ingredients and prescribed for more difficult cases.

Examples of the latter potions are the various concoctions used for warding off evil spirits or giving a man protection from his enemies. From northern Nigeria comes this secret formula:

Cut off the head of a snake and in it plant the seed of the swamp dock. Bury the head in a grave which must be seven days old. Pour water on it for three consecutive nights. When the plant has grown to a height of three or four feet, go again to the graveyard and strip naked. Pull up the swamp dock and use it as a girdle. If anyone attempts to attack you, the girdle will become a snake that will bite your enemy.

We can see from this formula that medicine

in Africa is more magic than science. Knowing nothing of bacteriology, the medicine-man relies to a great extent on psychology and faith, hence the hundreds of spells and charms, one for almost every contingency. Barrenness is supposedly cured by all manner of ju-jus; pregnancy safeguarded by others.

Men wear antelope horns, animal teeth, gourds, knives, iron bracelets and leather pouches. Both sexes in primitive Africa are often mutilated on the face or body as part of this all-pervasive charm cult. Mutilations, bizarre to Western eyes, take the form of scars, filing down of teeth, extending the lips or ears with discs or rings, and plugging the nostrils.

The more bizarre of these mutilations are seen less and less as Africans adopt the outward trappings of Western culture, including our clothes. But the individual still puts his trust in his favourite ju-ju which he will continue to wear in secret even when he has left his village in the forest for one of the large modern African cities.

Underlying Myths

Together with all religions, paganism has a collection of myths to explain the Creation of the World and the Fall of Man. While each tribe has its own account, the basic theme is nearly always the same — not unlike the Hebrew version as told in the first chapter of Genesis.

God is said to have made man and woman from clay. These two mortals lived for a time in Paradise, from which they were expelled due to some 'original sin'. A Nigerian legend blames the woman for annoying God by striking the sky with her pounding stick. A Congolese story says that her continual nagging became so intolerable that God lowered her down from heaven in a basket.

Whatever the reason for the expulsion from Paradise, man was alienated from God who, in most African myths, retires into his own domain where he grows older and, it appears, more maudlin. For according to some, his old eyes dribble with tears, which become the rain that falls upon the earth below. According to others, he spends a great deal of his time quarrelling with his wife. Claps of thunder are the Great God shouting.

The underlying notion of nearly all

African creation myths seems to be that God and man once lived on earth and conversed together. Then man — or more frequently woman — erred, and the Fall resulted. Ever since then, men have tried to climb back into heaven and have even built towers and ladders for that purpose, but without success. Consequently, when Christian missionaries arrived in Africa with the news that man could be saved through Jesus Christ, the appeal of the new religion was enormous, since no African myth explained how man was to ascend into Paradise.

(See also numerous articles on individual African tribes and ceremonies.)

JAMES WELLARD

FURTHER READING: the following are available in most large public libraries. They provide a good introduction to African religion and have extensive bibliographies: Daryll Forde ed., *African Worlds* (International African Institute, 1954); G. P. Murdock, *Africa, Its People and their Culture History* (McGraw-Hill, 1959); Geoffrey Parrinder, *African Traditional Religion* (S.P.C.K., 1962); Edwin W. Smith ed., *African Ideas of God* (Friendship Press, 1950); James Wellard, *Lost Worlds of Africa* (Dutton, 1967).

Possessed by Gods and Devils

Above left Ewe man of Ghana in trance cuts himself without loss of blood, to demonstrate the power of the war god who has possessed him
Above right Ubangi medicine-man beating a sick girl to drive out devils. Her back is daubed with herbs and warm water. The belief that all diseases are caused by evil spirits which have taken possession of the patient's body is found all over the world: in Africa 'a great deal of the medicine-man's treatment is psychological and belongs to the sphere of faith healing. Some Western observers of his methods, particularly in the case of neurotics, go so far as to say that he has as much success as our psychiatrists ...'
Facing page: above A Nigerian child, and a couple, in trance believing themselves to be possessed by the Holy Ghost
Below Zar priestess in Egypt. The priestess goes into trance to expel certain evil spirits, called zars, from her flock

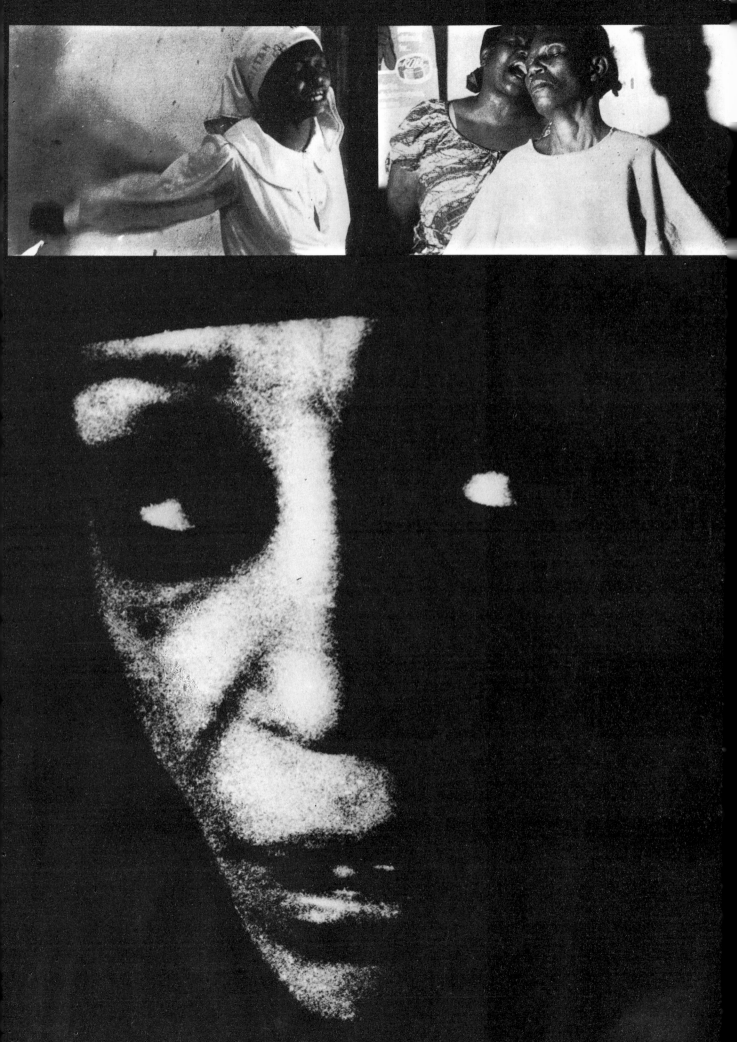

Afro-American Lore

Black America has created a highly influential folk tradition, in music, song, folk tales and legends: some of this tradition was affected in its early stages by white folkways but there are clear strands of African belief, brought by the slaves.

See NEGROES; UNITED STATES OF AMERICA.

Agriculture

Ploughing, sowing, reaping and other agricultural operations, depending for success on the regularity of Nature and the bounty of the gods, are associated with important rituals and myths.

See numerous articles, including CORN; EARTH; FERTILITY; HARVEST; MOTHER GODDESS; SPRING; VEGETATION GODS.

Agrippa gained a reputation in his own day as a great sorcerer who had dealings with demons but his real importance comes from his book Occult Philosophy, *in which he defended magic as the supreme path to the understanding of the world and God*

AGRIPPA

HEINRICH CORNELIUS AGRIPPA von Nettesheim was born at Cologne in 1486 and died in 1535, almost certainly at Grenoble. His books on magic and occultism were widely known and he was both famous and infamous at the courts and universities of western Europe. His real name was Heinrich Cornelis. After the fashion of the time, he latinized Cornelis into Cornelius and awarded himself the bogus noble title of Agrippa von Nettesheim, from the Roman founder of Cologne and the name of a place near Cologne.

Undisciplined, unstable and erratically brilliant, Agrippa was often forced to live by his wits and played at different times the roles of occult scholar and alchemist, faith healer and demonologist, court astrologer, theologian, lawyer and doctor, historian, town orator, financial adviser and secret political agent. He worked now for the Pope and now for his rival the Emperor, switching sides as opportunity offered. He founded secret societies whose members he was not above exploiting. He mixed with royalty at one moment, only to find himself in prison for debt the next.

Agrippa moved restlessly about Europe until his enemies caught him at Grenoble, imprisoned and tortured him, and left him so broken that he only survived his release a matter of weeks. Much of his career is shrouded in mystery and even before his death he had become the centre of stories in which he figured as a master black magician. Goethe drew on some of these stories for the title character of his play *Faust*.

Agrippa's best-known work, *De Occulta Philosophia* (Occult Philosophy) was published in three volumes in 1531 but had been written much earlier, in 1510, possibly during a visit to England. It is based on ideas current at the time: that man is a miniature copy of God, made 'in the image of God' as the Bible says; that the whole

universe, taken together, is God; and that man is therefore a miniature copy of the universe. The universe (the macrocosm or 'great world') is built on the model of man (the microcosm or 'small world') and so, like man, it has a soul. (See also MACROCOSM.)

Agrippa says that everything which exists has a 'soul' or spiritual component, part of the total world soul, which shows itself in the magical properties of herbs, metals, stones, animals and other phenomena of Nature.

For instance, the magnet attracts iron, whoever wears the stone called heliotrope becomes invisible, and a sure contraceptive for a woman is to drink mule's urine every month because mules are sterile.

Agrippa considers the relationship be-

tween matter and spirit in the light of various arts and sciences, including music, geometry and, especially important, astrology. Then he turns to the human soul and its relationship to the body, as revealed by necromancy – the summoning up of the spirits of the dead – and in the religions of all ages.

Agrippa builds up a system of the universe in which everything is part of a great spiritual whole, which is God. Magic is the way of investigating this system but magic is only for the initiated few, for men like Agrippa himself, members – as most of them were, in fact – of secret societies. He does not press the point fully home but his conclusion that man 'containeth in himself all things which are in God' is well in line with

Below left Portrait of Agrippa from the frontispiece of his *Occult Philosophy,* in which he defended magic
Right Agrippa's reputation as a magician lasted long after his death in 1535. In the mid-19th century he is 'the great Agrippa', who punishes three naughty boys by plunging them into his inkwell, in Heinrich Hoffmann's gruesome *Struwwelpeter,* which remained standard children's reading until quite recently

Man and God

Agrippa argues that man contains the whole world and God in himself:

Therefore man . . . hath in himself All that is contained in the greater world, so that there remaineth nothing which is not found even truly and really in man himself, and all these things do perform the same duties in him as in the great world: There are in him the four Elements with the most true properties of their nature, and in him an ethereal body, the Chariot of the soul, in proportion corresponding to the Heaven: There are in him the vegetative life of Plants, the senses of animals, of celestial spirits, the Angelical reason and the Divine understanding . . .

man, being made another world, doth comprehend all the parts thereof in himself but also doth receive and contain even God himself . . . Therefore man is the most express Image of God, seeing man containeth in himself all things which are in God . . . Whosoever therefore shall know himself, shall know all things in himself; especially, he shall know God, according to whose Image he was made.

Occult Philosophy
(17th century translation)

the magical theory that the magician can make himself God and wield the supreme power of God in the universe.

Agrippa's other main work forms a complete contrast to his first one. Written in 1526, at a time when his fortunes were at a low ebb, and published three years later. *De incertitudine et vanitate scientiarum et artium,* (The Uncertainty and Vanity of the Sciences and Arts) maintains that on balance the arts and sciences are harmful to man. Through an encyclopedic review of all the sciences and arts known to him, which provides a mine of information and holds up a fascinating mirror to the culture of the times, Agrippa contrasts the disillusion which all this knowledge brings with the spiritual strength gained through the only sure and beneficial thing on which man can rely — the divinely revealed word of God.

Agrippa is rarely an original thinker and his philosophy is a compilation of ideas from many sources. He ransacked the works of writers ancient and modern for ideas which he adapted in a tremendous display of erudition to his own magical system. But second-hand though much of his occult lore is, it is shot through with moments of genuine poetic utterance.

Of his contemporaries, Paracelsus was far the greater genius but Agrippa, with his virtues and vices, provides the best mirror to the social and intellectual ferment of his time.

D. G. DYER

Agrippa as Black Magician

One of the many stories told about Agrippa was that he went out one day, leaving the key of a secret room in the house with his wife. She foolishly lent it to the lodger, a student, who went into the room and found a huge book of spells, which he began to read. After a while he looked up and found a demon standing in front of him, asking why it had been summoned. He gaped at it in horror and the demon strangled him.

Agrippa returned and, fearing a charge of murder, made the demon restore the student to life for a few hours. The young man was seen walking in the street but when the demon's magic wore off, he collapsed.

Blackie & Sons/Michael Holford

'I have rent the sky, I have befouled it . . . I have befouled the waters, pierced open the earth' is the triumphal cry of Ahriman, the power of evil in the old Persian religion of Zoroastrianism. But his triumph brings its own defeat when evil has eaten up everything it can and has nothing left to destroy but itself

AHRIMAN

FOR 13 CENTURIES Persia has been a Moslem country but before the Moslem conquest the state religion was Zoroastrianism. Ahriman is the Zoroastrian Devil (not the Moslem one, whose name is Shaitan, more familiar to us as Satan). We first hear of Ahriman in the 7th century BC when he plays a significant part in the *Gathas*, or 'Songs', of Zoroaster, the prophet of ancient Persia and the founder of Zoroastrianism.

Zoroastrianism is generally held to be a classical form of religious dualism; that is to say, it holds that the universe is not the creation of one god or principle but of two — a holy power and an evil one. Some religions identify evil with matter, with what Christians call 'the flesh'; but in Zoroastrianism matter, far from being evil, is the creation of the holy god and is therefore in itself entirely good. Evil is a *spiritual* power, negative and destructive: it is called the 'Lie' and is the principle of disruption and death, the adversary of Truth.

In the *Gathas* there is the basic dualism between Truth and the Lie: these are principles which exist in opposition to each other for all time. Of the origin of the Lie nothing is said. Truth, however, is seen as an aspect of the One True God, or Ahura Mazdah, 'the Wise Lord': twice it is called his 'Son'. If the 'Lie' is the principle of evil, Ahriman is its personification. He is not yet the eternal Adversary of the One God but he *is* the eternal Adversary of an entity called the 'Holy Spirit'. From the beginning the two Spirits face each other in implacable hostility. But evidently there was a beginning, for the Holy Spirit, like God the Son in Christian theology, was born of the Father and it appears that he was also the twin brother of the Evil Spirit:

> In the beginning those two spirits who are the well-endowed (?) twins were known as the one good and the other evil, in thought, word and deed. Between them the wise chose rightly, not so the fools. And when these Spirits met they established in the beginning life and death that in the end the followers of the Lie should meet with the worst existence, but the followers of Truth with the Best Mind. Of these two Spirits he who was of the Lie chose to do the worst things; but the Most Holy Spirit, clothed in rugged heaven, (chose) Truth as did (all) who sought with zeal to do the pleasure of the Wise Lord by (doing) good works. Between the two the demons did not choose rightly; for as they deliberated delusion overcame them so that they chose the most Evil Mind. Then did they, with one accord, rush headlong unto Fury that they might thereby extinguish the existence of mortal men.

Above Lion-headed god of Mithraism (a religion which rivalled Christianity). He is believed to be identical with Ahriman, 'the most evil mind', ruler of death and destruction: now in the Vatican Museum
Right Ohrmazd, the principle of truth and light, riding on horseback, tramples on Ahriman's snake-covered head. Zoroastrians believed that the perpetual struggle between the two would end in the triumph of Ohrmazd. On the left a Persian king tramples an enemy. From a rock relief at Naqsh-i-Rustem, Iran

From this passage two facts emerge. First, the two Spirits are twins and since Ahura Mazdah, the Wise Lord, is the father of the Holier, it follows that he must also be the father of the Evil One. Secondly the Evil Spirit, though he is 'of the Lie' must *choose* evil: he is not evil absolutely but becomes evil by choice. Once the choice is made, however, he is no more capable of change than is Satan in the Christian tradition: he is forever committed to the Lie.

Declaration of War

Zoroastrianism is above all the religion of free will. Not only is Ahriman, the Evil Spirit, evil by choice and the Holy Spirit holy by choice, but the One Supreme God, Ahura Mazdah, has also to commit himself — has to choose between Truth and the Lie.

Ahura Mazdah chooses Truth. 'Holy and good Right-mindedness do we choose: let it be ours.' This is a declaration of war on the Lie and those who have chosen the Lie. On both sides this is an irrevocable decision and the battle must be fought to the finish.

In the *Gathas*, then, which are now generally admitted to be the work of the prophet Zoroaster himself, the supreme God

aligns himself with the Holy Spirit against the power of the Lie. The Evil Spirit, on the other hand, chooses to lead the powers of the Lie against the Holy Spirit and therefore against the Supreme God. But though he is the sworn enemy of the Holy Spirit, he is also his twin and must therefore also be the son of his father, the 'Wise Lord'. Would it not, then, be more true to say that the Zoroastrianism of Zoroaster is not a dualism at all but a form of monotheism (belief in one god), at least in the sense that the Wise Lord is the First Cause of all things? In later times the Zoroastrians became divided on this issue.

A purely dualist solution was favoured by the fact that in the course of time the Holy Spirit was simply identified with the Wise Lord. The name Ahura Mazdah took on its later form Ohrmazd, and Ohrmazd and Ahriman then appear as independent principles eternally separate and distinct, eternally opposed. This is the form of Zoroastrianism that we meet with in the Sassanian period, from the 2nd to the 7th centuries AD, when the Persian Empire was revived under the house of Sasan and Zoroastrianism became the official religion of the Empire.

By this time Ahriman had grown in stature: he had become an independent monarch who held undisputed sway in his own kingdom of darkness and death. But the myth of the two eternal twins lingered on because the problem of evil is at the very centre of Zoroastrianism.

Our experience of life seems to show that if God is all-powerful, he cannot be absolutely good — because he lets evil exist; and conversely, if he is absolutely good, he cannot be all-powerful — because he evidently cannot prevent evil. A cut-and-dried dualism absolves God from any responsibility for evil, however indirect, but he necessarily pays for his goodness at the price of his omnipotence. But if the old legend of the primordial twins was retained, and since the Wise Lord and the Holy Spirit were now identified in the single person of Ohrmazd, could it not be that these twin poles of good and evil themselves derived their being from a neutral principle which was the original Unity?

Such a principle some of the Zoroastrian theologians thought they had found in Infinite Time, which was also Infinite Space, and which they called by its ancient name Zurvan. The myth was therefore modified to suit this new theology. It has totally disappeared from the Zoroastrian texts of the period but it is preserved in Christian and other sources and is certainly authentic. The myth which has come down to us is a popular presentation of a far more subtle theological position, which seeks at all costs to preserve both the original Unity and the absolute goodness of God.

Zurvan and the Birth of Evil

The myth says that the great god Zurvan existed before there was anything else. He offered sacrifice so that he might have a son but after a long time he began to wonder whether his hopes were vain. As soon as this thought occurred to him, Ohrmazd and

The Evil Spirit must choose evil:
he is not evil absolutely
but becomes evil by choice

Ahriman were conceived – Ohrmazd because of Zurvan's sacrifice and Ahriman because of his doubt. Zurvan decided that whichever of them came to him first, he would make king.

When Ahriman heard this he ripped the womb open, emerged and advanced towards his father. Zurvan, seeing him, asked 'who are you?' And he replied: 'I am your son, Ohrmazd.' And Zurvan said: 'My son is light and fragrant, but you are dark and stinking.' And he wept most bitterly. And as they were talking together, Ohrmazd was born in his turn, light and fragrant; and Zurvan, seeing him, knew that it was his son Ohrmazd for whom he had offered sacrifice . . . And he said (to him): 'Up till now it is I who have offered sacrifice for you; from now you shall offer

sacrifice for me.' But . . . Ahriman drew near and said to him; 'Did you not vow that whichever of your sons should come to you first, to him you would give the Kingdom?' And Zurvan said to him: 'O false and wicked one, the Kingdom shall be granted you for nine thousand years, but Ohrmazd I have made a King above you, and after nine thousand years he will reign and do everything according to his good pleasure.' And Ohrmazd created the heavens and the earth and all things that are beautiful and good; but Ahriman created the demons and all that is evil and perverse. Ohrmazd created riches, Ahriman poverty.

Ahriman is born of Zurvan's doubt and rules the world, but only for nine thousand years.

This partial solution of the problem of evil which made the Evil One 'prince of this world', if only for a relatively short time, did not in the end satisfy the majority of Zoroastrians. The myth of the primordial twins was set aside and the universe was neatly divided into two separate halves, light and darkness, good and evil.

In the beginning, then, 'the Light was above and the darkness beneath; and between them was the void – Ohrmazd in the light and Ahriman in the darkness. Ohrmazd knew of the existence of Ahriman and of his

Ahriman in an Islamic miniature, as an old man who offers the fatal fruit to the first human beings. The Zoroastrians borrowed the story of Adam and Eve from the Bible

coming to do battle: Ahriman did not know of the existence and light of Ohrmazd.' He soon found out. Roaming around in his dismal kingdom, he reached the upper confines of his realm and saw a ray of light. He longed to get hold of it and to destroy it. Ohrmazd in his goodness offered him peace, which the Evil One summarily rejected, and leapt forward to attack the light. Ohrmazd repelled him, 'laid him low by the pure power of the Law and hurled him back into the darkness.' There he lay unconscious for over three thousand years.

Having foiled this first onslaught, Ohrmazd realized that he must create a bastion between himself and Ahriman, the eternal aggressor. For this purpose he first created a spiritual universe which is an 'ideal' model of the material universe, then the material world itself.

The ideal world was to remain forever free from the pestilential attacks of Ahriman, and at its summit were the souls of the human race. When Ahriman's attack on the material world took place, it was Ohrmazd's plan that these souls should acquire bodies and go to live in the world 'to do battle with Ahriman and the Lie'. But Ohrmazd demands the free co-operation of man, he does not and will not violate the freedom of man's will.

He took counsel with the consciousness and pre-existent souls of men and infused omniscient wisdom into them saying: 'Which seems more profitable to you, whether that I should fashion you forth in material form and that you should strive incarnate with the Lie and destroy it, and that we should resurrect you at the end, whole and immortal, and re-create you in material form, and that you should eternally be immortal, unageing, and without enemies; or that you should eternally be preserved from the Aggressor?' And the pre-existent souls of men saw by that omniscient wisdom that they would suffer evil from the Lie and Ahriman in the material world, but because at the end they would be resurrected free from the enmity of the Aggressor, whole and immortal for ever and ever, they agreed to go into the material world.

For the defeat and destruction of Ahriman, then, man's co-operation is essential. Man must become mortal and accept bodily existence in order in the end to annihilate the force of destruction, death and all evil.

Gayomart & the Lone-Created Bull

Once the souls have consented to this, Ohrmazd creates the material world: he creates the sky, water, plants, the animals in the shape of the 'lone-created Bull', and finally the first man, Gayomart 'shining like the sun'. All is now in readiness and Ahriman prepares his attack. It is devastatingly successful. Each of Ohrmazd's creations he defiles and corrupts; he slays the Bull and mortally wounds Gayomart. His triumph seems to be complete and he cries out in savage exultation:

Perfect is my victory; for I have rent the sky, I have befouled it with murk and darkness, I have made it my stronghold. I have befouled the waters, pierced open the earth and befouled it with darkness. I have dried up the plants and brought death to the Bull, sickness to Gayomart . . . I have seized the Kingdom. On the side of Ohrmazd none remains to do battle except only man; and man isolated and alone, what can he do?

But Gayomart's seed had fallen into the earth as he died and from his seed sprang up a rhubarb plant which split in two to form the first human couple: the human race was therefore saved to continue the long arduous battle against evil which it had already freely accepted.

Moreover, the material universe was bounded by the sky which Ahriman had rent open, forgetting that it was made of 'shining metal that is the substance of steel'. He has entered into his Kingdom but the Kingdom is his prison.

This does not matter so long as he and the vices he has brought in his train can prey upon the creatures of Ohrmazd; but in the end evil which is of its nature destructive, finding that Ohrmazd's creation is slowly slipping from its grasp, will be forced to disrupt and destroy itself.

Ahriman and the demons in the world are like wild beasts that have broken into a garden, but once they have wreaked all the destruction they can, they find that they have been trapped. They make frantic efforts to get out and in doing so they use their own strength against themselves and ensure their own destruction.

The End of the Lie

Ahriman's end comes about when Ohrmazd's creation has become so spiritu-

alized as to escape his power. Pandemonium then breaks out; demon attacks demon, each destroying the other until only Ahriman and Az, the demon of death, greed and lust, are left.

Az turns on Ahriman and threatens to swallow him, and Ahriman is forced to appeal to his eternal enemy to deliver him from his former ally. Ohrmazd will not relent. The Spirit of Obedience destroys the threatening demon Az and Ohrmazd himself lays Ahriman low.

Does this mean that Ahriman is finally annihilated? According to popular mythology, yes: 'he is dragged outside the sky and has his head cut off.' But according to more sophisticated accounts, he cannot be annihilated because he is the *substance* of evil and, according to the particular brand of philosophy the Zoroastrians had adopted, a substance by definition cannot be destroyed.

The technical term used means literally to 'put out of action': 'he is thrown out of the sky through the hole by which he rushed in; and at that hole he is laid low and knocked unconscious so that he will never arise again . . . He will be forever powerless and, as it were, slain and henceforth neither he nor his creation will exist.' With his destruction a new heaven and a new earth are created, all men are resurrected, and those who were confined to hell are released from their torments, and all enjoy perpetual bliss for evermore in the company of Ohrmazd, the Wise Lord.

While he still exists as a conscious being, Ahriman is intensely active in this world. He is the Adversary of both God and man, the Destroyer, the author of death, a 'liar and a deceiver'. His aim is to deceive men as to the true nature of God, and so to bring them to hate Ohrmazd and to love himself. By these means he entices them into hell of which he is the overlord. In fact he is not the equal of Ohrmazd and never really stands a chance because he 'comes to know things too late'. So he is defeated as much by his own stupidity as by Ohrmazd's wisdom and power.

(See also DEVIL; OHRMAZD; MANICHEANS; ZOROASTRIANISM; ZURVAN.)

R. C. ZAEHNER

FURTHER READING: R. C. Zaehner, *The Dawn and Twilight of Zoroastrianism* (Putnam, 1961).

Roger Wood, London

Ahura Mazdah

A name of Ohrmazd, the good god of Zoroastrian religion, twin brother and opponent of the evil god Ahriman, who will eventually be overthrown by Ohrmazd after ruling the world for nine thousand years.
See AHRIMAN; OHRMAZD.

Roger Wood, London

Air

Connected with 'life' and 'soul' in mythology, mysticism and magic, because living creatures cannot survive without it: connected with Maat, the Egyptian goddess of truth, and with the card called the Fool in the Tarot pack: control of breathing is an important technique in yoga.
See BREATH.

Rampant sexuality, torrents of filthy language and extraordinary bodily contortions are nowadays associated with hysteria and other mental disorders. In the 17th century they were put down to possession by devils

AIX-EN-PROVENCE NUNS

IN THE FIRST 25 YEARS of the 17th century the witchcraft delusion in France reached its high peak of intensity. A characteristic feature of the period was the prevalence of cases of demonic possession, involving priests and nuns. Demons were believed to be attacking the human race, obsessing the minds and controlling the bodies of victims into whom they had entered through the bodily orifices. In a reign of terror against every form of demonism, the Inquisitors attempted to withstand what they believed to be a mass assault levelled at Church and society by the Devil, working through his agents – sorcerers and witches.

In the year 1609 signs of diabolical invasion appeared at Aix-en-Provence in southern France, the victim being Madeleine de Demandolx de la Palud, a girl who had a history of emotional instability. In 1605 she had been admitted to the Ursuline convent at Aix but had been returned to the care of her parents, a well-established Provencal family, to recover from the attacks of depression which afflicted her when away from home. Unfortunately she fell under the influence of Father Louis Gaufridi, parish priest of Accoules in Marseilles and a friend of the family.

Like so many clerics of that age Gaufridi was far from ascetic in his way of life. Several women were known to be infatuated with him, and his services as a confessor were in particular demand among the wives of the citizens. The disparity between the ages of Gaufridi and Madeleine (he was 34, she was 13) was apparently no barrier to the priest. His visits became ever more frequent and he was often closeted alone with her for long periods. Inevitably, perhaps, she fell violently in love with him, and possibly he with her.

The story soon reached the ears of Catherine de Gaumer, head of the Ursuline convent at Marseilles, who warned the child's mother of the dangers to which her

Above Last page of the judgement against Louis Gaufridi, with the signatures of those who condemned him for bewitching the nuns of Aix. He was brutally tortured before being dragged on a hurdle through the streets and strangled. His body was then burned
Below Convents were often the scene of psychological disturbances which were put down to the action of devils. From *La Religieuse,* a film about a young girl who is forced into a convent against her will, and becomes the prey of demonic forces

daughter was exposed. A hint was conveyed to the priest Gaufridi that he should cease his attentions at once.

In the following year Madeleine was admitted to the Ursuline convent at Marseilles under the direct control of Mother de Gaumer, to whom she revealed the full story of her relations with Gaufridi, which she said involved sexual intercourse since her childhood.

Hordes of Demons

It was considered wise to move Madeleine out of danger of any further association with the priest by transferring her to the distant convent at Aix. The affair might have been forgotten had not Madeleine, two years later at the age of 16, suddenly fallen victim

to what in contemporary eyes was unmistakably demonic possession. Her body became contorted, hordes of demons surrounded her and in a fit of rage she destroyed a crucifix.

Such states of mind were not uncommon in convents and were usually cleared up very quickly by exorcism – a 17th century equivalent of modern psychiatric treatment. This case proved more obstinate, however, as the Jesuit Father Romillon discovered when his attempts to drive out the possessing demons failed.

Exorcism was an extremely complex ritual, requiring infinite patience and skill. It involved a violent verbal assault on the devil in possession, as well as prayers and the liberal use of holy water. The patient was often made to breathe in noxious fumes, to accelerate the departure of the devil from so inhospitable a habitation.

Father Gaufridi was questioned about his sexual relations with Madeleine and insisted that his association with her had been proper in every respect. Further exorcisms, however, brought from the mouth of the possessed girl damning accusations that Gaufridi was a devil worshipper and had copulated with her since she was 13. The situation at the convent was now getting out of hand, for three more nuns were possessed by devils; and by the end of the year the number had risen to eight. The most severely afflicted of these was Sister Louise Capeau whose ravings and contortions were, if anything, even more hideous than Madeleine's.

Reduced to desperation, Father Romillon sought the aid of one of the most famous witch-hunters of the age, the Grand Inquisitor Sebastian Michaelis. The Flemish exorcist, Father Domptius, was also called in and managed to produce from the mouth of Louise the harsh, blaspheming howls of three terrifying devils, by name Grésil, Sonnillon and Vérin, each of whom was high in the hierarchy of hell.

It was Vérin who accused Gaufridi of causing Madeleine's condition, revealing to the amazed exorcist that no less than 6666 ferocious evil spirits were now in possession of her body, the most eminent of these being the devils Leviathan, Baalberith, Asmodeus, Astaroth and the mighty Beelzebub, second only in authority and infamy to Lucifer himself.

Cannibalism and Perversion

Father Gaufridi was summoned from his parish and ordered to exorcize Louise Capeau. No expert in this highly specialized treatment, he failed miserably and heard himself denounced as a sorcerer and cannibal by the very demons he was struggling to expel. Typical of their denunciations was: Louis Gaufridi outside makes believe that he is a saint; however, inside he is full of iniquity. He feigns to abstain from flesh; nevertheless he makes himself drunk with the flesh of little children . . . whom he has eaten, the others whom he has suffocated and afterwards dug up all cry before God for vengeance upon crimes so execrable.' Gaufridi's reply to the dangerous charge of sorcery was not only curious but also damning, for he said: 'If I were a witch I would certainly give my soul to a thousand devils.' This statement was regarded as a confession of guilt by the Inquisitors, who flung Gaufridi into prison.

Meanwhile, the possessed nun Louise attempted to outdo Madeleine by loudly insisting that Gaufridi had committed every imaginable sexual perversion. The alarmed authorities immediately ordered the priest's rooms to be searched for magical objects or books but were surprised and disappointed to discover nothing of an incriminating nature. They learnt from those who knew him that he was well regarded in his parish. They released him and let him return to his parish. Here he clamoured for the vindication of his good name, and demanded that his accusers be punished.

Throughout this period the nun Madeleine never ceased to be wracked in body and spirit by the tormenting devils and the convent was in complete disarray as the result of her ravings, obscenities and accusations against Gaufridi. Overwhelmed by the 6666 furious demons within her, she sometimes neighed like a horse, while her bones creaked and groaned like a tree bending before a mighty storm.

The case of the possessed nuns of Aix was now rocking France. On the one side stood Gaufridi, insisting upon vindication, and on the other the Grand Inquisitor Michaelis, victor of a thousand battles with Satan, determined to bring Gaufridi to trial. The result was predictable. In 1611 the case came before a court in Aix and although he could not at first have realized it, the priest's doom was sealed.

The behaviour in court of the two nuns, Madeleine and Louise, was by 17th century standards typical of an advanced state of diabolical possession. Madeleine in particular was often demented, shrieking, crying and alternating between violent denunciations of Gaufridi as a devil worshipper and wizard, and the complete retraction of the same accusations. Then she would return to the charge of cannibalism. 'Much he cares for your salt fish or your eggs. He eats good smoking flesh of little children which is brought to him invisibly from the synagogue' (the meeting of the witches). Then she would expose her passion for him by pleading for a single word of kindness from his lips. Sometimes she would be overcome by the wildest

lust and it became painfully obvious to those in court that the girl was experiencing an orgasm before their eyes, her convulsions 'representing the sexual act with violent movements of the lower part of her body'.

In a frenzied reaction against life itself she twice attempted suicide. During the course of the trial it was discovered that she possessed 'Devil's marks' on her body, the secret brands by which Satan recognized his own. These marks later vanished in a mysterious fashion.

The Pact with Satan

Gaufridi was brought into court shattered by the mental anguish and physical tortures he had suffered in prison. His body had been shaved and searched for Devil's marks, three of which had been found as further evidence against him. To complete his misery, a pact with Satan signed in his own blood was produced in court, under the terms of which all women were to be made subject to his will.

It was common knowledge that the pact with the Devil required the surrender of the body and soul of a witch or sorcerer at the end of 20 years. But with true legalistic formality it was conceded that should the pact be written on virgin parchment or pre-

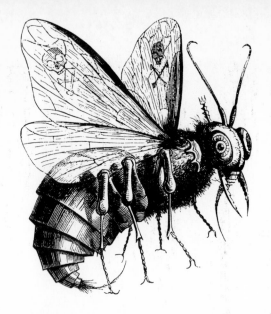

Beelzebub, Lord of the Flies, one of the demons which possessed Madeleine de Demandolx; from the *Dictionnaire Infernal*

pared outside the magic circle, the agreement was null and void. Such contracts between a sorcerer and Satan were sometimes written, and invariably signed, in blood. In return for his soul the sorcerer would receive some specific gift or power. There is no evidence that the agreement afforded any protection against the Inquisition, however, for Satan only rarely intervened on behalf of his dupes. The production of such a document in court was usually sufficient to secure a verdict of guilty from the witch-fearing judges of the 17th century.

Gaufridi's Confession

Gaufridi's confession, which he had signed in prison, reflected the morbid state of mind of his accusers rather than that of the accused. He said he had eaten babies and celebrated a black mass at the sabbath, where he held the rank of Prince of the Synagogue, sprinkling the witches with consecrated wine, and he had exercised his magical power over women. 'More than a thousand persons have been poisoned by the irresistible attraction of my breath which filled them with passion. The Lady of la Palud, the mother of Madeleine, was fascinated like so many others. But Madeleine was taken with an unreasoned love and abandoned herself to me both in the Sabbath and outside the Sabbath . . . I was marked at the Sabbath of my contentment and I had Madeleine marked on her head, on her belly, on her legs, on her thighs, on her feet . . .'

In court Gaufridi strenuously repudiated the confession, declaring it to consist of fantasies in the minds of the Inquisitors, extorted from him by torture. But protest was useless; the signed confession and the pact were sufficient to damn any man in the eyes of 17th century Christians, and Gaufridi was found guilty and condemned to suffer death by fire. He was to be burned slowly over a pyre of bushes instead of logs, so that his anguish would be prolonged. His tormentors gave him no peace, and even after his sentence he was pestered with demands for the names of his accomplices.

Exquisite Torments

On 20 April his spirit weakened and his mind gave way to despair. He cried out to his tormentors that since nobody would listen to the truth he might as well admit everything. On 30 April 1611, with head and feet bare and with a rope around his neck, he went through the official mummery of asking pardon of God. He was handed over to the torturers again to undergo certain exquisite torments that had been reserved for him — the strappado and squassation.

The strappado was an instrument used to interrogate criminals, to obtain confessions and the names of accomplices. With arms tied behind his back, the prisoner was hoisted to the ceiling by means of a pulley, while at the same time heavy weights were tied to his feet in order to dislocate his shoulders. During this ordeal it was custo-mary to apply the thumbscrews. This was regarded as a preparatory torture for the major torment that was to succeed it—squassation. This was an extreme form of strappado. The prisoner was hoisted to the ceiling with huge weights attached to his limbs, which were pulled from their sockets. The prisoner was allowed to hang for a time, when the rope was released, the fall being arrested with a fearful jerk a few inches from the floor, the shock of which was calculated to disjoint every bone in the body. Four applications of squassation were regarded as equivalent to a sentence of death.

After the torture, the shattered body of the still living Gaufridi was dragged on a hurdle through the streets for five hours, escorted by archers. Arriving at the place of execution, the priest was granted the unexpected mercy of strangulation before the fire was lit, thus escaping the ultimate horror of the original sentence. His lifeless body was then burned to ashes.

As if by the influence of a magic charm, the nun Madeleine suddenly became free of her tormenting devils, thus disposing of any doubts that may have remained about Gaufridi's guilt. Madeleine's fellow demoniac, Louise Capeau, was less fortunate, for she was harassed by demons to the end of her days, while the devil mania itself spread to the nuns of other convents before it finally subsided. Madeleine, however, never escaped from the watchful eyes of the Inquisition. Once the taint of diabolic possession had become associated with an individual, no one really knew what infamies the devils might venture on next.

A generation after Gaufridi's execution, the year 1642 saw her defending herself with difficulty against a charge of witchcraft. Ten years later she was prosecuted again and this time, incriminated by the Devil's marks which had reappeared on her body, was sentenced to perpetual imprisonment; she was released, at an advanced age, into the custody of a relative. Still under the eye of the Inquisition, Madeleine de Demandolx found freedom at last in death, in 1670 at the age of 77.

ERIC MAPLE

FURTHER READING: Louis Coulange, *The Life of the Devil* (Knopf, 1929); Eric Maple, *The Domain of Devils* (Barnes, 1966); R. H. Robbins ed. *Encyclopedia of Witchcraft and Demonology* (Crown, 1959).

Split Personality

The phenomena of *involuntary* possession are usually associated with pathological states of body and mind, such as are today diagnosed as epilepsy and hysteria. The main contributing factor, however, is a belief in the ubiquity of spirits, and in their power to enter into and take possession of human beings. The predisposing cause in all these cases is therefore psychical. Students of psychology are now familiar with the way in which within the one personality psychic states may arise which have all the appearance of separate personalities. The character assumed by these apparent alien personalities is largely determined by the nature of the current popular belief. Sometimes they are supposed to be animals. In Japan, for instance, possession by supposed foxes is prevalent. In other cases the possessing entities are held to be the spirits of departed ancestors or other relatives. In yet other instances the possessing entity is regarded as demonic.

Edward Langton
Essentials of Demonology

Jim Bamber

LIFE AFTER DEATH

The history of belief in a life after death runs from Neanderthal man to modern Spiritualism. This article introduces a subject whose many facets will be considered in detail in later entries

AT THE ROOT OF speculation about life after death is the powerful human urge to survive, to stay alive at all costs and against all odds. Beyond everything else, most of us want to live and so we hope that death is not the end. We also want those we love to live. A final parting is intolerable and we look for a reunion beyond death. It is particularly hard to accept that people of great gifts and personality can be snuffed out for ever, and among the early theories about an afterworld is belief in the survival of the powerful, the heroic or the wise.

'I am the resurrection and the life . . .' Christianity has comforted many severed by death from those they loved

Christians and other believers in a supremely good God draw the conclusion that he would hardly have given us life only to erase us again, like writing wiped off a blackboard. And many philosophers have suggested that there is a crucial difference between the body and the mind or the soul. The physical body disintegrates in the grave but we do not think of the mind, the soul, the personality of a man as a physical thing. If it is not physical, how can it disintegrate, and is there any reason for supposing that it ever comes to an end? But recent work on the brain, the nervous system and the

interaction of body and mind has made the distinction harder than ever to draw.

Dead Men's Shoes

Traces of these basic desires and ideas run all through the mass of human beliefs about an afterlife. At least 50,000 years ago, so long ago that man had not yet become fully man, the Neanderthals buried their dead with care. What they believed about life after death we have no way of knowing but that they believed something is suggested by the fact that they did not throw a corpse casually out of the way where it would not offend or annoy. They sometimes tied it with ropes into the position of a foetus in the womb, possibly to help it regain life by becoming an unborn child again,

Axel Poignant

or possibly to stop it from walking and plaguing the living.

The belief that the corpse retains life of some kind lies behind the widespread and very old custom of burying 'grave goods' with it — household objects, ornaments, weapons, food and drink to sustain the ghost through whatever adventures lay before it. In Germany and Scandinavia long ago shoes were placed on the dead man's feet to save him from stumbling painfully barefoot on the paths of the next world.

When those who had been powerful in this life were buried, the grave offerings could be extremely elaborate. The royal tombs at Ur in Mesopotamia, dated c 2250 BC, contained quantities of rich grave goods, including furniture, musical instruments and gambling equipment. Courtiers, soldiers and servants were killed and buried with the rulers they had served in life and as there is no sign of any violence or struggle, they apparently went to their deaths consenting, to continue their accustomed duties in the afterlife.

Besides supplying the dead with equipment they will need in a future life, it is also a worldwide practice to tend their tombs, surviving with us in attenuated form in our habit of putting fresh flowers on graves. This care of graves was originally based on the belief that the dead know what we are doing, are pleased when we do not forget them and will resent it if they are neglected.

The worship of the dead ancestors, the forbears to whom we owe our lives and our environment, and who watch us from the other world, is a vital element in the religions of the majority of people alive at this moment. The ancestors have their shrines in China, they are honoured in Japan, offerings are made to them in India. All over Africa and in simpler societies everywhere, they help or hinder their living descendants.

Heaven and Hell

The oldest religious writings we have, dating from before 2000 BC, are the Egyptian Pyramid Texts, cut into the walls of pyramids at Sakkara. They are rituals, prayers and spells to help a dead pharaoh to reach a happy life in the afterworld. Later the use of these spells spread to the upper classes and then to anyone who could afford them. Some of them enabled the dead man to go to the sky, flying as a falcon or climbing up a ladder. There he would live in eternal happiness with the sun god. Others gave him everlasting life by magically identifying him with the god Osiris, who had himself risen from death.

By contrast in Greece, the Homeric heroes who loved life on earth and revelled in physical action, saw the underworld where the soul had lost its physical body as a wretched place of insubstantial shadows. The powerless dead, squeaking like bats, lived without everything that makes existence worthwhile. When they were offered blood, the carrier of life, they rushed to lap it greedily.

The Homeric underworld was not a hell, a place of punishment for the wicked, but the home of all the dead, good and bad alike. Only a few great heroes escaped death altogether and lived immortal in happy Elysium. But by the 6th century BC the Eleusinian Mysteries had begun to promise a happy life after death to those who were initiated, while those who were not would go down into darkness and gloom. In the *Frogs* of Aristophanes a chorus of initiates sing of the afterworld that awaits them where the lovely meadows lie, where the living waters flow, where the roses bloom and blow.

Jesus promised his followers eternal life: 'I am the resurrection and the life; he who believes in me, though he die, yet shall he live.' He was also quoted as promising a final judgement and the eternal punishment of the wicked in the fire prepared for the Devil and his angels. Much earlier, the Egyptians had believed that each soul is judged after death and rewarded or punished. The Papyrus of Ani, c 1320 BC, has a famous illustration of the dead man's heart being weighed against a feather, the symbol of Truth. In the 4th century BC the judgement of the dead and the punishment of the unjust appears in Plato, and after 200 BC the Jews developed a belief in the fiery torment of the worthless dead in Gehenna, named from a valley outside Jerusalem where the city's rubbish was burned.

Christians built up a terrifying picture of the Day of Judgement, when Christ would return to judge the living and the dead, who would rise from their graves at the sound of the last trump. The righteous would be taken up into heaven and the wicked hurled down to the fiery tortures of hell. The human mind often finds it easier to imagine hell

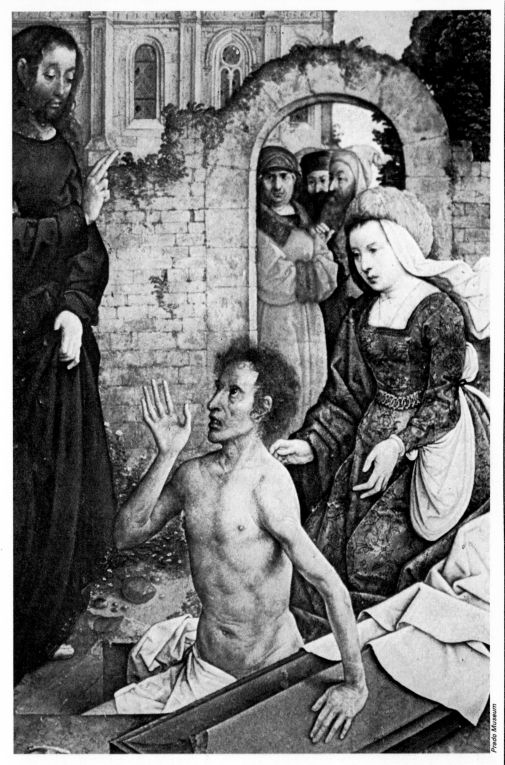

than picture heaven, so much so that in the 12th century Hugh of St Victor said that one of the reasons why the wicked burn is to allow the saved to watch their anguish and so realize more fully the joy of being in heaven. Earlier, a Jewish commentary on Leviticus had described the saved gloating over the damned. But most modern Christians and Jews either reject hell altogether or think of its agony as the pain of separation from God rather than as physical torture.

The joy of the Christian heaven consists of being eternally close to God, and the Christian emphasis is not on mere survival but on resurrection, the lifting up of man to God's level, symbolized by the soaring arches and spires of Gothic churches. Others

have believed in more sensuous paradises, like the Valhalla of the Norsemen where the great god Odin lives on wine and warrior-heroes fight each other enjoyably by day and feast together on pork and mead in the evening. The Mohammedan paradise contained the beautiful black-eyed houris whose embraces delighted the faithful. The Eskimo saw the dead in the splendour of the Aurora Borealis, cheerfully playing football with the head of a walrus.

Reincarnation and Release

Ideas of heaven and hell generally imply the survival of each human soul as a separate individual. The great Indian contribution to beliefs about life after death is that the soul loses its individual personality and becomes

Some psychical researchers maintain that communications coming through genuine mediums point clearly to human survival

part of a larger whole. Most people are re-born to live fresh lives, over and over again, not always as human beings but sometimes as animals, each person falling to a lower form of life or rising to a higher as a result of his actions. Release from the prison of this succession of existences comes through self-denial and austerity, through the techniques of yoga or by following the Eightfold Path of Buddhism. When you gain release, you are merged into a greater and non-personal reality, in Hinduism Brahman, the un-changing, the One which is the basis of all things and which is also the innermost being of each one of us, 'the self within the heart'; or in Buddhism Nirvana, the snuffing out of the flickering flame of life and the attainment of eternal changelessness.

The theory of reincarnation has been adopted by many in the West, including Pythagoras, Plato and the Druids. The 'myth of Er', with which Plato's *Republic* ends, is a story about a man who returned from the dead and described his experi-ences. He and other departed spirits had been told that they were now to choose new lives. Samples of lives were placed before them, 'lives of every animal and of man in every condition', lives mingling fame and infamy, wealth and poverty, health and disease and every other quality in different proportions. The souls chose, some wisely and others not. Plato told the story to drive home the moral that 'a man must take with him into the world below an adamantine faith in truth and right, that there too he

may be undazzled by the desire of wealth or the other allurements of evil . . . but let him know how to choose the mean and avoid the extremes on either side, as far as possible, not only in this life but in all that which is to come. For this is the way of happiness.'

Belief in reincarnation is widespread among primitive peoples, who take it as the obvious answer to the question, where do human souls come from? Australian aborigi-nes say that the soul waits at a certain place, perhaps a waterhole or a rock, for a woman to come by, when it enters her body to be reborn. Some Pacific islanders expected to live a second life as white men and their word for 'ghost' and 'white man' was the same. The general belief in Africa is that many of the dead are eventually reborn again, and far from wanting an Indian 'release' from the burden of earthly existence, the dead are delighted to return to this warm and lively world of human sensation.

The Medium and the Message

Modern Spiritualism is usually dated from investigations of mysterious rappings, sup-posedly made by the spirit of a murdered man, in the house of the Fox family at Hyde-ville, New York, in the late 1840s. Spiritual-ists believe that the dead can pass messages to a medium, who is usually in a state of trance or semi-trance which sets her apart from the normal world. The messages often come to her through a 'control', who is also thought to be a departed spirit but who may in fact be a secondary personality of the medium, acting almost independently of her.

Mediums have produced many other unusual phenomena besides verbal messages, including knocks and rappings, moving lights and moving furniture; bodily appear-ances of spirits and photographs of them.

Camera Press, London

Left Spiritualists believe that they can make contact with their dead relatives and friends. These spiritualists, typical of hundreds all over the country, meet weekly at a flat in north London. The flowers are important, as the departed spirits are said to like them
Right Seeing that in this world the good often suffer while the wicked flourish, people have concluded that there must be rewards and punishments after death. In this medieval Christian picture the damned are being literally carted off to hell, where they are punished with hideous torments.

ectoplasm, a whitish substance exuding from the medium's body and usually turning out to be cheesecloth; and objects which appear to have entered the room supernaturally through the walls or the ceiling.

The history of Spiritualism is riddled with trickery, fraud and folly. The sadly depressing triviality of what so many of the dead have to say, their saccharine piety and the inanities of 'controls' masquerading as Red Indians or children have long been matters of cynical comment. But there have also been some serious mediums whose good faith has never been successfully challenged in spite of rigorous investigation and some striking cases of 'automatic' painting and writing, supposedly inspired by the dead and hard to explain away entirely.

The human tendency to want to believe in life after death makes objective appraisal of the evidence peculiarly difficult but some psychical researchers maintain that communications coming through genuine mediums point clearly to human survival. Others believe that the information contained in these communications probably does not come from the dead but is picked up by the medium, unconsciously, from the minds of living people through extra-sensory perception. This explanation becomes harder to accept when the living people are miles away from the medium at the time and runs into serious difficulties with some very complicated cases in which a communication has been received, not by one medium but in fragments by several different mediums,

making sense only when the fragments are pieced together; especially when the communication contains obscure scholarly allusions, as in the case of the 'cross-correspondences'. These were communications received by a number of mediums early in this century from what appeared to be a group of friends, including F. W. H. Myers and Edmund Gurney, who in life had been prominent members of the Society for Psychical Research.

The uncertainty of the evidence and the difficulty of evaluating it have caused the trend in psychical research towards investigation of ESP and away from the question of survival. Despite all the centuries of enquiry, the verdict on life after death has still to be 'not proven'.

ALCHEMY
A secret language of the mind

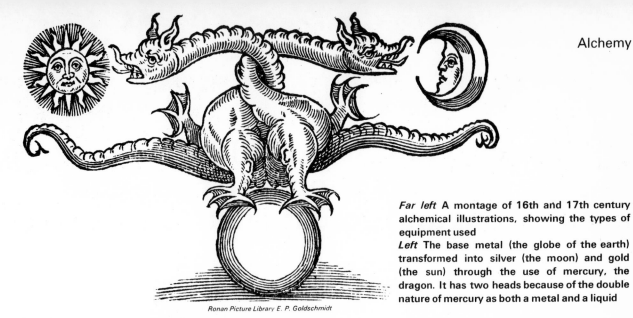

Far left A montage of 16th and 17th century alchemical illustrations, showing the types of equipment used

Left The base metal (the globe of the earth) transformed into silver (the moon) and gold (the sun) through the use of mercury, the dragon. It has two heads because of the double nature of mercury as both a metal and a liquid

The alchemists moved along two tracks, which to most of us will never meet — one mystical and the other chemical. But to the adepts these were one track, for they believed that through the processes of the art they could both perfect themselves as human beings and perfect metals by turning them into gold

IN MOST BOOKS OF REFERENCE, even today, alchemy is described as a false science, based on the pretence that gold could be made from other metals, and it is still often referred to as nothing more than a fraudulent or inefficient forerunner of modern chemistry. These are misguided descriptions, which fail to take account of modern advances in the study of the philosophical and psychological side of the subject.

Alchemy was more an art than a science and its most important and most interesting aim was the spiritual transformation of the alchemist himself. For the mystical alchemists, the art involved both a chemical process and a spiritual process, both the turning of lead into gold and the transmutation of the alchemist from a state of 'leaden' earthly impurity to one of 'golden' spiritual perfection.

The Alchemical Labyrinth

Whether we are ever likely to gain a full understanding of the details of alchemical operations is doubtful, because of the obscure language of so many of the old texts. This obscurity of language and symbolism was deliberate. The medieval alchemist was uncomfortably close to heresy because, for the redemption of his soul from earthly bondage, he relied on his own efforts combined with devout and direct appeals to God, rather than on an approach to the divine through the conventional medium of the Church.

This spiritual position near the brink of heresy was one reason for the cryptic mystery-mongering of alchemical writers. They also recognized that the forces of nature involved in the 'great work' could be dangerous: violent explosions were a frequent accompaniment of alchemical operations. But above all they were determined to keep powerful mysteries of material and spiritual progress out of the hands of the greedy and the unworthy. As Thomas Norton of Bristol puts it in the 15th century, in his

The Mysterious Stone

Comments by alchemists on the Stone which turns all things to gold:

From a man and a woman make a circle, then a square, then a triangle, finally a circle, and you will obtain the Philosopher's Stone.

Michael Maier

But when we marry the crowned king with the red daughter, she will conceive a son in the gentle fire, and shall nourish him through our fire . . . Then is he transformed, and his tincture (tinge of colour) remains red as flesh. Our son of royal birth takes his tincture from the fire, and death, darkness and the waters flee away. The dragon shuns the light of the sun, and our dead son shall live. The king comes forth from the fire and rejoices in the marriage.

Tractatus aureus

Take the serpent and place it in the chariot with four wheels and let it be turned about on the earth until it is immersed in the depths of the sea, and nothing more is visible but the blackest Dead Sea. . . . and when the vapour is precipitated like rain . . . you should bring the chariot from water to dry land, and then you have placed the four wheels on the chariot, and will obtain the result if you will advance further to the Red Sea, running without running, moving without motion.

Tractatus Aristotelis ad Alexandrum Magnum

Out of other things thou will never make the One, until thou hast first become One thyself.

Gerhard Dorn

poem called *Ordinal of Alchemy:*

> This art must ever secret be,
> The cause whereof is this, as ye may see;
> If one evil man had thereof all his will,
> All Christian peace he might easily spill,
> And with his pride he might pull down
> Rightful kings and princes of renown.

To put off the incompetent and unworthy, alchemical writers veiled their directions behind a tangled code of symbols — the dragon, the king, the king's son, the grey wolf, the black crow, the lepers, the lion and the unicorn, the slaughter of the innocents, the royal marriage, the Ethiopian, the tree, the peacock, the bath and many more. An unusually simple example is that the spherical glass vessel used in many alchemical processes was called 'the philosophers' egg', not only because of its shape but because the Philosophers' Stone — which turns all things to gold — would emerge from the vessel just as, in an old legend, the universe was hatched from an egg.

The 'great work' laid a heavy burden on those who attempted it. It involved hours of prayer for God's grace and help, and the reading of almost impossibly difficult books — a task which had to be repeated many times until, slowly and painfully, their hidden meaning loomed up through the mists of symbolism. It meant months and years of toil over stills and furnaces, difficult processes being repeated over and over again with inadequate equipment. The experimenter wound his way through a labyrinth of false starts, misleading side tracks, dead ends, false hopes, disappointments, disasters and delays. Whether we believe that any of the alchemists ever reached the heart of the maze or not, those who devoted themselves body and soul to the art cannot all be dismissed as fools or swindlers.

Gold and the Stone

The aim of alchemy — on the physical plane at least — was to take a raw material (usually but not always a metal) and through long and complicated chemical processes to manufacture the Philosophers' Stone. The Stone had in itself the power of perfecting matter and when a small quantity of it was mixed with other materials, it would turn them into gold.

Many of the descriptions of the Stone do not suggest a real object at all. It is made of

'I answered that it looked yellow, like gold Yes, he said, it is supposed to be gold I took it out and gold it was'

fire and water; it is a stone but not a stone; it comes from God but does not come from God; it grows from flesh and blood, and yet is made of animal, vegetable and mineral; unknown and yet known to everyone, it is generally considered worthless and yet supremely valuable.

These descriptions sometimes refer to the Stone, the final step in the 'great work', and sometimes to the raw material with which the alchemist was supposed to begin, the first step in his operations. This curious meeting of the opposite ends of the work was symbolized by a snake swallowing its own tail, called the Ouroboros. From the spiritual point of view, the snake probably meant that alchemy begins and ends with man: the alchemist himself is the raw material of the work and he is also its final product – himself perfected. *Ars totum requirit hominem*, the alchemists said, 'the art requires the whole man'.

Despite the rhapsodical and paradoxical descriptions of the Stone, which relate to the alchemist himself – the true 'egg' in which the spiritual Stone was hatched – many alchemists evidently believed that the Philosophers' Stone did exist as a real physical object, that it did in reality turn things to gold, and that some great masters of the art had succeeded in manufacturing it.

One adept who was believed to possess the Stone was Paracelsus, the famous 16th century doctor and theorist. An account in a book by Michael Neander published at Leipzig in 1586 *(Orbis Terrae Partium Succinta Explicatio)* describes how Paracelsus heated a pound of mercury in a crucible. When it began to smoke, a piece of wax containing grains of the 'red lion' – the Stone in the form of red powder – was dropped into the crucible. The crucible was covered. Half an hour later, Paracelsus asked what the mixture in the crucible looked like. 'I answered that it looked yellow, like gold. Yes, he said, it is supposed to be gold. I took it out and gold it was. He said: Take it to the goldsmith who lives above the pharmacy and tell him to pay me for it. I did as he said and the goldsmith weighed it. Its weight was a pound minus half an ounce. And he went for money. . . .'

As late as 1782 there was a tremendous sensation in England when James Price, chemist and Fellow of the Royal Society, mixed a white powder with fifty times its own weight of mercury, added borax and nitre, and heated the mixture in a crucible, stirring it with an iron rod. The result was an ingot of genuine silver. When the same operation was repeated with a red powder, the result was genuine gold. However, when the Royal Society insisted that the experiments be repeated before observers chosen by the Society, Price reluctantly agreed and then committed suicide by drinking prussic acid, collapsing and dying before the observers' eyes. It was assumed that he had introduced silver or gold into the crucible through a hollow stirring rod.

Various medals and coins were struck to commemorate supposedly successful transmutations. There is the great medal of 'alchemical gold' dated 1677, for instance, struck for the Emperor Leopold I by the alchemist Wenceslaus von Reinburg; a medal of 1609, showing alchemical symbols for mercury and gold; another struck by the Baron Pfenninger with the inscription *Aurea progenies – plumbo prognata parente*, 'golden progeny begotten by lead as the father', which shows Saturn, the symbol for lead, with the head of the rayed sun (gold); and there are many others.

Gold from Pesos

In 1899 an American scientist performed what appeared to be a successful 'transmutation'. According to the New York *Herald*, Dr S. H. Emmens not only succeeded in making gold but sold his product regularly to the United States Assay Office. But Dr Emmens was no alchemist. His process involved the use of Mexican silver *pesos*, the metal of which already contained some tiny fragment (about one ten-thousandth part) of gold – 'argentaurum gold', as Dr Emmens called it. Still, the process itself might have pleased some ancient alchemists with its very complexity – though its central feature was a special press which hammered the silver powerfully while blowers kept the metal cooled. (Attempts to imitate Emmens's technique failed, usually because pure silver, not Mexican, was used.) Apparently Emmens professed some metallurgical theories that might also have interested alchemists, including the idea that gold and silver are chemically alike – so that silver could turn into gold by a form of long-term *natural* chemical transmutation.

Did Alchemy Work?

Few modern scientists would accept the truth of the alchemists' claim: that metals could be turned into gold through the use of a secret substance, the Philosophers Stone, and with little more equipment than a furnace and a crucible. Most investigators have concluded that the alchemists were either fraudulent or mistaken. That many swindles were perpetrated is beyond any doubt but no serious historian of alchemy has ever tried to explain away *all* the evidence as the product of deliberate deception.

Mercury was a material used constantly in alchemy and it has been suggested that vapours from heated mercury may have caused hallucinations. Alternatively, A. Siggel and other historians of chemistry have pointed out that the alchemists lacked the knowledge of the modern chemist and that for them any yellowish material was virtually the same as gold. In many cases they may have succeeded in giving some other metal a golden colour and then concluded that they had made gold. Alchemical manufacture of silver has been explained by reference to arsenic compounds like orpiment and realgar which together with copper form 'silvery' alloys. Siggel has suggested that the yellow brass which, before zinc was known as a metal, was sometimes made in the Middle Ages by treating calamine and copper, could be taken for the alchemists' 'gold'.

The main objection to these theories is that alchemical gold was apparently quite frequently tested and accepted by professional goldsmiths. Brass might perhaps have been mistaken for gold in antiquity but probably not in Europe of the 15th and 16th centuries.

One powerful argument against the validity of alchemy is the fact that its supposedly successful practitioners do not seem to have become wealthy men. When Paracelsus made his will – signed on 24 September 1541, three days before his death – he made no mention of gold and silver. All he had to leave was books and ordinary personal property, and his most valuable single possession was a silver

Alchemists made important contributions to the study of chemistry. In this 18th century painting by Joseph Wright of Derby, an alchemist named Hennig Brand is shown discovering phosphorus

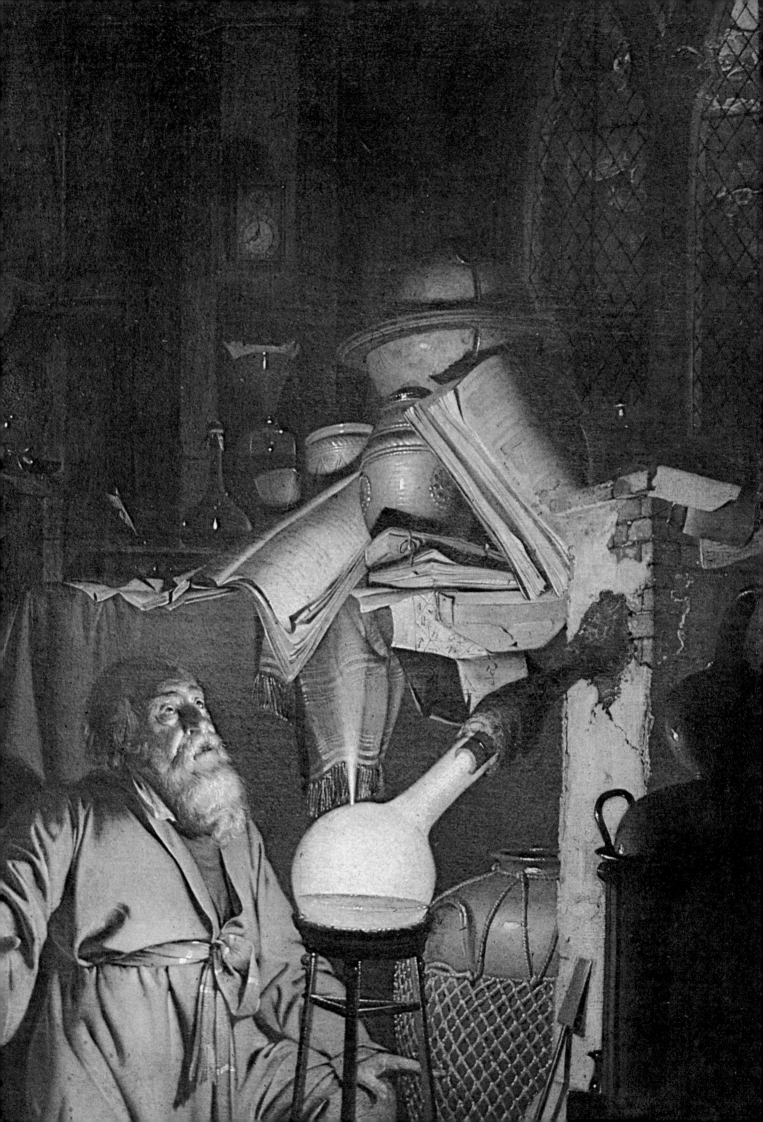

Top left The theme of rebirth was important in alchemical theory: the spiritual rebirth of the alchemist after the killing of his old self, and the rebirth of the base metal after the alchemist had 'killed' it by stripping it of its qualities. The Bath of Rebirth, from the 16th century *Splendor Solis* of Salomon Trismosin *Top right* Another illustration from *Splendor Solis*: the black figure, which has been killed, is rising from the waters of rebirth and beginning to glow with the blood-red hue of new life *Bottom left* Symbols of the materials used in the work, from *Cabala Mineralis*, in the British Museum *Bottom right* More symbols of death and resurrection, from an alchemical MS in the British Museum

To a basis in practical metallurgy, mystical and magical doctrines were added...

chalice decorated with lions' heads and weighing little more than 4 ounces. If Paracelsus could make gold in large quantities, he seems to have been strangely uninterested in doing so.

The 'Parachemical' Explanation

The following suggestion is put forward tentatively for what it may be worth as a possible interpretation of evidence which is confused and inadequate.

Investigators in the field of parapsychology have suggested that there are cases of 'psychokinesis' or 'telekinesis' in which a person causes changes in his physical surroundings — by causing objects to move about, for instance — without physical action on his part and apparently by means of some 'psychic' force. It is possible — though certainly not proven — that the long and intense concentration of an alchemist on his materials and operations, and the physically exhausting toil of the work, might induce an unusual condition of mind in which the alchemist was able to cause abnormal chemical reactions in his materials. These might be termed 'parachemical' reactions, possibly accounting for the alchemist's success.

If this were so, we would expect it to occur only very rarely and for very short periods of time — which would explain the inability of successful adepts to grow rich by making large quantities of gold.

On this hypothesis, the 'grace of God' for which alchemists devoutly prayed and without which, they said, the work could not succeed, would be interpreted as the rare and fleeting psychic ability to cause parachemical change in the alchemist's materials — an ability which in a pious age seemed to be something coming from outside the alchemist himself, as a gift from God. The reading and re-reading of mysterious books, rich in symbolism, might create a suitable mental atmosphere for this ability to show itself, a condition of mental exhaustion and 'headiness', a kind of drunkenness of the imagination. And the same mental condition might also be contributed to by the exhaustion produced by long concentration on the chemical operations themselves, performed over and over again.

In this light, it is not surprising that so many alchemical writers insist that guidance from a 'master', a successful adept, was essential for success. The adept's experience

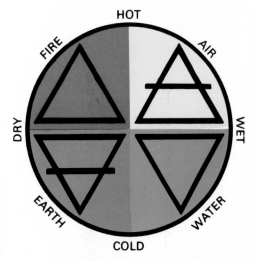

would enable him to guide and train the experimenter in the development and control of parachemical ability.

First Matter and the Elements

Western alchemy originated, so far as we know, in Egypt in the last centuries before Christ. In the East there is another old nucleus of alchemical doctrine in China, connected with Taoist philosophy and magic. The highest stage of enlightenment there was designated by the symbol of the Golden Flower, and there seem to be parallels and even connections with occidental alchemy. But our knowledge of Chinese alchemy is still very limited.

In Egypt, part of the basis of early alchemy came from the metalworking techniques of the ancient world. Craftsmen had reached a high level of competence in producing silver and copper alloys which looked like gold, so much so that a large number of technical terms had to be invented for the numerous different varieties of 'gold' which were available. A papyrus found at Thebes in Egypt, written in Greek c 300 AD, contains recipes for changing the colour of a metal so as to make it resemble gold or silver, and claims that the results will successfully pass all the tests for natural gold or silver. (This emphasis on changing the colour of a metal supports the theory of Siggel and others, mentioned earlier, at least so far as the early history of alchemy is concerned.)

To this basis in practical metallurgy,

mystical and magical doctrines were added, often put out under the name of Hermes Trismegistus, 'thrice-greatest Hermes' — hence the later references to alchemy as the 'hermetic' art or philosophy. Some of the essential alchemical doctrines had been formulated before 400 AD.

It was accepted that all things are made of a primeval substance called 'first matter', the substance from which the world was originally made; with the implication that an experimenter could strip a material of its ephemeral qualities — such as colour, size, shape, weight — and get back to the irreducible element of first matter. He could then add to first matter the qualities needed to make it into gold. And there was the parallel implication that the alchemist could do the same thing in the inner reaches of his own being.

The prevailing theory of the elements, which was worked out by Greek philosophers and reigned almost unchallenged until the 17th century, also gave the alchemists support for their belief that the 'base' metals — lead, copper, tin, iron — could be changed into the precious metals, silver and gold. The theory was that all things are made of differing mixtures of four basic elements — fire, air, earth and water. These elements were the first stage in the 'growth' or development of first matter, and each combined two of the four primary qualities — hot, cold, dry, wet. Fire was hot and dry, earth was dry and cold, and so on (see diagram).

Now, if one of the qualities in an element alters, it changes into a different element. If water (cold and wet) is heated, it changes into air (hot and wet) in giving off vapour. If a burning fire (hot and dry) dies down and loses its heat, it changes into earth (cold and dry) in turning into ashes.

The theory suggested that if alchemists altered the elemental structure of, say, lead, they could turn it into gold. The theory also determined the pattern of their chemical processes, which consisted mainly of heating and cooling, drying and liquefying.

Metals and Planets

Another theory, which was the basis of much alchemical symbolism, connected the seven principal metals with the seven planets known to the ancient world. The two precious metals were assigned to the two most

GOLD	☉	SUN
SILVER	☽	MOON
MERCURY	☿	MERCURY
COPPER	♀	VENUS
IRON	♂	MARS
TIN	♃	JUPITER
LEAD	♄	SATURN

'valuable' heavenly bodies, those which gave light – the sun (gold) and the moon (silver) – and the remaining metals to the other planets (see diagram).

It was assumed that metals developed in the earth, each under the influence of its own planet; that metals had a natural tendency to 'grow' or develop into the noblest and most perfect of their kind – gold; but that owing to the accidents of Nature the metals reached this desirable end all too seldom. The alchemist, theoretically, could take the 'lowest' of metals, lead, and develop or 'ripen' it through the stages of the planetary chain until it became gold. A medieval work called *The Investigation of Perfection* says of alchemy (in a 17th century translation) that 'This *Science* treats of the *Imperfect Bodies* of *Minerals*, and teacheth how to perfect them'. And again there was the parallel with the successive stages in the 'perfecting' of the imperfect alchemist himself.

The Sex of Metals

To the alchemists, metals and minerals were 'alive'. They grew in the belly of the earth and were endowed with sex. A German handbook on metals, printed in 1505, says, 'It is to be noted that for the growth or generation of a metal ore there must be a begetter and some subject capable of receiving the generative action' and that 'in the union of mercury and sulphur in the ore, the sulphur behaves like the male seed and the mercury like the female seed in the conception and birth of a child.'

Underlying these various theories, from very early times, was the belief in the unity of the universe: that all the varied phenomena of the world are parts of one harmonious whole, and that just as a man's body contains his soul or spirit, so the 'body' or matter of the world is permeated by a universal 'spirit'. Alchemists came to believe that the universal spirit could be compressed or concentrated into the marvellous Philosophers' Stone, and that in this form it would 'ripen' or 'perfect' the other metals and turn them to gold.

In the alembic are the three stages of the work, shown by the black, white and red birds; the body, soul and spirit in man; mercury, sulphur and salt in chemistry; the elements which have to be united to produce the Philosophers' Stone

British Museum

The Stone in California

In 1910 Mr and Mrs Richard Ingalese, both occultists and authors, began a study of alchemy in their Los Angeles home – hoping to find the Philosophers' Stone and Elixir.

Years passed while they worked to isolate the 'spirits' or 'virtues' of metals. Then, in 1917, Mrs Ingalese claimed success: she had created the White Stone of alchemy. They tried it on their cat, then on themselves, with what they called 'energizing' effects.

More years passed, then these modern alchemists proclaimed their achievement of the Red Stone. A writer for the *Occult Review* described it as a 'cinnamon-coloured powder', with an intensely bitter taste.

Mrs Ingalese claimed to have performed some astounding cures with the Stones – including the restoration to health of a woman who had been dead for half an hour.

While never claiming the power of rejuvenation for their elixir, the two alchemists did imply that the Stones could arrest the physical deterioration of old age. In 1928, when Mrs Ingalese was 73, she was apparently still slim, graceful and lively.

The Alchemy of the Mind

In this century psychologists, notably C. G. Jung, have begun to pay serious attention to the symbolism of alchemy. Jung's interpretations are often not much easier to understand than the obscure texts of the old alchemists themselves but his investigations focused attention on 'esoteric' alchemy, on the symbolism as opposed to the chemistry, on the alchemist's attempt to perfect himself as contrasted with his attempt to make gold. Though it must be remembered that the two sides of alchemy are like two faces of one coin and cannot properly be separated. The search for the Stone was *both* a search for gold and a search for spiritual perfection.

Jung's approach to alchemy was based on his discovery of alchemical symbolism in the dreams of some of his patients – patients who themselves knew nothing of alchemy at all.

This suggested that the symbols – the snakes, dragons, lions and wolves, the springs and fountains, the trees, castles and the rest – were not chosen deliberately by mystery-mongering authors out to impress the gullible or cheat the greedy, but that they correspond to ageless realities of the human mind.

Jung believed that the 'great work' of alchemy was very close to what he called 'individuation', the shaping of an integrated personality. The symbols are a secret language of the mind, which stand for psychological processes and stages in the 'work'. The alchemist, he explains in *Psychology and Alchemy*, was really exploring not the nature of matter but his own unconscious mind.

The real nature of matter was unknown to the alchemist: he knew it only in hints. Inasmuch as he tried to explore it he projected the unconscious into the darkness of matter in order to illuminate it. In order to explain the mystery of matter he projected yet another mystery – namely his own psychic background – into what was to be explained: *Obscurum per obscurius, ignotum per ignotius!* This procedure was not, of course, intentional; it was an involuntary occurrence.

The Latin words in this quotation are an alchemical maxim, meaning that the obscure is to be explained by the more obscure, the unknown by the more unknown.

Another favourite maxim of the alchemists was *Solve et coagula*, 'dissolve and combine'.

Alchimia vera ('The True Alchemy'), a German work of 1604, says that the whole secret of the art is hidden in these three words. To 'dissolve' refers to the old belief that the characteristics of a substance could be stripped away from it, to reduce it to first matter. To 'combine' meant to build up a new substance by adding desirable characteristics to the first matter.

Psychologically, to dissolve means to break down and destroy surface mental characteristics and attitudes which surround and obscure a man's basic self. To combine is to build up a new integrated personality.

Death and Resurrection

The details of alchemical processes are extremely complicated and vary from one alchemical textbook to another. But, broadly speaking, the first steps in the 'great work' were concerned with the 'dissolution', the reduction of the material in the alchemist's vessel to first matter. The parallel in the mind is the destruction of attitudes, ideas, complexes, of the whole outer shell of the personality.

In alchemy this process ended with what was called *nigredo*, the 'black' stage, when the material in the vessel had been broken down to first matter and was said to be 'dead' and 'putrefying'; when the alchemist himself had subjected his own personality to the fiery furnace of self-questioning and self-doubt, had gone down into his own inner abyss, had apparently destroyed himself and lay 'dead', 'rotting' in the slime which was all that was left of his ideals, his hopes and ambitions, his defences against the outer world.

The nigredo corresponds to the mock death found in many rituals of initiation. Among some primitive tribes, a magician's initiation involves a sleep of 'death' from which he is 'reborn'. In the *Golden Ass* of Apuleius, written in the 2nd century AD, the hero describes his initiation into the mysteries of the goddess Isis and says that he approached the very gates of death but was allowed to return. The alchemists often drew a parallel between the nigredo and the Crucifixion, the death from which Christ rose to new life. (See also INITIATION.)

The remaining processes of the work constituted the 'combination' or 'putting together again' after the 'dissolution' had been completed. After the nigredo came the rebirth, which is described in an alchemical version of the mass written by Nicholas Melchior, astrologer to the king of Hungary in the 16th century. The 'Ethiopian' or black man is the alchemist's material, black in the 'death' of the nigredo.

Then will appear in the bottom of the vessel the mighty Ethiopian, burned, calcined, bleached, altogether dead and lifeless. He asks to be buried, to be sprinkled with his own moisture and slowly calcined till he shall arise in glowing form from the fierce fire. . . . Behold a wondrous restoration or renewal of the Ethiopian!

This is the 'bath of rebirth', in which a new inspiration, a new life, revives the alchemist after the 'death' of the nigredo. From here on, often through a long succession of complicated processes, the alchemist built up the Stone, or the perfected personality, which, to quote Nicholas Melchior, is 'the treasure of treasures, the supreme philosophical potion, the divine secret of the ancients. Blessed is he that finds such a thing'.

We know now that the alchemist's dream of turning base metals to gold is theoretically possible, though the cost of doing so would make the operation distinctly uneconomic. Modern nuclear physics has, in a sense, reached the alchemical goal but has totally neglected its non-material aim of perfecting the soul. When we consider its fell possibilities we may feel that perhaps Thomas Norton of Bristol was not so naive after all. 'This art must ever secret be. . . . If one evil man had thereof all his will, all Christian peace he might easily spill.'
(See also ELIXIR OF LIFE; MERCURY; PHILOSOPHERS' STONE.)

HANS BIEDERMANN

FURTHER READING: Excellent introductory books are C. A. Burland, *The Arts of the Alchemists* (Macmillan, 1968), E. J. Holmyard, *Alchemy* (Penguin, 1968) and J. Read, *Prelude to Chemistry: An Outline of Alchemy* (MIT Press). For C. G. Jung's theories, see his *Psychology and Alchemy* (Princeton University Press, 1967) and *Mysterium Coniunctionis* (Princeton University Press, 1963). For the experiences of a modern alchemist see A. Cockren, *Alchemy Rediscovered and Restored* (Rider, 1940). See also Mircea Eliade, *The Forge and the Crucible* (Allenson, 1956).

Sonia Halliday

ALEXANDER THE GREAT

*One of his eyes was black and the other yellow;
he went to the end of the earth and the bottom of
the sea, and flew through the air; he encountered
all kinds of monsters and wonders*

ALEXANDER THE GREAT led his trium-
phant armies from Greece to the Nile and on
into India, created a vast empire which no
one afterwards could hold together, and
died before he was 33. Deified in his own
lifetime – he was recognized as a god by the
Greek cities of the League of Corinth – his
astonishing career caught the imagination
of succeeding generations. Four hundred
years after his death at Babylon in 323 BC,
the Emperor Trajan, one of the ablest of
Roman generals and rulers, went to ruined
Babylon and offered sacrifice to Alexander's

spirit in the room where he had died.

Legendary stories clustered round
Alexander's memory like limpets on a rock
and were retold for hundreds of years with
alterations, additions and shifts of emphasis. They spread across Europe and Asia,
as far west as Ireland and as far east as Java.

The core of the later romance of
Alexander was a book written in Greek at
Alexandria after 200 BC by an unknown
writer now called pseudo-Callisthenes
(because the book was originally wrongly
attributed to a real Callisthenes). The
original is lost but four revisions of it have
survived. It combined accurate historical
material with legend. Later authors
expanded it and translated it into other
languages, with liberal additions in which

they mingled material from reliable historians with imaginative fictions of their own
invention and fables which were originally
independent of Alexander. They often
quoted letters supposedly, but not really,
written by Alexander or to him.

Just as many of us now cannot feel any
bond of sympathy with a character in fiction
who is too far from our own likeness – a monstrous Martian or Venusian, for instance –
so each different audience for the tales of
Alexander made him one of themselves by
giving him their own setting, nationality and
outlook. As a result, he appears as an object
lesson in the workings of fate, or as a saintly
Christian, though he lived long before Christ;
as a benefactor of the Jews, an emissary of
Allah, a noble medieval knight, or even as an
incarnation of the Devil because he was a
predecessor of the 'Antichrist' Antiochus IV
Epiphanes (see ANTICHRIST).

At the World's End

The extent of Alexander's travels – he only
stopped, reluctantly, when he had invaded
India because his soldiers refused to go any
further east – inspired stories about him
reaching the end of the earth, where paradise, the fountain of life and other marvels
were to be found.

Some of these stories were told to draw a
moral. A Jewish tale in the Babylonian
Talmud (before 500 AD) says that Alexander
reached the earthly paradise but was turned
back at the gate because 'only the just can
enter here'. But he was given a mysterious
ball as a present, which turned out to be an
eyeball. The eye, like Alexander himself, is
restlessly insatiable and tries to encompass
the whole earth and yet only a handful of
dust dropped on it, blinds it and blots it out;
the dust, of course, being death to which all
men come, even the most successful.

This story was expanded later and
appears in the 12th century in the German
Lay of Alexander and the Latin *King
Alexander's Journey to Paradise*. Alexander
and his companions voyaged up the Ganges
(or the Euphrates) till they came to the wall

**Alexander's career of conquest seemed so
superhuman that he became the hero of many
legends *Left* Detail from a portrait in mosaic,
found at Pompeii and now in the Museo
Nazionale, Naples *Right* Alexander examines
the talking tree**

Over the castle's gateway was written, 'No man may go in to the greatest and least treasure of the world until he has passed the night of fear'

of a great city. There was no opening in the wall and they sailed on beside it for three days before they found a small window. When an old man came to the window, Alexander's lieutenants imperiously demanded tribute from the city. The old man sent them away, telling them that the city was the earthly paradise, the home of the blessed, but gave them a stone of mystic meaning as a present for Alexander.

Alexander took the stone back to Babylon, where various wise men puzzled their wits to find its meaning. At last an aged Jew demonstrated with scales that the stone was heavier than any quantity of gold but if a little dust was sprinkled on it, it was lighter than a feather. The stone stood for Alexander himself. The greatest of monarchs in life, a feather would outweigh his value once dusty death had claimed him.

There is the same motif in the story of how, on the way to the Wells of Life, Alexander came to a lake in which was an island, and on the island a castle and over the castle's gateway was written, 'No man may go in to the greatest and least treasure of the world until he has passed the night of fear:' Alexander and his men spent the night beating off the terrifying and dangerous attacks of tigers and dragons, monstrous crabs, lions the size of bulls, mice the size of foxes, foul bats and an army of wild men with six hands each.

In the morning the castle's drawbridge was lowered. They went in and saw a niche in the wall, above which was written, 'The greatest treasure and the least.' In the niche was a rich cushion and on it a stone shaped like an egg. When they looked into the stone they saw everything that a man could desire in this world, and when they weighed it against gold and silver it was heavier than all their treasure. But when a

The extent of Alexander's victorious travels inspired stories about him reaching the ends of the earth, where he found all kinds of marvels. He also explored the limits of height and depth, flying in the air and descending to the bottom of the sea
Above **The first submarine voyage, from a manuscript in the British Museum**
Below **Alexander flies through the air in a basket drawn by six griffons. He was supposed to have steered them by dangling a piece of liver on a spear in front of their beaks**

pinch of dust was put in the other pan of the scales, it outweighed the stone.

Within a hundred years of his death Alexander was already said to have gone to the world's end looking for the water of life which conferred immortality − like other heroes. What was originally a separate story about 'the green one', who drank the water of life and became immortal, was tacked onto Alexander in the tale of his cook. Nearing the world's end, Alexander's expedition came to an area of many wells. The cook washed a dried fish in one of them and the fish came to life and swam away. The cook drank some of the water, became immortal and promptly turned green, the colour of vegetation which is reborn every spring. But the cook could not find the right well again. Furious, Alexander tried various methods of killing him − which all failed because he was immortal − and finally threw him into the sea, where he lives to this day as a sea-spirit.

Marvels and Monsters of the East

. . . we came to a wood inhabited by wild men with faces like ravens. We arrived at the country of the people whose feet are twisted, and next we came to the land of the lion-headed men. We came to a river where we saw a tree which grew from dawn to the sixth hour of the day, and which diminished from the sixth hour until night. We marched through a wilderness and arrived at the ocean. We saw what appeared to be an island and twenty of my men tried to swim there, but beasts came up out of the water and devoured them. We came to the land of the people having their eyes and mouths in their breasts. We saw the 'palm-bird' (phoenix). After a march of 65 days we arrived at Obarkia and saw two birds, one of which spoke Greek.

. . . we marched towards the east and after ten days arrived at a high mountain where a dragon lived. I caused the dragon to be slain. We marched on and arrived at a river called Barsatis and a high mountain. I left my troops and with two hundred of my friends marched to China in 25 days. . . .

From a fabricated letter of Alexander the Great to his former tutor, the philosopher Aristotle, in the Syrian version of pseudo-Callisthenes (translated by E. A. W. Budge).

Fiction from Fact

Many of the stories were built up around a grain of historical truth, like a pearl in an oyster. The daughter of a Scythian king, offered in marriage to the real Alexander but declined with thanks, turned into a Queen of the Amazons who visited the legendary Alexander with amorous intent. Another example is the famous story of Alexander's birth which represented him as the son of a god.

The real Alexander was the son of King Philip of Macedon, in northern Greece, and his queen, Olympias. When he drove the Persians out of Egypt, he was accepted as Pharaoh and when he visited the oracle of the god Ammon in the desert, as Pharaoh he was formally hailed by the priest as 'son of Ammon'. On this basis, apparently, pseudo-Callisthenes and other Egyptian authors said that Alexander was not really the son of Philip of Macedon. They said that the wise Nectanebus, King of Egypt, skilled in magic and astrology, fled before the invading Persians to Macedon and told Olympias that Ammon would father a child on her. Which Nectanebus, pretending to be the god and disguised as a dragon or a snake, duly did.

The legend may not be as cynical as it looks at first sight. Nectanebus may have been meant to be both himself and the vehicle of the god, for in Egyptian belief a pharaoh was a god. Plutarch, who lived at the turn of the 1st and 2nd centuries AD, suggested that the snake came into the story because Olympias was a devotee of Dionysus and danced with snakes twined round her in the frenzy of his worship.

The Sky and the Sea-Bed

Alexander's rule of the West (Greece) as well as the East greatly impressed posterity and may account for the notion that one of his eyes was black (the West, sunset) and the other yellow (the East, sunrise). It may lie behind his Arabic title Dhul-Karnain, 'the two-horned', meaning that he had subdued both horns of the sun, or the horns may be those of Ammon, whose animal was the ram. It was not unfitting to suppose that he had also gone to the limits of height and depth; and so in legend he goes down to the bottom of the sea in a green glass box banded with iron, and flies through the air in a chariot drawn by birds or griffons, which he steered by dangling a bit of liver enticingly on a spear

in front of their beaks.

His other legendary feats included shutting up the savage tribes of Gog and Magog behind a wall of iron and brass, from which they will pour out to wreak havoc in the last day, a story which appears in the Koran. He made love to the beautiful Candace, Queen of Ethiopia (or of India). He tamed a vicious man-eating horse which became his favourite war-charger and which was called Bucephalus, 'the bull-headed', because it had horns. He met and defeated innumerable monsters and peculiar humans, gigantic ants, female cannibals, giants with six heads, dwarves with one leg, horses with the faces of men, men with the faces of dogs, and in the English *King Alysaunder* the people who stand on one foot all day gazing steadfastly at the sun.

In the 14th century Chaucer said that the tales of Alexander were so common 'that every wight that hath discretion hath heard somewhat or all of his fortune', and Philip the Bold of Burgundy took Alexander for his hero and model in much the same way that Alexander himself had conceived a great admiration for the Homeric hero Achilles.

It was not until the revival of classical scholarship in the Renaissance that the legend of Alexander began to go out of fashion and to be replaced by sober history. He has not lasted as well as King Arthur, about whose real life far less is known, and few of the stories about him are still common currency. He wept because there were no more worlds to conquer. When at the height

Detail from the 'Alexander Sarcophagus' of the 4th century BC, showing him in battle wearing a lion's skin, the attribute of the great hero Hercules

of his power he asked the philosopher Diogenes what he could do for him, Diogenes replied, 'You're standing in my light'. He cut the Gordian knot which no one had been able to untie; when he was told that whoever undid the knot would rule the East, he slashed it with his sword. But you may be reminded of him when you hear 'The British Grenadiers' – 'Some talk of Alexander . . .'

FURTHER READING: For the literary history of the legend, see G. Cary, *The Medieval Alexander* (Cambridge Univ. Press, 1967).

Algol

Bright white star in the constellation Perseus, widely regarded as evil because a dark star, which revolves round it, dims its light at intervals and gives it the look of a malevolent winking eye; named Demon's Head by the Arabs, by the Jews Satan's Head and later Lilith, a demoness of the night; classical authors said it was the head of Medusa the gorgon, hanging from Perseus' belt.

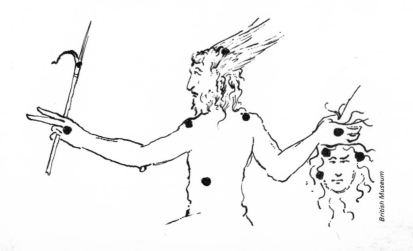

Algonquin myths inspired both Longfellow's Hiawatha and the Brer Rabbit stories. Their religion centred on Nature – the sacred plants, the Great Rabbit, the young girls walking through the fields naked

ALGONQUIN INDIANS

THE ORIGINAL ALGONQUINS, or 'fish spearers', lived in a single village in Canada, in the area now covered by the city of Ottawa. Later on the name was used for a group of small tribes who allied themselves with the French settlers in Canada against the Iroquois Indians. But these tribes were in fact only the northern division of a larger group of Indian tribes speaking similar languages called the Algonquin (or Algonkian or Algonquian) linguistic group. They ranged along the eastern seaboard of North America and inland to the prairies. They did not realize that they were probably all related and were in a constant state of inter-tribal warfare, which was later complicated by the arrival of the white man.

It was the Algonquin-speaking Indians with whom the first European colonists made contact in the 16th century. The Elizabethan painter John White met them in Virginia and left an invaluable collection of paintings of them. The delightful and intelligent princess Pocahontas, who married an English settler, was one of them. They taught the Pilgrim Fathers to grow maize and hunt turkeys. It was one of their women praying to the manitous (spirit beings) in the cornfields who unwittingly set off the Salem witchcraft tragedy (see SALEM). It is an Algonquin mythology which Longfellow used in his *Song of Hiawatha*; the name Hiawatha is that of a great Iroquois Lone Pine chief, but everything else in the narrative poem is Algonquin.

The Holy Fireplace

The Algonquin-speaking tribes practised agriculture and lived more on the produce of their fields of maize and pumpkins than by hunting. Their villages were usually near rivers and good fishing grounds. Houses were made from saplings bent into arches, which supported walls and roofs made from sheets of bark. In some villages each house held a single family, in others there were long-houses, large constructions used by several related families, each of which had an individual screened compartment and, very important, a family fireplace. There was something holy about the fireplace, for all the tribespeople understood that fire was the gift of God and in itself was holy. Thus the family fireplace was something of a shrine. In addition, all food was given by God and all food-plants and animals had a living soul.

All villages included sacred dancing grounds where the shamans (medicine-men) met and conducted ceremonies during which they made contact with the spirit world, putting the living people of the tribe in touch with the world of their ancestors, and with the great spiritual powers. The Algonquins do not seem to have evolved a special type of building as a temple, but many of the

Brompton Studio

'The Flyer', an Algonquin medicine-man, by John White. He is acting out the myth of the bird which carries messages between the earth and the world of spirits. He has a dried bird on his head, and the otter skin at his belt contains magic charms

medicine-men, and women too, were inspired by the spirits in their own houses. Such places were regarded with awe but the power was associated with the shaman and not with the building. The real holy places were usually out in the open air, and they were

---

The Singer of Paradise

Chipiapoos, protector of the Land of the Dead in Algonquin myth, is the gentle singer of *Hiawatha*.

Most beloved by Hiawatha
Was the gentle Chibiabos,
He the best of all musicians,
He the sweetest of all singers.
Beautiful and childlike was he,
Brave as man is, soft as woman,
Pliant as a wand of willow,
Stately as a deer with antlers . . .
All the many sounds of nature
Borrowed sweetness from his singing;
All the hearts of men were softened
By the pathos of his music;
For he sang of peace and freedom,
Sang of beauty, love and longing;
Sang of death, and life undying
In the Islands of the Blessed,
In the kingdom of Ponemah,
In the land of the hereafter.

Longfellow, *The Song of Hiawatha*

---

marked by rings of wooden posts carved with heads of ancestors and spirits, as John White drew them in 1587.

The Shaman and the Great Rabbit

The Algonquin tribes as a whole, in common with most American Indians, believed that human contact with the unseen powers came through specially selected individuals. These shamans, or medicine-men, were usually marked out in childhood by some unusual psychological features. They might experience visions, suffer epileptic fits, show homosexual tendencies, dress in women's clothes, or go away alone for long periods. No doubt a modern psychiatrist could have made them normal citizens; but in their own culture they were regarded as facing difficulties sent from the spirit world to which they were thought to be closer than ordinary men. They were usually sent to study further as assistants to well-known shamans. Sometimes they lost their strange magical personalities when they reached puberty; but many passed on to become shamans of importance.

The medicine-men were intermediaries between the people and the spirits, which at times took possession of them. Each had his own branch of magic in which he specialized, and could call on brother shamans to help on special occasions. They were expected to help the tribespeople in all seasons of difficulty. They healed the sick, found lost property, smelled out evil magic, forecast the weather, and consoled the family in time of death. Yet they never became great chiefs. They were too unstable to be trusted with power, but their ability to see into the future was used to assist a chief to assess the value of his line of policy (see also SHAMAN).

John White painted a picture of a shaman in 'The Flyer'. The shaman is dancing and lifting himself as if he were a bird. His balletic action is magically aided by a dried bird attached to his hair, and no doubt by the magic charms in the otter skin tucked in his belt. But for all the apparent freedom of his dance, he is expressing part of a well-defined group of religious myths. He is the bird which arises from earth, as it did once from the waters before the earth was born. He rises to the world of the manitous (spirit beings) from which he will return bringing messages to the people.

The shaman's dance was most likely a round dance, just as the ceremonial posts around the sacred ground were set in a circle. This was natural enough, because he was concerned with the circuit of the heavens. The circular movement of the zodiac constellations around the sky was seen as a procession of the heavenly powers. Among them moved the sun, who was not only a manitou of power but a form of the strange creator spirit, who was also conceived as a great rabbit or a white hare.

In the more recent days of Negro slavery in America, some of the slaves from Ashanti in West Africa mixed with Indians of Algonquin stock, amalgamated their own spirit Anansi, famous as a trickster, with the Algonquin Great Rabbit, and so produced the world of the Brer Rabbit stories.

Algonquin Indians

The Battle of the Brothers

Important among the Algonquin-speaking tribes were the Cree of the western plains and forests, and their neighbours to the south-east, the Chippewa (Ojibway). Among these tribes, who to a large extent escaped the colonial wars between the Europeans, the old mythology survived long enough to be recorded by scientific scholars. The survival of the old ideas was greatly helped by the secret society of the shamans known as the Midewiwin. This society had a method of writing in pictorial code. Their pictures scratched on birch-bark or painted on skin recorded the legends of the gods, and also notes on tribal history.

It is from the Cree in particular that we have the most complete form of the myths of the Algonquin-speaking peoples. Before the earth existed, there was water, on which a few floating sticks were placed by two ducks. The animals came along and could find no solid ground to stand on; those who could joined the ducks and dived to find more sticks. They made a raft on which they all lived. Then the Great Manitou placed some sand on the raft. It grew and spread out. In his form of a white hare he is still making the raft which is the earth bigger, and you hear him shaking the raft whenever there is an earthquake.

It came about that Death was sent to earth. As different groups of animals died, the Creator took their bodies and changed them so that the first races of men came into being. There was a daughter of the children of men and she gave birth to four divine sons. They were Nanabozo, the protector of humanity; Chipiapoos who died to become the protector of the Land of the Dead; Wabosso the maker of white, the magician and guardian of the North; and Chakekenapok, the flint-stone and maker of fire but also the winter. At his birth, the mother died. Thus Nanabozo and Chakekenapok were destined to be enemies.

It was not until Nanabozo had grown up that the two opposed brothers met. Then they stormed around the earth, wrestling and tearing at each other. The magic deer-horn which Nanabozo carried broke pieces off the body of Chakekenapok. These fell to the ground as pieces of flint, and at last Nanabozo won the battle. Chakekenapok was torn to pieces and thrown over the earth. His bones became the ranges of mountains and his intestines turned into the pleasant grapevines.

There was a power granted by the Creator, which the Indians knew as a kind of magic breath called orenda (see also AIR; BREATH). This was available to all the manitous, who were the secret life of every created thing. Seeing that Nanabozo and his most beloved brother Chipiapoos had become so powerful and beautiful, the various manitous planned to kill them. Nanabozo knew all things and was able to elude the spells, but Chipiapoos walked on the thick ice of the Great Lakes and the manitous used their orenda to melt the ice. So Chipiapoos drowned and the manitous hid his body at the very bottom of the lakes, from which it could never be recovered.

For six years Nanabozo wept for his brother in seclusion, and sent out his magical powers to destroy the manitous. At last they managed to pacify him by sending their orenda in bags to blow on him like soothing winds. They brought peace to his heart. Four of the greater manitous brought mourning gifts, tobacco and magical medicine pouches made from animal skins. Nanabozo welcomed them as messengers of peace and accepted their invitation to visit their sacred house. There they gave him a drink which brought him peace and happiness. Then they combined to form the society of the Midewiwin and Nanabozo was the first initiate. Then they all summoned up the spirit of Chipiapoos and before sending him back to the underworld, they invested him with the powers of Lord of the Land of the Dead and Guardian of Souls.

The Sacred Plants

It was Nanabozo who discovered the magical virtues of the plants which were to be the food of the future human race of our own kind. He stored them in his magical hut, and put the Grandmother of Humanity, Mesakkummikokwi, in charge of them. And so, when the Algonquins picked the food plants, they put a portion of their reaping on the ground as a thank-offering to the ancient lady, 'Our Grandmother'.

Left The Algonquin village of Secoton, from a water-colour by John White. In the foreground are the holy ring of posts and the sacred fire — the place of solemn prayer

Among the Algonquin tribes these and other myths were re-enacted at ceremonies on the anniversary of each event; in other words, at the appropriate seasons for planting maize, hunting deer or reaping the harvest. The timing of the ceremonies was calculated by counting moons and days, so that a practical calendar was linked with the religion. The passage of the stars marked the six great seasons of the year.

The dancing and chanting of the myths at these ceremonies were linked with Nature's progress through the seasons of the year. It was a kind of magical drama. The power summoned up and released in the ceremonies helped the people to enjoy the fruits of earth and protected them from the dangerous powers of manitous.

Agriculture was always a holy thing. The little garden plots which went to make up the village farmland were given magical life by young women silently walking around them on a given night in spring, quite naked and so expressing the fertility of Nature which they were summoning to help them.

• The Indians understood well enough that they depended on the powers of Nature for their existence; if there was a poor harvest, a drought, an earthquake – they died. They taught this to the early white settlers but found that the newcomers rewarded good with evil. Though the tribes detested any central authority, the pressure of the white man who seized their lands drove the chiefs to organize large confederations for resistance. On the eastern seaboard the struggle ended with the war of 1675–6 when the Algonquins were decisively defeated, massacred and driven from their heartland.

C. A. BURLAND

FURTHER READING: C. A. Burland, *North American Indian Mythology* (Hamlyn, 1967); H. B. Alexander, *North American Mythology* (Cooper Square, 1964); F. W. Hodge ed, *Handbook of American Indians North of Mexico* (Scholarly Press, 1968).

Below Religious dance of the Algonquin Indians, by John White. Their holy places were usually in the open and were marked by a ring of wooden posts, carved with heads of ancestors and spirits. The rattles and corn are symbols of fertility

Brompton Studio

Paul Watkins

Allah

Supreme Being of Islam, 'the god', worshipped by the Arabs from before the time of Mohammed, who proclaimed him as the only god; pictorial representation of Allah is forbidden but Arab artists have made graceful play with designs using letters of his name. See ISLAM.

Hallowe'en now is mainly celebrated by children, especially in the United States. But their weird and grinning masks echo the terrors inspired by the old festival of All Hallows, when the dead came out from their graves to walk the earth.

ALL HALLOWS' EVE

ALL HALLOWS' EVE, or Hallowe'en, was originally a festival of fire and the dead and the powers of darkness. It is the evening of 31 October, the night before the Christian festival of All Hallows' or All Saints' Day. All Hallows' Day commemorates the saints and martyrs, and was first introduced in the 7th century. Its date was changed from 13 May to 1 November in the following century, probably to make it coincide with and Christianize a pagan festival of the dead. All Souls' Day in the Roman Catholic calendar is 2 November. It is marked by prayers for the souls of the dead.

It is only in recent times that Hallowe'en has been reduced to a minor jollification for children. Before the coming of Christianity, the pagan Celts in northern Europe held two great fire festivals each year – Beltane on the eve of 1 May and Samhain on the eve of 1 November – to mark the beginning of summer and winter. These dates have no connection with the equinoxes or solstices, or with sowing and reaping, but seem to date from very early times when Celtic society depended heavily on cattle for subsistence. Samhain marked the beginning of winter and was the time when the cattle were brought in from pasture to spend the winter under cover. It was also the beginning of a new year. Because the Celtic day started at sunset, and ran to the following sunset, the festival began on the eve of 1 November.

Sir James Frazer said in *The Golden Bough* that 'throughout Europe, Hallowe'en, the night which marks the transition from autumn to winter, seems to have been of old the time of year when the souls of the departed were supposed to revisit their old homes in order to warm themselves by the fire and to comfort themselves with the good cheer provided for them in the kitchen or the parlour by their affectionate kinsfolk. It was, perhaps, a natural thought that the approach of winter should drive the poor shivering hungry ghosts from the bare fields and the leafless woodlands to the shelter of the cottage with its familiar fireside.'

Bonfires on high hills were a conspicuous feature of the old Hallowe'en rites, though in England they have been gradually transferred to 5 November to mark the arrest of Guy Fawkes. In the 1860s a traveller in Scotland counted 30 fires on the hilltops between Dunkeld and Aberfeldy, each with a circle of people dancing round it. Down to the end of the 19th century fires blazed on the hills in Lancashire on the eve of All Hallows. In north Wales every family built a

bonfire and each person threw into the ashes a white stone which he had previously marked. Prayers were said round the fire and next morning if a stone was missing, it was thought that its owner would die before he saw another Hallowe'en. The same belief existed in the Scottish Highlands and many forms of fortune telling were a traditional feature of Hallowe'en – probably because it was the Celtic New Year's Day and so a suitable time for predicting the events of the coming year.

In Aberdeenshire and Buchan in the 19th century, boys collecting fuel for the bonfire would ask for 'a peat to burn the witches'. When the fire was lit, the boys danced round it shouting 'Fire! Fire! Burn the witches.' When the fire died down, the

> ## Hallowe'en
>
> The mouth of the night is the choice hour of the *Sluath*, the Host of the Dead, whose feet never touch the earth, as they go drifting in the wind till the Day of Burning; of the *Fuath*, the Spirit of Terror that frightens folk out of the husk of their hearts; of the Washer, who sits with herself in the twilight; of the slim green-coated ones, the Water-Horse, and what not. The light that is shadowless, colourless, softer than moonlight, is ever the light of their liking. At the mouth of the night, along the water-courses by ways that at the hour of dusk and of lateness you had best be shunning, you are like to meet them; to west of houses they pass – what to do, who shall say? their ways being nowise human.
>
> Amy Murray *Father Allan's Island*

ashes were scattered and when the last spark had gone out, the cry went up in the ominous darkness 'The devil take the hindmost' and they all ran for their lives. In Wales 'the cropped black sow' would take the hindmost.

From the Wintry Grave

Originally the bonfires were probably meant to provide light and heat which would help the sun through the winter, when it seemed to grow feeble under the attack of darkness and cold. Winter called to mind the chill blackness of the grave and in many parts of Europe – not only in Celtic countries – All Hallows' Eve, as the beginning of winter and the dying time of the old year, was a night when the dead stalked the countryside. Offerings of food and drink were put out for the ghosts. They passed by to the west always, the direction of the dying sun at sunset.

The fairies could also be seen on All Hallows' Eve, moving from one fairy hill to another with the music of bells and elf-horns. They were sometimes identified with the dead. There is an old Irish story about a young man who incautiously stayed out on Hallowe'en and met a band of fairies. They welcomed him cheerfully and gave him wine and fairy gold. But when he looked closely at them, he saw that they were neighbours who had died – some of them many years before. They shrieked with laughter when he recognized them and tried to tug him into their dance. Terrified, he struggled against them until he dropped unconscious. He woke in the morning lying inside a stone circle, his

Hallowe'en, originally a festival of fire and the dead is still celebrated by children and witches *Left* Witches and demons on their way to the sabbath *Right* Sugared skulls at the feast of All Souls, Mexico

Snark International

Jacqueline Mackay

Michael Busselle

arms black and blue with the marks of fingers.

Darker and colder creatures still roamed through the night on Hallowe'en — demons and hobgoblins, witches who straddled broomsticks or shankbones, flew in sieves or egg-shells, or rode on coal-black horses. The fires helped to keep them off and at Balmoral in Queen Victoria's time the effigy of a hideous old witch was ceremoniously burned on a bonfire at Hallowe'en.

The guisers went from house to house, singing and dancing. Their blood-curdling masks and grotesque costumes may have been meant to keep evil at bay or, more likely, were a visible representation of the ghosts and goblins that lurked in the night. The masks have now been transferred to the children who, in the United States, visit the neighbours for the food-offerings which once belonged to the dead — or play tricks akin to the legendary destructiveness of witches and imps abroad on this night.

Witches' Revels

Real witches held high revel on All Hallows' Eve and this was one of the ways in which they preserved pagan customs. The witches of Aberdeen in 1596 said that they had danced round the market cross at midnight on Hallowe'en and also round an old grey stone at the foot of the hill at Craigleuch, the Devil himself playing music before them.

Modern witches have kept up the tradition. In 1963, for instance, a journalist watched the Hallowe'en festivities of a coven

Above left 'Double double toil and trouble, Fire burn, and cauldron bubble': modern witch ceremony with cauldron *Above right* Children with Hallowe'en pumpkin masks or 'Jack o' Lanterns (a name for Will o' Wisp)

of witches at St Albans. The high priestess, naked except for a string of beads and watched by the other 12 members of the coven, drew a circle on the ground with the point of her magic knife. A candle burned in each quarter of the circle, with a fifth candle on an altar in the middle. The reporter did not reveal the details of the ceremony but he did record a remark of the high priestess. 'We are not anti-Christian', she said, 'we just have other means of spiritual satisfaction. It's hard to describe that satisfaction.'

Alligator

Indian tribes of the tropical Americas have many gods in the form of alligators, native to those regions. In North America the Choctaws venerated the alligator and would not kill it; the Chickasaws devoted a major ceremonial dance to it: in the southern United States, alligator teeth were used to help a baby's teething, to cure snake-bite and to keep witches away; an old North Carolina superstition says that alligator gall helps sore eyes, and that the fat can cure cancer. See LIZARDS.

Aloes

Fragrant wood, valued in antiquity for its pleasing smell and recommended in magical textbooks for operations connected with Jupiter and the sun: bitter aloes, made from a different plant, is a purgative drug and therefore a symbol of spiritual cleansing, purgatory.

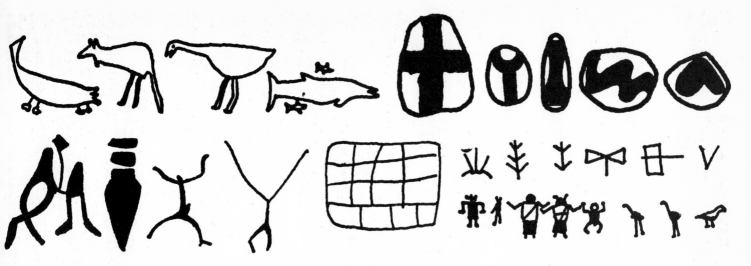

Christian priests forbade the use of runes, the letters of the old northern European alphabet, because the runes were so closely connected with paganism and magic. This is one example of the age-old belief in the magic power of letters, which survives to this day in numerology, a way of telling your fortune from the letters of your name

ALPHABET

WRITING IS a mysterious and magical art. In many primitive and ancient societies it was assumed that the gods must have invented this marvellous method of capturing speech and turning it into visible form. In the ancient world the fact that most people could not write, or read what was written, and that those who could were usually priests, brought writing a reputation as a great hidden wisdom. And its use in inscriptions on the tombs of the dead gave it a close connection with the other world.

The Egyptians called the picture-writing which they carved on the walls of tombs and temples, 'the speech of the gods'. The Greeks called the Egyptian letters hieroglyphics, 'sacred carvings'. Because they came from the gods and because they were pictures, the hieroglyphs had magical powers. One of the basic laws of magic is that a picture or a symbol does not merely refer to the thing it represents; it actually *is* the thing.

In Egypt, for instance, a hieroglyph which was a picture of an animal sometimes had to be used in an inscription inside a tomb. It was feared that it might come alive and the animal might eat the food provided for the dead man, or even eat the dead man himself. To prevent this, the hieroglyph would be left incomplete or drawn in two halves, so that the whole animal could not appear.

The Whispering Runes

The letters used in northern Europe in the early centuries after Christ were also powerful in magic. They were called runes, which comes from a root meaning 'mystery, secret', surviving in the modern German word *raunen,* 'to whisper'. The art of writing with a pen did not reach northern Europe until Christian missionaries brought it with them from the south, and the runes were carved – on wood, tombstones, jewels, swords and armour and other equipment.

Inside a tomb, it was thought runes would keep evil forces away from the dead. Or sometimes they were meant to stop the corpse from creeping out of its grave. They were cut on tombstones to prevent people from destroying them or stealing them for their own dead. Part of an inscription on a Swedish gravestone says, 'This is the meaning of the runes; I hid here magic runes undisturbed by evil witchcraft. He who destroys this monument shall die in misery by magic art.'

This inscription would serve by itself to bring the gravestone's destroyer to a miserable end. Because in magic a symbol *is* what it stands for, to write down a wish or a curse in symbols automatically gives effect to what is written. In the same way, runes were engraved on swords to make them irresistible in battle, as in the case of a sword named Marr – 'may Marr spare nobody'.

The poem called *Havamal* (Utterance of the High One) says that runes have the power to bring the dead to life.

> A twelfth (spell) I know; when I see aloft upon a tree
> A corpse swinging from a rope,
> Then I cut and paint runes
> So that the man walks
> And speaks with me.

To win mastery of the runes, the god Odin had to hang for nine days and nights in agony, transfixed by a spear to the World Tree – the ash Yggdrasill. At the end of this torture, he saw the runes and seized them.

> I peered downwards,
> I took up the runes,
> Screaming, I took them –
> Then I fell back.

Christian priests condemned the use of runes because they were so closely linked with pagan religion and magic. As late as the 17th century in Iceland, people were burnt to death because they had been found in possession of runes.

Development of the Alphabet

The earliest known forms of writing go back to about 20,000 BC and were drawn on the walls of caves. They were pictures of animals and men, and also geometric shapes and patterns. Nobody can be sure of their meaning but they probably had some religious and

Prehistoric forms of writing from Australia, Italy, Crete and California. They were probably connected with magical and ritual practices

magical significance.

Broadly speaking, the development of systems of writing runs through three main stages. First comes *pictographic* writing, which means simply drawing pictures. For instance, ⊙ means 'the sun' and ★ means 'star'. Next, in *ideographic* writing the picture's meaning broadens out to include ideas associated with the thing shown. Now ⊙ means not only 'the sun' but also 'light' and 'heat' which come from the sun, and 'day' over which the sun presides. And ★ means not only 'star' but 'heaven' and 'god'.

The trouble with ideographic writing is not merely that the same picture may have several different meanings, which causes confusion, but also that there are a great many words in any language which cannot easily be represented in pictures. The next step is the introduction of *phonetic* symbols, which stand for sounds.

Phonetic writing can be extraordinarily complicated. There are some 50,000 Chinese symbols which stand for different sounds or combinations of sounds. The triumph of the development of an *alphabet* – a triumph of simplicity – is the use of a small number of symbols which can be used in combination with each other to represent all the words of a language. 'For this achievement,' David Diringer says, 'simple as it *now* seems to us, the inventor, or the inventors, are to be ranked among the greatest benefactors of

Your Name and You

Why were your parents so anxious to select a suitable name for you at the time of your birth? Because your name signifies your destiny and is the medium through which your character is expressed. It is the sign-board or blueprint along your road to success. Your parents sensed this and unconsciously named you for the particular character you were destined by birth to express.

J. Walton-Jordan
Your Number and Destiny

mankind.' It is not surprising that this brilliant invention was regarded long ago as sacred and magical.

Diringer's theory is that all the world's alphabets are descended from one original alphabet, invented somewhere in the area of Syria and Palestine, the land-bridge between the great civilizations of Egypt and Mesopotamia, in the period 1750–1500 BC.

Hebrew and the Making of the World

In the European magical tradition, far and away the most important of all alphabets is the Hebrew, which was written from right to left and had 22 letters, all of which were consonants. No vowels (our a, e, i, o and u) were represented. The same is true of the Phoenician alphabet, from which our own alphabet is descended – by way of the Greek, Etruscan and Latin alphabets.

The importance of the Hebrew alphabet comes from the fact that God is described in the Bible as creating the world by expressing commands in words – 'God said, Let there be light; and there was light.' It was believed that when God pronounced the word *light*, light itself instantly sprang into existence. And all the other things which God made came into existence as he pronounced their names.

But what language did God speak? Obviously, Hebrew. And so the 22 letters of the Hebrew alphabet came to be regarded as supremely powerful magical instruments, through which the whole universe had been created and which contained the secret of the structure of all things.

This belief was one of the basic ideas of the Cabala – a complicated web of mystical and magical theories, originally Jewish but adopted with enthusiasm by non-Jewish occultists from Reuchlin and Agrippa in the 16th century to Aleister Crowley in the 20th (see CABALA).

The cabalistic *Sefer Yetsirah* (Book of Creation) written by an unknown author probably between the 3rd and 6th centuries AD, describes – if its obscure and at times impenetrable language can properly be said to 'describe' anything – how God created the world by means of numbers and letters; the numbers from 1 to 10, and the 22 Hebrew letters, 'the foundation of all things'. God 'drew' the letters, 'hewed them, combined them, weighed them, interchanged them and through them produced the whole creation and everything that is destined to be created.'

In cabalistic theory, God created the world by extending his own being. The *Sefer Yetsirah* says that 'the production of all things from the 22 letters is the proof that they are all parts of one body.' In other words, the letters are parts of 'one body' – the alphabet – and all created things, made by means of the letters, are also parts of 'one body' which is God.

It is not a long step from this to reach the equation, God = the universe = the Hebrew alphabet. Some theorists saw the Hebrew letters as parts or aspects of God, and so they were suitable objects of meditation; for a full understanding of the letters in all their innumerable combinations, if such a thing were possible, would be a full understanding of God. Arranged in different combinations

The Björkertorpstone, Sweden: the inscription in runes, the letters once used in northern Europe, is intended to kill whoever disturbs the monument

with each other, the letters threw light on the complexities of God's nature, and equally on the complexities of the universe.

To magicians, Jewish -and non-Jewish, the Hebrew letters were sources of power – the divine power, which created the world. Magicians employed them in suitable combinations to bring the power of God to bear on summoning up a spirit or reviving a corpse or finding buried treasure.

An example is the powerful word Agla, which is made of the initial letters of the Hebrew phrase *Aieth Gadol Leolam Adonai*, 'Thou art mighty for ever, O Lord.' Agla was written inside magic circles to give the magician mighty power to control spirits, and it had a special use as a fire-extinguisher. If written on a wooden plate and thrown into a fire, it would put the fire out. Medieval German Jews explained this use of the word by expanding it into the initial letters of *Allmächtiger Gott, Lösch' Aus*, 'Almighty God, extinguish it.'

Though the Hebrew alphabet was particularly important, the older principle of the magic of letters applied to other alphabets as well. The word Azoth for mercury, a metal frequently used in alchemy, comes from the Arabic name of mercury, *al zauq*, but some alchemists thought that Azoth was a peculiarly effective name for the metal because it combines the first and last letters

of the Hebrew, Greek, Roman and Arabic alphabets, and so contains the total magic power of all four. (See also GEMATRIA; NAMES.)

Letters and Correspondences

Observing that God had used the 22 Hebrew letters to create the world, some Jewish and Christian commentators succeeded in calculating that in the first chapter of Genesis God is said to create 22 things, obviously corresponding to the 22 letters. Because the letters were used to make everything that exists, they contain all truth and all wisdom, and Josephus, a Jewish historian of the 1st century AD, and other commentators calculated that the Old Testament, through which God reveals himself to men, has 22 books – though it required some ingenious juggling to reach this figure. It is probably not by chance that there are 22 principal cards or 'major trumps' in the Tarot pack, which are also believed to contain all the secrets of the universe. (See TAROT.)

Following up the theory that the universe was created by means of the letters, the *Sefer Yetsirah* classifies various phenomena of the world in terms of the letters they belong to. Twelve of the Hebrew letters are connected with the 12 signs of the zodiac, the 12 months of the year, 12 organs of the body and 12 'properties' (including sight, hearing, smell, sexual love, work, anger, laughter and sleep). Seven other letters are assigned to the 7 directions (east, west, north, south, above, below and the centre), the 7 planets known in antiquity, the 7 days of the week, the 7 'gates of perception' (the mouth, plus two eyes, ears and nostrils), and 7 pairs of opposites (including life and death, peace and war, riches and poverty, wisdom and folly).

The three remaining letters – mem, shin and aleph – are called 'mother letters'. They are connected with 3 elements or basic materials of which everything is made – water, fire and air; with 3 divisions of the universe – earth, heaven and the atmosphere between them; with 3 seasons of the year – winter, summer and spring; and with 3 parts of the body – belly, head and lungs.

A system of 'correspondences' of this kind, a classification of different phenomena into a set number of categories – as if, to use Aleister Crowley's analogy, you had to sort all the papers on your desk into a given number of pigeonholes – may seem peculiar but it is part of the old attempt to make sense of the world by classifying things in groups; just as we classify animals by species for a better understanding of how the animal world works. And there was a logic to the connections. The letter aleph (our A) was not a vowel in Hebrew but a 'breathing', a rough exhalation of breath, and it was natural to connect it with the lungs, which breathe; and with air – especially as it was thought that the shape of the letter came from an Egyptian hieroglyph representing an eagle, the lord of the air. Similarly, mem (our M) was connected with water because the letter was adapted from the Egyptian hieroglyph for 'water'.

In magic, correspondences are used not merely to understand the world but to con

The young Napoleon Buonaparte and the old. Modern numerologists turn your name into a number, which supposedly reveals your character and future. A change of name means a change of destiny, and Napoleon is the stock example. When he dropped the u from Buonaparte, he altered his number from 1, standing for power and victory, to 4 – the number of defeat

trol it. A commentary on the *Sefer Yetsirah* assigns the letter kaph (our K) to Venus, the planet of the love-goddess. A magician who accepted this might wear the letter embroidered on his robes or hold it drawn on parchment in his hand during a magical operation to make a woman submit to him — particularly if he noticed that in Greek k is the first letter of the word for the female genitals, *kteis,* which he would say was no accident. (See also CORRESPONDENCES.)

Fortunes by Letters and Numbers

The idea that the Hebrew alphabet enshrines the secrets of the universe is one basis of modern numerology, a method of analysing your character which depends on the belief that the letters of your name contain the essential truth about you.

You start by turning each letter of your name into a number (using the name by which you normally think of yourself), as follows:

1	2	3	4	5	6	7	8
A	B	C	D	E	U	O	F
I	K	G	M	H	V	Z	P
Q	R	L	T	N	W		
J		S			X		
Y							

These letter-number equivalents come from the Hebrew alphabet, in which the letters also stood for numbers – aleph (A) for 1, beth (B) for 2, gimel (G) for 3, and so on. Noughts are disregarded so that S (shin – 300) is 3, K (kaph – 20) is 2. There is no 9

in the table because the Hebrew letters which stood for 9, 90 and 900 have no equivalents in our alphabet. Numbers for letters like E and X which do not exist in Hebrew are taken from the Greek alphabet, where the letters also stood for numbers.

You write down your name with the number equivalents and add up the numbers. If the total has two or more figures, add these together and go on in this way until you reach a single figure. For example:

W I L L I A M   B A T E S O N
6 1 3 3 1 1 4   2 1 4 5 3 7 5
Total 46 = 10 = 1

The number 1 is the number of the name William Bateson and is supposed to reveal the truth about him.

More details will be given in later articles on the individual numbers which will also consider how each number got its particular meaning but, briefly, if your number is *one* you are thought to be an exceptionally powerful, positive and dominating person, forceful, aggressive and ambitious. You lead, pioneer, originate and invent. Self-reliant, obstinate, authoritative, you tolerate no rivals and you have few close friends. You can be kind and generous to people who do what you want but you have a violent temper and no scruples if opposed. All this follows from the fact that 1 is the number of the god of the Old Testament.

The number *two* – an evil and female number – has all the opposite characteristics. People whose names add to 2 make good subordinates and are obedient, quiet, help-

ful, gentle, modest, tidy and self-effacing. Sweet-natured, sympathetic and persuasive, they are also over-sensitive, easily depressed, unsure of themselves. And since 2 is the number of the Devil, they may be subtly malicious, deceitful and cruel.

Three is traditionally the luckiest of numbers and belongs to fortunate, lively, sparkling, charming people who easily make money and conquests in love, who are talkative and like to show off, highly talented, witty and gay. They tend to be unduly anxious for other people's approval and lavish their efforts wastefully in too many directions. An American numerologist says that they prefer opera to jazz 'when living true to their higher nature'.

Four, number of the earth, is distinctly gloomy and is the number of people who are solid but uninspired, hard-working but plodding, steady, cautious, conservative and conventional. Calm and composed on the surface, there may be violent eruptions of feeling underneath and also severe indigestion (earthquakes). They are excellent organizers and administrators but as 4 is essentially the number of poverty, disappointment and defeat, it does not hold out much prospect of success.

Those whose number is *five* are clever, jumpy, energetic, optimistic, versatile, impulsive, erratic and irresponsible. Nervous and highly-strung, lovers of risks and excitement, they are boastful, quick-tempered, resilient and bouncy. Because 5 is the number of sex (the word 'sex' adds to 5, incidentally), they have lurid love-lives.

Six is the number of well-balanced, peaceful, worthy but rather unexciting people, who are warm-hearted, reliable and kindly but also fussy, gossipy and narrow of outlook. Loyal and affectionate, their interests are centred on home, family and friends; wholesome and conventional, they dislike upsets or rows of any sort. They work hard but rarely have any flair for business.

Seven, one of the great magical numbers, belongs to people who tend to retreat from the world around them into the privacy of their own reflections. Philosophical and scholarly, they value the things of the mind. They are reserved, serious and dignified, self-controlled, uninterested in money and material pleasures, sometimes sarcastic and aloof. Their ideas are profound but they find it hard to explain them and are impatient of contradiction or opposition.

By contrast, *eight* stands for involvement in the rush and bustle of the everyday world, in money-making, business, politics. People with this number have the capacity for great worldly success but also, unfortunately, for disastrous failure. They do not forge ahead easily but by long effort, strain and concentration. They can be hard and selfish, grim and determined on the surface, sometimes wildly rebellious and eccentric underneath.

The Sacredness of Vowels

Nothing therefore is more excellent than the mysteries which ye seek after, saving only the mystery of the Seven Vowels and their forty and nine Powers, and the Numbers thereof. And no name is more excellent than all these (vowels), a Name wherein be contained all Names and all Lights and all Powers.

Pistis Sophia
(3rd century AD)

Referring to the seven Greek vowels; a, short e. long e, i, short o, u and long o.

Finally, *nine* is the number of high achievement, not in the worldly sense but in spiritual matters. It belongs to people who are high-minded, visionary, energetic, emotional and passionate, who have a sense of duty to others and an intense hatred of poverty, old age and ugliness, for themselves

Magical alphabets, frequently made by combining symbols from the Hebrew, runic and other alphabets thought to contain power

and everyone else. Often condemned as wild and impractical, they are easily imposed on and are always falling in and out of love. Cheiro, the celebrated palmist, says in his *Book of Numbers* that 'as a general rule they undergo many operations by the surgeon's knife', which may have something to do with the fact that 9 is the number of initiation, which in primitive societies frequently involves mutilation of the body.

Other Numbers in Your Name

As well as the number given by your whole name, you can add up the *consonants* in it, this number referring to your outer personality and the impression you make on other people. The total of the *vowels* in your name is supposed to indicate the person you are at heart. (Y is treated as a vowel only if there is no other vowel in the word: in Lynn it is a vowel, in Henry a consonant.)

This distinction follows from the fact that written Hebrew and other early alphabets had no vowels. So the consonants which were written down show your outer shell, and the vowels which were concealed your hidden, inner personality.

The same fact probably also accounts for the old idea that vowels are particularly sacred and magical, more mysterious and important than the consonants which everyone could see written down; the 'soul' hidden in the 'body' of the consonants. Gnostic mystical theorists of the eastern Mediterranean area in the early centuries after Christ – Gnosticism originated in the same area and at the same period as the Cabala – were sometimes peculiarly addicted to vowels. One of their versions of the name of God was, in English letters, Iaoouee.

There are many obvious objections to numerology, of which numerologists take little notice. One of them is that all who share the same name also share the same character (including, of course, the same vowel and consonant totals). However, this is modified by the fact that numerologists bring in another number, the Birth Number, which is found by adding up your date of birth thus, 18.5.1935 adds to $32 = 5$.

The Birth Number is meant to show your basic, underlying characteristics, 'the foundation on which you stand' or 'the reason for which you came on earth, how you can develop yourself and what you should do'. This number has to be considered as well as the other numbers in analysing your character. And if you find yourself really fascinated you can take the number of each letter in your name one by one and consider its influence on your life and fortunes.

(See also NUMEROLOGY; and articles on the numbers from ONE to NINE plus ELEVEN; TWELVE; THIRTEEN and FORTY.)

RICHARD CAVENDISH

FURTHER READING: For the history of the alphabet, see David Diringer's fascinating books *The Alphabet* (Funk and Wagnalls) and *Writing: Its Origins and Early History* (Praeger, 1962). For runes, see Ralph W. V. Elliot, *Runes* (Philosophical Library, 1959); for words of power and for numerology, Richard Cavendish, *The Black Arts* (Putnam, 1967).

The Misterious Characters of Letters deliver'd by Honorious call'd the Theban Alphabet.

B C D E F G H I K L M

N O P Q R S T V X Y Z

The Characters of Celestial Writing

Lamed Caph Jod Theth Cheth Zain Vau He Daleth Gimel Beth Aleph

Tau Shin Res Kuff Zade Pe Ain Samech Nun Mem

The Writing call'd Malachim.

Caph Jod Theth Cheth Zain Vau He Daleth Gimel Beth Aleph

Pesh Kuff Zade Pe Ain Samech Samech Schin Tau Nun Mem Lamed

The Writing call'd Passing the River

Lamed Caph Jod Theth Cheth Zain Vau He Daleth Gimel Beth Aleph

Tau Schin Resh Kuff Zade Pe Ain Samech Nun Mem

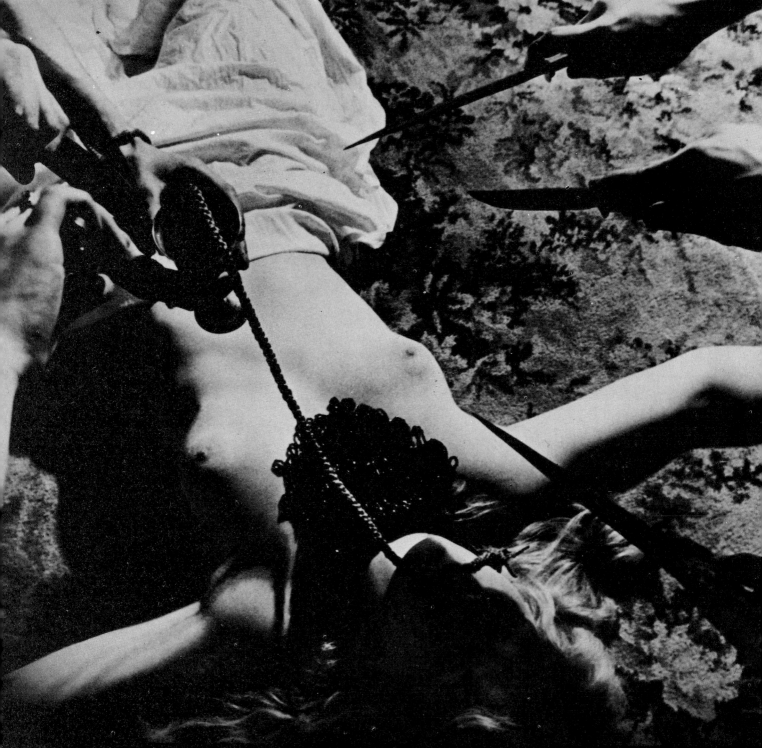

BLACK MAGIC AND WITCHCRAFT

What are the methods of black magic? Is there a difference between a black magician and a witch, or between black magic and white? This introductory article sets the scene for later, more detailed entries

MAGIC ATTEMPTS TO make use of mysterious forces which most people cannot control or do not believe in. A black magician is one who does this for evil purposes. His operations may vary from things as trivial as afflicting somebody he dislikes with lice, as in the case of a Suffolk witch named Alicia Warner who confessed in 1645 that she had sent evil spirits to carry lice to two women, and the court found that 'the said women were lousy according as she confessed'; to much more serious crimes, blighting crops or cattle, or

committing rape or murder, like the Celtic poet-magicians who were said to rhyme their victims to death by declaring literally blistering satires against them, in verses which caused black, red and white blotches to erupt on the skin, followed sooner or later by death; up to the ultimate aim of the master black magician, which is to wield supreme power over the entire universe, to make himself God.

Power is the black magician's guiding light. It is the hope of obtaining limitless power which spurs him on and the exercise of power which he enjoys. He exalts dominance, cruelty, hatred, lust, all fierce and hard emotions. He scorns kindness, humility, sympathy, self-sacrifice. He often takes a double-edged attitude to his own activities,

In a modern witch ceremony, the High Priestess breathes power along an 'umbilical cord' into a wine chalice, which will then be fertilized by the male (phallic) knives. The wine will be shared by the witches at a ritual feast

convincing himself that his intention to kill or terrify is the highest good, while simultaneously wriggling with glee at his own delicious evilness.

Black magicians exist today, as in the past, but they are few and far between. The number of people so dedicated to the total reversal of the accepted rules of the society they live in that they consistently practise evil magic is, and always has been, very small. But human reluctance to believe in a universe so disorderly, and so out of

In the Ozark hill country of the United States the ceremony of initiating a witch ends with the recitation of the Lord's Prayer backwards

...mpathy with man that important events ...n occur by mere chance has caused all ...rts of misfortunes, deaths, illnesses and ...ccidents to be put down to hostile magic. ...nd so the term 'black magic' includes ...oth the practices of a limited number of ...al sorcerers and the much wider field of ...lusory practices and powers attributed to ...n-existent ones.

The Left-Hand Path
...oth in fact and in popular belief, black ...agic is intensely anti-social, rejecting all ...ccepted values and proclaiming their ...pposites. This is why it is connected with ...ings which are inverted, upside down or ...e wrong way round. In the Ozark hill ...untry in the United States the ceremony ...initiating a witch ends with the recitation ...the Lord's Prayer backwards. In southern ...ance in 1932 an American writer, W. B. ...eabrook found a witch-doll, pierced with ...ns and smeared with toad's blood, intended ...kill the person it represented. Near it, ...sting on a Bible, was an inverted crucifix ...which a toad had been crucified head ...wnwards. Today, California hippies who ...bble in Satanism wear inverted crosses.

...Black magic is called 'the Left-Hand Path' ...cause right-handedness is normal and left-...ndedness is reversal of the normal. ...itches were accused of dancing widder-...ins, to the left, at their meetings. And the ...incipal charge against witches in Europe ...s that they had leagued themselves with ...e Devil, the arch-enemy of God and man, ...e rebel against divine order.

...ove **Consecrating oil at a witches' altar on ...e Yorkshire moors. The oil, a descendant of ...e Flying Ointment of the Middle Ages, is used ...day to protect the body against cold during ...tdoor ceremonies**
...low left **Modern ritual magician at his altar**
...low right **Modern witches with the para-...ernalia of their art — horns, wand, candle, ...rd, scourges, censer, pentacle. Similar ...uipment is used by both magicians and ...tches but where the magician seeks to ...minate supernatural forces, witches worship ...em**
...r right **Both black magicians and witches, ...ditionally, are in league with demonic ...wers. The demon of 'ingenious discoveries ...d inventions', Belphegor, from Collin de ...ncy's** *Dictionnaire Infernal*

The same connection between black magic and the reversal of accepted values appears outside the European tradition. Navaho Indians say that to obtain his power a black magician must murder one of his younger brothers or sisters. In the Congo the Logo and Keliko people say that witches walk about upside down. The night-dancing witches of the Kaguru in Tanganyika go about naked, walk on their hands, and turn their black skins white with ashes.

Black magicians, real or alleged, are sexually perverse and they love dirt. In Africa the Azande associate lesbianism and witchcraft together. The Mandari of the Sudan say that wizards practise homosexuality, bestiality with cows and goats, and intercourse with immature girls. Filthy habits, like urinating in drinking vessels, are taken as indications that a person is probably a witch.

In Europe witches were accused of committing every conceivable sexual perversion, with each other and with demons, and the words 'filthy', 'lewd', 'unnatural', appear constantly in descriptions of their behaviour. Aleister Crowley, a notorious modern black magician, performed perverse rituals with male and female partners, and took a marked interest in human excrement.

Incest and cannibalism are commonly associated with black magic, and so are unnatural relationships with animals. European witches were said to keep familiar spirits in animal form which sucked their blood; like Jane Bussey of Kent, accused in 1583 of keeping three imps, 'Pygine resembling a mole; Russell resembling a grey cat; and the other called Dunsott resembling a dun dog, with intent that she might enchant and bewitch as well men as beasts and other things.'

The Methods of Black Magic
The black magician's armoury is as various as his purposes. He may use his own inner powers; spirits, demons or forces outside himself; mimicry, words and gestures; 'weapons' like the magic wand or circle, and 'medicine'.

Evil 'medicines' can be herbs or plants, roots, parts of the bodies of animals or human beings, pieces of paper with words or symbols written on them, knots tied in string, stones or almost anything else. Whether they are actually harmful, like

---

snake venom, or outwardly harmless but having sinister associations, like bat's blood, they are not usually expected to work by themselves. There must be a link between the charm and the victim. His nail clippings or hair, clothes he has worn or bedding he has slept in, are believed to retain a connection with him, so that what is done to them is done to him. Less tangible things, a man's name or his shadow or his footprint, are also linked with him and can be used against him. An 18th century French magical textbook, the *Grimorium Verum*, says that you can harm an enemy by driving into his footprint a nail from an old coffin, saying *Pater noster upto in terra*, which seems intended to mean 'Our father which art on earth', parodying the Lord's Prayer and appealing to the Devil. You hammer the nail well in with a stone and say, 'Cause harm to so-and-so until I remove you.'

If there is no natural link with the victim, the magician must create one. He may bury an evil charm in a path where his victim will walk over it, or he may hide it in his enemy's house. When the Roman general Germanicus died in 19 AD, under the floor and behind the walls of his room were found human bones, rotting bits of dead bodies and pieces of lead, the metal of death, with his name written on them.

Another way to create a link is simply to state in words that one exists. The witches of North Berwick tried to kill James VI of Scotland by making a doll to represent him and roasting it in a fire. But first they passed it from hand to hand, saying 'This is King

James the Sixth . . .'

Language is one of the great magical weapons because of the belief that words, infused with the power of the magician's will, make what is stated in the words happen: 'Cause harm to so-and-so until I remove you.' In some societies, as among the Maori in New Zealand, the words which make a particular spell work must never be altered. The correct forms are handed down from magician to magician, for the words themselves have magical force. But more often a magician is free to vary his incantations and he experiments with them until he finds those which seem to work best.

The link with the victim, like the electric wiring in a house, is the channel through which the spell hits its target. To make the spell effective, a black charge of energy must be propelled through the link, and this energy comes from the magician himself or from forces outside him.

Through mimicry, words and gestures the magician works up his own inner fury or hatred or lust to a frenzied pitch, and through them he externalizes his frenzy and directs it at his target. The sorcerers of the central Pacific islands list all the parts and organs of the victim's body, saying over and over again in a torrent of rage, 'I break, I twist, I burn, I destroy'. When a bone or a stick is pointed at a man to kill him, the magician jabs it in the air with an expression of violent hatred, and turns and twists it as if in the wound.

In the same way, a European black magician acts out hatred for his victim, stabbing the air with a sword or a knife and whipping or wounding an animal or another human being, filling his mind with images of blood and pain, and working himself into a state of frenzy in which, he believes, he draws into himself all the forces of violence and destruction in the universe. He becomes these forces, he masters them, and he launches them against his enemy with scarifying force.

Black magicians and modern witches in Europe frequently work inside a circle, which is both a barrier against hostile forces and an enclosure in which the magician's power can be built up and concentrated. They also use great quantities of symbolic paraphernalia, which bring the magician power and with which he gives effect to his will. When he stabs in mimicry with the sword, he pierces his enemy with agony, when he strikes with the scourge, he flails his enemy's flesh.

To what extent a magician's magical power comes from inside himself or from outside is a matter which magicians themselves are often vague about. They are frequently believed to be able to harm a victim by concentrated malice alone, by ill-wishing him. For instance, a Suffolk witch, Elizabeth Hobart, was said to have 'wished her cousin Hobart harm and he fell lame and so continued till he died.' But usually they also claim to evoke and use forces from outside themselves. The European magical textbooks are mainly concerned with rituals for summoning up spirits and demons which will obey the

The Witches' Sabbath by Goya: witches were believed to hold orgiastic revels at which their god appeared to them, sometimes in human form, sometimes in the form of an animal frequently a goat

magician's orders. Quiché Indians in Guate mala say that a man who wants to become witch sleeps in a cemetery for nine night and prays to the Devil, from whom he ca obtain power. In Africa the Nyoro blac magicians send evil spirits to attack peopl and the Lele sorcerers force the spirits dead babies to foretell the future.

When Magic Works

When magic works, as it sometimes doe it usually appears to be explicable in term of its effects on the minds of the magicia and his victim, without any necessity t assume the presence of mysterious ou side forces. A black magician of dominatin personality can have a terrifying effec even on the sceptically inclined, and when sorcerer puts a fatal spell on a man wh believes in his power it is not unknow for the victim to fade away and die. But it probably the belief which kills him, not th spell.

In European ritual magic a small group magicians perform a long and exhaustin ceremony in which they attempt to conjur up to visible appearance a spirit or dem or occult power of some kind. During th ceremony they gradually whip themselve up into a state of intense excitement. The have a clear mental picture of the dem

they expect to see, and often a drawing or painting of it. It is not very surprising if at the climax of the ceremony they actually see it, but the demon seems more likely to be a creation of their own minds than something existing independently.

Black Magician and Witch

Some anthropologists studying African beliefs have drawn a rough distinction between a sorcerer and a witch. A sorcerer uses 'medicine', plants, roots, nails, hair and the rest. A witch, on the other hand, possesses inner magical power and can injure a person by concentrating malice upon him. Anyone who takes the time and trouble can become a sorcerer but not everyone has the innate power of a witch.

This distinction is not always clear in practice and is not accepted as generally true by all anthropologists. Certainly it does not fit the European tradition, in which both black magicians and witches are credited with innate power and both use noxious substances and potions. In Europe the distinction between them is based on the difference in their characteristic attitudes to the forces with which they deal. Broadly speaking, the black magician seeks to dominate and control occult powers, while the witch worships them. This is reflected in the fact that the majority of European black magicians have been men and the majority of witches women, for it is an old tradition that man is essentially dominant and woman subordinate.

According to the accusations made against them in the time of the persecutions, witches worshipped the Devil. They met at their sabbaths to pay homage to Satan, expressing their subjection to him by kissing his backside. It was he who taught them how to work evil magic and gave them their familiar imps, he who whipped them if they were disobedient, he who led their orgies. He was their master and their god.

Modern witches have continued the tradition of the witch as a worshipper. They worship 'cosmic forces' which they see personified in the gods of pagan, pre-Christian Europe. They believe that their predecessors were misunderstood and misrepresented by Christian persecutors, and they claim to practise white magic, not black.

Black Magic and White

The distinction between black and white magic is simple enough in theory: a black magician works for evil ends and a white magician for good. But in practice the distinction is frequently blurred. For one thing, it rests in the eyes of the beholder and very often white magic is what you work and black magic is what other people work. For another, a man who believes he has magical powers is likely, being human, to use them sometimes to help and sometimes to harm.

Among North American Indians the medicine-man who can cure a disease can also inflict it. A Papago Indian recalled a year in which 'we lynched a medicine-man. He had been killing people.' Similarly, modern witches and white magicians will usually admit their readiness to turn their powers against rival occultists who attack them.

For magicians themselves, magic is morally neutral. It works automatically, like a tap. If you turn the taps on in the bath, you get water. You may be filling the bath to wash the baby or to drown him, but your motives do not affect the water supply.

The most startling thing about the European grimoires or magical textbooks, is their use of fervent and sincere prayers to God, asking his help in operations intended to kill people, to cause pain or to stir up hatred. One example from many is the long process in the *Grimoire of Honorius*, dating from the 17th century or earlier. It purports to have been written by a pope and the magician who uses it should be a priest. It involves the slaughter of a lamb which is ritually identified with Christ as the Lamb of God, and it bristles with impassioned appeals to God and solemn sayings of Mass. But its purpose is to summon up the Devil.

The authors of the grimoires inherited an old magical tradition that the power of a god can be captured and 'turned on' like a tap, regardless of the magician's motives. They also inherited a deeper tradition still, that the true goal of the magician is to find and identify himself with an ultimate unity, underlying and pervading all things. All things are grist to the magician's mill and all experiences are necessary to him. He must experience and master hatred as well as love, cruelty as well as mercy, evil as well as good. This is the path of the 'magus' and it is the magus perverted who makes the master black magician.

The altar is usually the most sacred part of any church or temple. It has a double origin, as the platform or table on which offerings to a deity were placed but also sometimes as the throne or home of the deity itself

ALTAR

FROM THE DAWN OF human culture there is evidence that man was moved to make offerings, probably of a sacrificial kind, to supernatural powers. Even the sub-human precursor of mankind, Neanderthal man about 100,000 BC seems to have practised a cult which involved the sacrifice of bears. In caves, for example, at Drachenloch, Switzerland, the Petershöhle near Nuremberg, bear skulls have been found carefully arranged in niches and on stone slabs which the prehistorian J. Maringer has described as 'the oldest altars of sacrifice so far known'. But this interpretation of problematic material of such remote antiquity must necessarily be treated with reserve. More certain is the later evidence from about 6000 BC at Catal Hüyük in Turkey, where a shrine was used for fertility rites, associated with a Mother Goddess and a bull cult. A low mud-brick platform formed a kind of table before a wall adorned with representations of bulls' heads, women's breasts, and human hands. Human skulls were on the 'altar'.

These prehistoric examples indicate that from very early times places have been specially used or constructed for the purpose of offering sacrifice. The need to show that the offerings were specifically presented to supernatural beings doubtless caused the 'altar' to be raised above ground-level, thus suggesting the idea of a 'table of the gods', though this analogy must not be pressed too far. The words for 'altar' in Semitic languages merely indicate a place where a victim was slaughtered, while in some Indo-European languages the terms used denote a place where a sacrifice was burned. Their association with deity gave altars an aura of holiness and the altar could even be regarded as the throne of a deity.

Altars and Sacrifice

Altars are frequently represented in ancient Egyptian art, and the remains of some still survive in temples. It would seem that the Egyptians regarded altars only as necessary adjuncts to ritual worship. Their altars generally appear to have been light tables, holding food and jars. Temple altars could be large stone erections, with steps, such as the sun-altar in the temple of Hatshepsut at Deir el-Bahiri. Tall stands, containing fire, served for burnt offerings. In ancient Mesopotamia two types of altar generally seem to have been used: large structures of brick for burnt offerings and small altars of various shapes, for burning incense.

Altars figured prominently in ancient Jewish worship. Significant examples of early practice occur in Genesis. In chapter 8 Noah builds an altar and offers burnt offerings, and God 'smelled the pleasing odour'; chapter 22 describes how Abraham built an altar for the sacrifice of his son Isaac. Exodus (chapter 20) records divine instructions for making altars of earth, and of unhewn stone (unhewn because the use of tools on the stone would profane it). Altars of bronze and gold and their equipment, made by Solomon for the Temple in Jerusalem, are described in 2 Chronicles (chapter 4). A notable feature of these altars were the 'horns', which projected at the corners; they appear on a stone altar found at Megiddo, but their origin and significance are uncertain. Exodus (chapter 21) implies that the altar of God was a place of refuge for criminals; the gospel of Matthew (chapter 23) indicates that in the 1st century AD Jews were accustomed to swear by the altar of the Jerusalem temple.

Altars for public and family worship abounded in the ancient civilizations of Greece and Rome. The Greeks distinguished between two kinds of altars. The *bomos* was used for sacrifices to the Olympian gods, the essence of the victim ascending in the smoke of its burning. The *eschara* (hearth) served for the cults of divine heroes and chthonic (underground) deities. This was a low structure, but often the sacrifice was performed over a pit, so that the victim's blood descended into the earth.

In the Greek temple, the image of the deity, not the altar, was the focus of attention. Altars varied in kind and form. On the Athenian Acropolis the great altar of the goddess Athene was an outcrop of

The altar on which Christ's sacrifice was re-enacted became the focal point of Christian worship: Gothic altarpiece

natural rock, and at Delphi Apollo's altar was reported to be made on the bones of sacrificed victims. Public altars were sometimes of immense size: that of Zeus at Pergamon in Asia Minor was 40 feet high. In both Greece and Italy small altars were set up in homes and market-places, at graves, groves and springs. Offerings included fruit, flowers and libations of wine. Shapes varied and the Romans often favoured cylindrical altars. The altars of Hestia in Athens and Vesta in Rome, where a perpetual fire burned, were essentially the 'hearths' of these cities. Roman tombs frequently took the form of altars, dedicated to the cult of the dead.

In ancient Persia the cult of fire, later associated with Zoroastrianism, stemmed from that reverence for fire which characterized Aryan religion and had its Indian counterpart in the worship of Agni, the Vedic god of fire. Persian fire-altars comprised a massive base, surmounted by a stone slab on which stood the fire-container. This fire-cult has been preserved by the Parsees, whose altars follow the ancient pattern.

The Sanskrit word for altar, *vedi*, originally denoted a trench in which the sacrificial fire burned, and was closely associated with the domestic hearth in ancient India. Early Hindu literature describes other vedis of different shapes for various kinds of offerings. Great importance was attached to the shape, and special Sanskrit manuals deal in great detail with the matter. Brick altars were constructed in the form of a falcon, heron or tortoise. A Hindu text, the *Satapatha Brahmana*, compares the shape of an altar with that of a woman. In modern Hinduism altars are simpler affairs: a square-shaped structure of earth or clay, on which a fire is kindled for offerings of butter.

The Altar of Heaven

Altars were essential to the religions of China. There were two kinds: those used in the public worship of the cosmic powers and those required for the ancestor cult. The most impressive of Chinese altars is the Altar of Heaven in Peking, at which the Emperor of China, the Son of Heaven, offered sacrifice, the most crucial occasion being at the winter solstice.

Japan provides a unique example of an altar, or rather of an ideal altar. The Shinto sect of Tenri-kyo reverence a spot in Tamba-Ichi as the centre of the world and the place where creation culminated. There an unfinished altar is located, which will achieve completion when the teaching of the sect has been preached in all lands and universal brotherhood established in the service of God. Apart from this, Japanese altars have only a practical significance as tables of offerings or incense in Shinto and Buddhist shrines.

In Aztec religion the altar was adapted to the slaughter of human victims. The altar in the great temple of Huitzilopochtli, god of war, in Mexico City, was a block of green stone five feet in length and three feet in height and width. Its convex top was so fashioned as to present the breast of the victim to the stone knife of the sacrificing priest, who cut out the heart and

Roger Wood London

Above Zoroastrian fire altar at Naqshe-Rustam, near the site of Persepolis, Iran
Below Nigerian chieftain's bronze 'altar of the hand' symbolizing the power of the hand; it would be placed on a mud altar during religious ceremonies: British Museum

Michael Holford

presented it to the deity.

The Christian altar, from earliest times, has been essentially associated with the celebration of the Lord's Supper or Mass. In the early Church the rite was doubtless celebrated on wooden tables but the custom of celebrating it on the tombs of martyrs led to the tradition that stone was the proper material for altars. According to Roman Catholic practice today, even where the structure is mainly of wood, a stone *mensa* ('table') must be inserted. In Catholic Christianity, both in the Eastern and Western Churches, the status of the Mass or Eucharist as the supreme act of public worship has made the altar the focal point of church and cathedral.

The development of the doctrine of the sacrifice of the Mass invested the altar with a sacrificial significance: at each Mass the original sacrifice of Christ is re-presented. The doctrine of transubstantiation (that the bread and wine become the body and blood of Christ) and the custom of keeping the consecrated sacrament in a receptacle on the altar, encouraged the idea of the altar as a throne or local abode of Christ. Reaction against medieval abuses of the Mass was one of the causes of the Reformation, and it led to the abolition of altars in most Protestant churches. The placing of a cross and candles on altars dates from the 10th century; the location of the high altar is usually at the eastern end, but in some modern churches it is placed in the centre of the church.

S. G. F. BRANDON

On the fringes of the Classical world lived a mythical race of warrior women who had declared war on men and relegated them to slavery. The memory of their fierceness and bravery cast a potent spell on the Greek imagination

AMAZONS

THE AMAZONS were a mythical race of warrior women, whose battles with a number of Greek heroes were recorded in various local legends. Their original home was in the gorges and forests of the Thermodon valley in Pontus in Asia Minor, and their capital city was Themiscyra on the coast of the Euxine (modern Terme, on the Black Sea coast of Turkey). According to one tradition, men were excluded altogether from their country, but for purposes of propagating the race the Amazons made an annual visit to the Gargareans in the Caucasus. Girls born of these unions were then brought up by the Amazons, each one having her right breast either burnt or cut off to make it easier to hurl a javelin or stretch a bow. Boys were either put to death or sent back to their fathers. Another version has it that a number of men were kept for mating purposes, but had the status of slaves, and were allowed to perform only those tasks executed in other countries by women.

Legend also has it that the legs and arms of these men were mutilated to prevent their challenging the Amazons' power.

Whether men were or were not included in the Amazon state, only women bore arms, not only defending their own country, but making expeditions of conquest into neighbouring territories. They fought both on foot and on horseback, carrying crescent shields and wielding spears, bows and battle-axes. Their life consisted mainly in hunting and war-like exercises and the training of the girl Amazons. They were ruled by a queen and they worshipped Ares, the god of war from whom they were believed to be descended, and Artemis, goddess of the hunt.

Stories about the Amazons belong to the

Below The Amazons were legendary women warriors descended from Ares, the god of war. From a silver panel in the British Museum

earliest Greek sagas. Homer mentions them in a way which shows that they were familiar to his audience. When in historical times the Greeks got to know the Thermodon region and found no Amazons there, they supposed either that Hercules had destroyed them all, or that they had been driven away. Thus in later legends, the Amazons were moved further and further away from their original homeland, but they were always located on the fringe of the world as it was then known to the Greeks. They were said to be of Scythian origin from Colchis (south of the Caucasus), and there was also supposed to be a race of Amazons in Africa. They were in any case, always foreign to the Greek homeland, and in Greek eyes — like all foreigners — they counted as barbarians.

Hercules, Theseus and the Amazons

Two of their queens, Hippolyta and Penthesilea, figure in widely told Greek myths. The ninth labour imposed on Hercules by his master Eurystheus was to take from Hippolyta her girdle, symbol of her royal power, which had been given to her by the god Ares. According to one version of the myth, Hercules withstood a cavalry charge of Amazons single-handed and routed their whole army, killing Hippolyta at the same time.

Later legends linked the name of Theseus, mythical King of Athens, with Hercules' expedition against the Amazons. Theseus carried off Antiope whose sister Oreithyia, sworn to vengeance, led an invading army into Attica. The Amazons were defeated by the Athenians after four months fighting. Some say that Antiope was killed in the fighting, but others that she survived to make a scene at Theseus' wedding (she being the mother of Theseus' son Hippolytus, though not his lawful wife), where she threatened to murder all the guests. Theseus killed her, to prevent her carrying out her threat.

In another legend, Hippolyta brought yet another Amazon force against Theseus after this wedding, and in the ensuing battle was killed accidentally by her sister Penthesilea. Pursued by the Furies of her dead sister, Penthesilea sought refuge in Troy, where she obtained purification from her blood-guilt at the hands of the aged King Priam. In gratitude she enrolled in the Trojan army, where, as the war-god Ares' daughter, she fought bravely until Achilles killed her. Achilles then wept for the lost

Amazons in the Old World

We are told, namely, that there was once in the western parts of Libya, on the bounds of the inhabited world, a race which was ruled by women and followed a manner of life unlike that which prevails among us. For it was the custom among them that the women should practise the arts of war and be required to serve in the army for a fixed period, during which time they maintained their virginity; then, when the years of their service in the field had expired, they went in to the men for the procreation of children, but they kept in their hands the administration of the magistracies and of all the affairs of state. The men, however, like our married women, spent their days about the house, carrying out the orders which were given them by their wives; and they took no part in military campaigns or in the exercise of free citizenship in the affairs of the community by virtue of which they might become presumptuous and rise up against the women. When their children were born the babies were turned over to the men, who brought them up on milk and such cooked foods as were appropriate to the age of the infants.

Diodorus Siculus,
Bibliotheca Historica

Amazons in the New World

Sir Walter Raleigh, the famous Elizabethan adventurer, explored South America in the 16th century and was told of Amazons:

But they which are not far from Guiana do meet with men but once in a year. At that time all the Kings of the borders assemble, and the Queens of the Amazons, and after the Queens have chosen, the rest cast lots for their Valentines. This one month they feast, dance and drink of their wines in abundance, and the Moon being done, they all depart to their own Provinces. If they give birth to a son, they return him to the father, if a daughter they nourish it and retain it. It was further told me, that if in the wars they took any prisoners that they used to accompany with those also at what time soever, but in the end for certain they put them to death; for they are said to be very cruel and bloodthirsty, especially to such as offer to invade their territories.

Sir Walter Raleigh,
The Discovery of the Empire of Guiana

beauty, youth and courage of the dead queen and made love to her corpse. Thersites, reputed to be the ugliest Greek at Troy, jeered at Achilles' grief and accused him of unnatural lust, whereupon Achilles killed him. This enraged some of the Greeks and Diomedes, a cousin of Thersites, threw Penthesilea's corpse into the River Scamander.

The Greeks continued to circulate stories about the Amazons down to a late period. One very popular story was that the Amazon queen Thalestris visited Alexander the Great (356–323 BC) during one of his Asian campaigns, wishing to have a daughter by such a famous general. She stayed with him for 13 days before returning to her own country. Writing more than 400 years later, Plutarch lists no less than 14 authorities who mention this tale, though nine of them, he says, dismissed it as 'complete fiction', and it was laughed at after Alexander's death by his successor in Thrace, Lysimachus.

Slave-Girls or Matriarchs

The Amazons were a favourite subject for Greek sculptors and painters. In art of the earliest periods, they are dressed exactly like Greek warriors, but usually with one breast bare. After the Persian Wars (499–448 BC), for example on Greek vases of the great classical period, they are represented in oriental garb, wearing caps and trousers, and pictures of them relate more and more to known legends about them. They are never depicted as having lost one breast, in spite of the Greek belief that their name meant 'breastless'.

Various explanations of the origins of the legends about the Amazons have been put forward. Some writers trace them to the armed slave-girls who were dedicated to the service of certain Asian deities, and the association of the Amazons with Artemis supports this theory. But the story is more likely to be an imaginative Greek embroidery of reports about matriarchal tribes in south-west Asia, or of tribes in which the women led a freer and tougher life than they did in Greece. Certainly the persistence of the legend right up to the 2nd and 3rd centuries AD, and its perennial popularity as a theme in the arts show that it had a deep appeal to some area in ancient Greek fantasy.
(See also HERCULES; THESEUS.)

The Japanese Buddhist deity Amida offers entry into heaven to all his followers, in return for the faithful repetition of a short prayer – 'I adore thee, O Lord of Boundless Light'

AMIDA

THE WORD AMIDA originally denoted merely an abstraction — the ideal of unlimited light. But this abstraction, like others in Buddhism, came slowly to be personalized, first as a mere Bodhissatva (one assiduously undergoing the disciplines necessary to become a Buddha) and then as an actual Buddha.

Amida had 48 wishes, one of which was to let the dead pass into Jodo, or the Pure Land of the afterlife in which he would reign, and another that if any single mortal who had offered prayers to him failed to obtain salvation, then he, Amida, would never be a Buddha. These wishes were fulfilled, with the result that anyone with sufficient faith in Amida was assured of a place in Jodo.

The formulation of this doctrine of Amida as a personage rather than an abstract concept dates back to India in the 2nd century BC, but it was in Japan that it found its most enthusiastic devotees, who eventually formed the Jodo (Pure Land) and other similar sects. Perhaps the first

Japanese individual to be granted a vision of Jodo was the student priest Genshin (942–1017), who retreated to Mt Hiei, near the old Japanese capital of Kyoto, in order to live in solitary meditation aloof from the luxury and depravity of his day. His most famous work, *Ojo-yoshu*, is usually quoted as the source of Japanese Amida worship. Certainly it contributed greatly to the foundation of the Jodo sect and had a profound effect on later literature and art.

Genshin maintained that for most people the Nembutsu or repetition of the phrase 'Namu Amida Butsu' ('I adore thee, O Lord of Boundless Light') could, without any other aids, ensure entry into the heaven that awaited the soul after death.

The actual founder of the Jodo sect was not Genshin but Honen (1130–1212). After studying at a monastery on Mt Hiei and finding no satisfaction there, he formulated a doctrine based on a remark of Zendo Daishi, a Buddhist priest of an earlier Epoch, to the effect that man's salvation does not depend so much on his own strength as upon the grace of Amida. Honen thought that men should not trouble themselves about whether their hearts were good or bad, or their sins light or heavy, but should only believe that they would be born into the Pure Land and repeat the invocation 'Namu Amida Butsu' with total conviction.

To people of small intellectual capacity and little education, it was natural that a form of Buddhism that required merely a simple act of faith accompanied by a single phrase should have a strong and instantaneous appeal. To people who lived precariously, decimated by wars, famines and plagues, to be able to look forward not to the annihilation of self in the Buddhist Nirvana but to existence in a paradise far from this world of trouble, was a most potent source of consolation. Here, beyond the grave, was Amida offering something unobtainable in mortal life; an existence devoid of pain, sadness, hunger or anxiety.

Amida of the Phoenix Hall

In Buddhist art Amida may generally be recognized by the hands lying in his lap, with the thumbs placed end to end. Very often the halo (in Japanese goko) forms a background not only to the head but to the entire body. There is a gleaming spot on the forehead, emblematic of wisdom. The two images waiting on either side of Amida are Kannon (goddess of mercy) and Seishi (Lord of Might).

Probably the most beautiful sculptured representation of Amida is in the 'Phoenix Hall', part of the Byodoin Temple in the suburbs of Kyoto. Carved in the 11th century, this Amida rests in a building that indeed resembles the phoenix from which it takes its name, so lightly does it appear to

Amida in the paradise to which those who believe in him are sure of entry. The gleaming spot on his forehead symbolizes wisdom and his forehead is encircled by a halo

hover over the water that surrounds it. This, the weary, harassed and despairing believers of that time must have thought, was indeed the Lord Amida himself, sitting there in repose, his eyes lowered, as he compassionately promised salvation to all who believed in him. This offer of a future life of bliss is not dissimilar to that offered by depictions of Christ on the Cross; and the self-sacrifice of Amida, renouncing the possibility of becoming a Buddha unless all believers can join him in paradise, is not dissimilar to that of the Christian Saviour.

In most religions there is a conflict between the belief in salvation through works (the idea that it is a man's good actions which bring him to heaven) and the belief in salvation through faith. Those who accept the doctrine

of rebirth in a paradise over which Amida presides and who believe that rebirth can be achieved merely by the repetition, in faithful submission, of a single invocation, maintain that all men are possessors of a 'Buddha nature' and that to make an intellectual or spiritual effort at self-improvement is illogical since by doing so one denies that one is already Buddha – and it is only by accepting one's Buddha nature that Buddhahood can be won.

Others, perhaps more self-exacting, deplore the way in which the Jodo and similar sects have turned what was at first no more than an abstraction into an actual personage. But if Buddhism was to be made accessible to the ordinary people of Japan, it was perhaps inevitable that the abstract

should be made concrete, the unreal real; so that by seeing the walls of their temples covered with hosts of greater and lesser deities, they should be able to embrace a faith made personal enough to grasp. The promise of a future life may in part explain Japanese willingness to seek out death, even by suicide.
(See also JAPAN.)

FRANCIS KING

FURTHER READING: D. T. Suzuki, *Zen and Japanese Buddhism* (Japan Pubn, 1962); E. Conze, Buddhism: *Its Essence and Development* (Harper Row); Sir C. Eliot, *Japanese Buddhism* (Barnes and Noble, 1935); E. Dale Saunders, *Buddhism in Japan* (University of Pennsylvania Press, 1964).

Amulet
An object worn or carried to ward off evil or to attract good luck; usually a jewel, a stone, or a piece of metal or parchment, inscribed with magic signs.
See TALISMAN.

Michael Holford

Mary Evans Picture Library

Anabaptists
Protestant revolutionaries of the 16th century, persecuted for re-baptizing converts from other Christian sects; produced many small splinter groups such as the Old Order Amish, numbers of whom emigrated to America where they still adhere to traditional ways of life.
See COMMUNISTIC RELIGIOUS MOVEMENTS; ENTHUSIASM.

Anandamayi Ma is venerated in India for her ability to take on the appearance and personality of gods and goddesses and also for her extraordinary bodily contortions when in trance, sometimes bouncing up and down like a rubber ball

ANANDAMAYI MA

EARLY ONE MORNING in spring 1896, a girl was born in a rural village named Kheora, situated in what is now called East Pakistan. Her parents named her Nirmala Devi. She received no formal education and as a child began to experience peculiar states of intense and brooding abstraction. As she grew older these moods often developed into positive ecstasies of mystical exaltation.

She was married at 13 and sometimes, while preparing meals for her husband, her consciousness would be slowly indrawn to such an extent that she became totally oblivious of her surroundings.

By the time she was 18 it was felt by many who met her that her freshness and simplicity concealed a strange and unpredictable personality which seemed to come and go unaccountably.

It was not long before the power that appeared to use her body as a vehicle through which to show itself was recognized as being not only charming and benignant, but also peculiarly solicitous and motherly in its attitude to those it attracted. Nirmala drew people to her by the sheer magnetism

of this radiant and indwelling presence and some people felt they discerned in her an embodiment of divinity.

Among these was a saintly man named Bhaiji, who became one of Nirmala's first devotees. He was the first to call her Anandamayi Ma, or Blissful Mother, the name by which she is now generally known throughout India and in many other countries.

Most of the great mystics of whom we have reliable record are known to have had spiritual guides, some of whom appeared in ordinary human form, and some not. Unlike them, however, Anandamayi Ma – or Mother as she is often called – claimed no direct initiation from a particular guru or spiritual guide.

When asked about this she said, 'In earlier years my parents were my guides; in household life, my husband; and in all the situations of life, now, all persons and things of the world are my guru. But know it for certain; the one Supreme Being is the only Guide for all.'

And, something which is probably unprecedented among Indian holy sages, Anandamayi Ma says she has not undergone any previous births. Which means that she does not claim to be the outcome and final flowering of a series of human incarnations in which she has striven to arrive at spiritual perfection. On the contrary, she has stated on various occasions that she has appeared on earth as the direct result of the profound yearning for God on the part of certain individuals, who – in their ardour to know God and realize their spiritual identity

with the Supreme Being – have caused that Supreme One to respond and assume human form.

It is a tenet of oriental belief, particularly in India, that such yearning creates a similar yearning in the Supreme Being; and because of the limitations of his devotees he (the Supreme) shows himself to their external senses in a seemingly human embodiment.

This manifestation of divinity is not confined in Anandamayi Ma to the appearance of a single human embodiment. Whichever god or goddess has been worshipped intensely by any of her devotees, that particular image or aspect of divinity appears to them to play through Mother's form. The spectral semblance of one deity after another has been seen by them to flow out of her being, each image the perfect original of some traditionally recognized god-form. Kali, Krishna, Shiva, Brahma, it matters not which aspect of divinity; its form duly appears when Mother enters one of her moods of mystical ecstasy.

She once said, 'The personality and figures of gods and goddesses are as real as your body or mine.'

A Vision of Kali
Some time in 1925, while in Dacca (about 200 miles north-east of Calcutta) Mother was asked to perform Kali Puja, the worship of the image of Kali.

During preparations for the ceremony, which required an image of the goddess, flowers, incense and sandal paste, Mother saw – about 130 yards distant – the ethereal form of the actual goddess, floating in the air towards her, with hands out-stretched as if eager to come to Mother's lap. Later another apparition appeared to Mother as a little girl of infinite sweetness. This also was Kali, she said.

During the rite itself the celebrants not only noticed the unusual effect which these occult experiences had upon Mother, but they were also swept by a wave of bliss which so engulfed them that they lost consciousness of externals. Each felt divine emotion greater than had been experienced when the ceremony was performed by priests.

In earlier years, during the celebration of kirtan (religious chanting and dancing) Mother would often go into a state of trance during which her body underwent the most amazing contortions. Her devotees claimed that her body, rolling on the ground, would appear to grow unusually large and then, as suddenly, contract almost to nothing. At other times her body behaved as if it were boneless, bouncing up and down like a rubber ball.

These and similar powers are mentioned in certain statements in manuals of yoga, particularly the Shiva Sanhita, where they are listed under the Eight Siddhis, or Magic Powers, that may be developed by yoga practice. But since Mother did not practise yoga, it was claimed that these supra-normal powers manifested themselves in response to the thoughts and emotions of her devotees, being, so to speak, the visible outer tokens of intense inner devotion.

On one occasion a devotee of Anandamayi

Above Anandamayi Ma: her devotees believe that the Supreme Being has shown himself to them on earth in her apparently human form
Right Indian print of Kali, goddess of time, holding symbols of war, raising one hand in peace and grasping for power with the fourth. Anandamayi Ma believed she saw Kali, once floating in the air and once as a little girl of infinite sweetness

Ma said to her in all good humour: 'You are credited with great power. If you have such power, just burn me to ashes.' He then set out to return to his own home.

It was an extremely hot day and he had put up his umbrella. Anandamayi Ma suddenly decided to join him and they walked a few paces together.

The devotee then became conscious of a fierce and unbearable heat beating down on him, despite the umbrella. He panicked and said: 'From where is the fire raining down on my head? Please stop the fire. I have ample proof of your power.' He lowered the umbrella just as the overpowering heat abated. But he noticed that some of the fabric had been consumed, as if by flame.

Anandamayi Ma is famous throughout India for her untiring devotion to the poor and the helpless. She has helped many homeless and starving people.

She teaches that knowledge of God alone constitutes true knowledge; that God alone is real, all else unreal; and that by knowing God one comes to a knowledge of all else besides.

In 1931 Bhaiji decided upon a site for the construction of an Ashram, or place of worship, centring round Mother, where her devotees could meet together, receive her blessing and conduct divine service in her name. When a trench was dug so that foundations could be laid, four or five tombs were uncovered. They each contained a human skeleton, and Mother declared these to be the mortal remains of Sannyasis (saints or holy men) who had once formed a community which had been housed on that particular site. One of them, she said, had been Bhaiji himself in a former incarnation.

Since the establishment of that first Anandamayi Ma Ashram in Dacca more than 20 others have been built by devotees in Mother's name.

KENNETH GRANT

Ananse
Spider-trickster of West Africa, hero of many fables in which he cleverly deceives animals, men and even God himself; the stories were taken to the West Indies by Negro slaves.
See SPIDER.

Ancestor Worship
Veneration of dead forbears who are believed to see and influence events on earth, and to whom prayers and offerings are made by their descendants: still an important element of religious belief in many parts of the world.
See CULT OF THE DEAD.

Anchor
In early Christian symbolism, an emblem of salvation and hope, partly because it stands for security and partly because it is shaped like a cross; it was often depicted upside down to emphasize its resemblance to the cross.

Anchorite
Originally, a Christian who abandoned human company and the clamour of the world to live alone and silent in a cell attached to a church; later used more generally as another word for a hermit.
See SELF DENIAL.

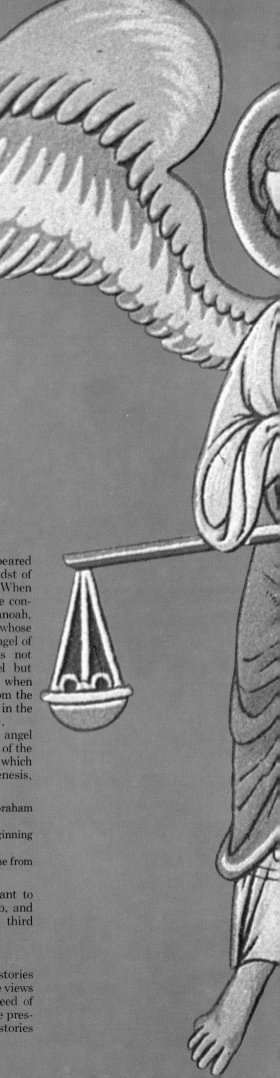

The angel who weighs souls at the Last Judgement, a detail from the medieval Psalter of St Louis. 'It is a member of that family of wondrous beings who, ere the worlds were made, millions of ages back, have stood around the throne of God . . . and served him with a keen ecstatic love' (Cardinal Newman, *The Dream of Gerontius*)

In Jewish and Christian theory, angels are God's courtiers and are sent as messengers and helpers to men. They are usually described as beautiful, winged creatures and sometimes said to be of enormous height; as in the case of a female angel 96 miles high

ANGELS

BEHIND THE PASTEBOARD Christmas card angel and the stylized angels of many Christian hymns, there lies a long tradition. The term 'angel', from the Latin *angelus*, entered the English language in very early times when it denoted a supernatural being of kindly qualities. In the Bible it translates Hebrew and Greek words meaning 'messenger'. It first appears in the Old Testament in the phrase 'angel of the Lord', the title given to the divine messenger who told Hagar that she would give birth to Ishmael (Genesis, chapter 16). It is significant that Hagar identifies the angel with the Lord himself. Evidently the writer believed that when God wishes to make his will known to man, he can assume a visible human form and can speak.

Sometimes in the early accounts there was no visible appearance. The angel of the Lord calling from heaven restrained Abraham from killing Isaac (Genesis, chapter 22) and was invisible to Balaam, though he was seen with his drawn sword by Balaam's ass, which repeatedly took evasive action till at last his rider's eyes were opened (Numbers, chapter 22).

It was the angel of the Lord who appeared to Moses in a flame of fire in the midst of a burning bush (Exodus, chapter 3). When the angel of the Lord announced the conception of Samson to the wife of Manoah, she described him as a man of God whose countenance was like that 'of the angel of God, very terrible'. Again, he was not immediately recognized as an angel but Manoah made a burnt offering, 'and when the flame went up toward heaven from the altar, the angel of the Lord ascended in the flame of the altar' (Judges, chapter 13).

The most exalted use of the word angel in the Pentateuch (the first five books of the Bible) occurs in the Blessing of Jacob which equates 'the angel' with God (Genesis, chapter 48):

The God before whom my fathers Abraham and Isaac walked,
the God who shepherds me from my beginning to this day,
the angel who as my kinsman saves me from all evil. . . .

Perhaps here the writer was reluctant to speak of God as a kinsman of Jacob, and substituted 'angel' for 'God' in the third line.

The Helpers of Men
The role of angels in these early stories seems to have been connected with the views of theologians who recognized the need of human forms and voices to convey the presence of the unseen God. In these stories

it is through angels that divine help comes to men. Abraham could promise his servant, about to set out on his search for a wife for Isaac, that 'the Lord, the God of heaven . . . will send his angel with you . . . and prosper your way' (Genesis, chapter 24). Jacob in his dream at Bethel saw 'a ladder set up on the earth, and the top of it reached to heaven, and behold the angels of God were ascending and descending on it', almost as though their primary function was to take earthly news to heaven (Genesis, chapter 28).

In the historical books of the Old Testament, to the angels are ascribed power to discern good and evil, the wisdom that knows everything, and the certainty of choosing aright. Belief in the goodness of angels is attested by the writer of Job, when he gives as an extreme instance that God charges 'even his angels' with error (chapter 4), and persists into New Testament times, as when it is said that the Jews in council saw Stephen's face 'like the face of an angel' (Acts, chapter 6).

Michael and Gabriel

In Daniel, the latest Old Testament book, a heavenly figure important in later doctrine about angels is introduced as 'Michael, one of the chief princes'. Michael is described as 'your prince' and 'the great prince who has charge of your people' (chapters 10, 12). This is the earliest biblical evidence of the belief that certain angels had charge of certain nations.

Another divine being named in the visions

of Daniel but also not called an angel is Gabriel, who was sent to Daniel to interpret a vision. Afterwards 'the man Gabriel' came 'in swift flight' to give Daniel wisdom and understanding (chapters 8, 9). Seraphim and cherubim are presented in the Old Testament as winged but this flying man is the biblical basis for later presentations of angels wearing wings. Michael and Gabriel became important in later thought as angelic leaders. In Revelation, Michael leads the angels against the Devil in the war in heaven.

Origins of Angels

The beginnings of the biblical belief in angels must be sought in very early folklore. Our stories come from what are regarded as the early pentateuchal sources, the later writers in the Pentateuch making no mention of angels. The courts of the great kings of the Near East also were a model for the idea of a heavenly court. The gods of the Hittites and Canaanites had their supernatural messengers, and parallels to Old Testament stories of angels are found in Near Eastern literature.

In the Old Testament the functions of angels are to worship God and attend on him, standing ready to do his will; they announce coming prosperity or destruction, guard holy places, and guide and protect individuals and peoples. They manifest no personality separate from the God whose message they bear. They appear unsummoned, perform their appointed task and vanish.

After the Old Testament period, many

Jewish writings, such as Ecclesiasticus, ignore angels but others give them prominence. In Tobit Raphael guides Tobias throughout his adventure. More details are given about angelic intercession for men and their control of nations. Many more angels have personal names, they are organized in ranks, and are assigned the new function of controlling Nature and the stars.

Angels and Jesus

In the New Testament as clearly as in the Old, God may choose to communicate with man through an angel. It is interesting that at the beginning of the first gospel there appears in Joseph's dream 'an angel of the Lord' telling him of the conception of Jesus (Matthew, chapter 1) reminding us of the ancient story of Manoah in Judges. An angel of the Lord announced Jesus' birth to shepherds on the Bethlehem hills (Luke, chapter 2). Gabriel, whom we have already met as the man coming in swift flight to Daniel, is now an angel standing in the presence of God, sent to announce to Zechariah in the temple the conception of John the Baptist, and six months later to Mary at Nazareth to announce the conception of Jesus (Luke, chapter 1). Again as in the Old Testament, individual angels bring help to men.

The warm interest of angels in man's welfare is vividly expressed in the saying of Jesus that 'there is joy before the angels of God over one sinner who repents' (Luke, chapter 15), and that children have their guardian angels standing as favoured envoys near to God himself (Matthew, chapter 18).

Such beliefs are part of angelology, which shows a steady development since its presentation in the later books of the Old Testament. Some trace Babylonian and Persian influence on this development but it must be remembered that the angels of Zoroastrianism were abstract principles, in this quite unlike the messenger angels of the Old Testament. Others see in the number seven, which often recurs in Jewish and Christian angelology, the influence of Assyrian beliefs in seven planetary gods. But in any case there is firm evidence in the New Testament of Jewish traditions existing after the period of the Old Testament writings.

It was through Jewish Christians that angelology, based on the Old Testament and other Jewish writings, entered the teaching of the Church. Angels were set over the life of Nature, and over human communities. God was Israel's portion but Michael was her protector, taught her Hebrew and gave the law on Sinai. Every individual had his guardian angel and babies exposed or aborted were cared for by guardian angels. There continued to be angelic intercessors and messengers of revelation or warning, but further functions were more specialized. There was an Angel of Repentance who brought to man consciousness of sin and the promise of forgiveness, and an Angel of Peace received the soul as it left the body and bore it to paradise. The Angel of Death in Sheol was a good angel and guardian of

Moslems pray only to God but also ask angels to intercede with God on their behalf. Mohammedan dwellers in the presence of God, from a Turkish manuscript which is now in the British Museum

Wing Measurements

Crawford H. Greenewalt in his book Hummingbirds *considers how large an angel's wings would need to be, assuming a weight of about 150 lbs:*

The wing from wrist to tip would be about four feet long, its total length between six and seven feet. When folded neatly into the body, the end of the wing would come just below the knee – comfortable enough for perching and walking. The wings would beat about once every second – a nice easy rhythm – not too far from a normal walking pace. The wings would, however, be heavy, perhaps a quarter the weight of the body and, alas, here lies the rub: the human frame hasn't the pectoral muscles to drive such formidable gear. Human pectorals are barely five per cent of the total body weight and a reasonable aerial job would call for at least fifteen per cent.

souls. Good and bad angels, of light and darkness, all were under God's control.

The Seven Heavens

Angelic rank was associated with speculation about the universe which increased to seven or eight the three heavens known to St Paul. All these were thought to be above the firmament where fallen angels were imprisoned, and all were inhabited exclusively by angels, the lower heavens by those in charge of human affairs, the upper by Angels of the Presence. According to some speculation these heavens were successive stages through which souls must pass, encountering their guardian angels to whom account must be given.

Corresponding to the seven heavens were

seven archangels, this number sometimes including Christ and sometimes being additional to him. Angels continued to be given superhuman status, but were clearly distinguished from God. They were God's first creation, formed from fire. They were sometimes described as of enormous height, symbolic of their greatness. In the Gospel of Peter the heads of the two angels who bore Christ's body to heaven actually touched the skies, and the Elkesaites (an unorthodox Christian sect) knew of two angels, one of them female, 96 miles high.

The early Christian church was helped by concepts of angelology to formulate its doctrine of the Trinity, and especially of the nature and work of Jesus the Christ. By some writers Michael was equated with 'Word' and 'Son', and Gabriel with 'Spirit' and the Angel of the Spirit who entered Mary and became flesh. But from the 5th century, care was taken to avoid any heretical doctrine that Jesus was only an angel and subordinate to the Father.

Through the Middle Ages, speculation continued in angelology, and there was even learned argument as to how many angels could dance on the point of a pin. In modern theological thought angels still present concepts of 'pure spirits without physical bodies' or 'mirrors of God's mind and will'. Belief in them remains in varying degrees an article of faith, but speculations as to their origin and nature, and interpretation of human experiences of their help, are still matters of considerable debate. Throughout the centuries there have been accounts of angelic visitations – to the Celtic saints, the young Joan of Arc, and the soldiers at Mons.

Angels were sung of in carols and represented in illuminated manuscripts, sculpture and stained glass. It is consistent with the biblical record that Hamlet confronted by his father's ghost cries 'Angels and ministers of grace defend us!' and when he is killed Horatio exclaims 'Flights of angels sing thee to thy rest!'

Angels are figures of light. It was because of the fairness of the English boys in the Roman slave market that Pope Gregory said that the Angles had faces of angels, and Bunyan liked to call them Shining Ones. The kindly angels of the Old Testament are behind Crashaw's description of the heavenly welcome to St Teresa:

Angels, thy old friends, there shall greet thee,
Glad at their own home now to meet thee!

As long as the biblical record continues to be known and loved, the term 'angel' will still be used for a figure coming unsummoned, bringing from God revelation directly affecting the life of the one who receives him. (For the fallen angels, see DEMONS; DEVIL.)

J. N. SCHOFIELD

FURTHER READING: Gustav Davidson, *Dictionary of Angels* (Macmillan, 1967).

ANIMALS

Teeth and claws of the Gods

Early men recognized a close link between themselves and the beasts which they feared, used or admired. They designed magical rituals to obtain the animals' powers and many animals were elevated to the realms of the gods

AFRICA IS STILL sometimes troubled by outbreaks of the leopard men, who disguise themselves as leopards with masks and metal claws, pounce on a victim who they kill by piercing the jugular with their claws, and part of whose body they eat. In India sacred cows wander the streets unmolested. Long ago an Egyptian mob murdered a Roman for killing a cat. The early Christians were accused of worshipping a donkey. Norse berserkers in the skins of bears or wolves were feared for their crazed ferocity in

battle. Finn mac Cumaill, a great Irish hero of legend, could turn himself into a deer or a dog at will. His two faithful hounds were the sons of his sister, who had been magically transformed into a bitch. American Indians often ascribed the Creation to 'trickster' animal gods such as Coyote on the Plains, Raven in the north-west and Rabbit in the south-east.

In folklore there are talking animals and animals which marry human husbands or wives. Some animals are said to sense the presence of ghosts. It is lucky to see a white horse. A black cat can be either a good luck charm or an omen of evil. The Devil frequently appeared in animal form to witches, who were also accused of suckling familiar spirits in animal shape. In South America

The hippo-crocodile goddess Taurt in a sacred procession, shown on the walls of the burying place of the Apis bulls at Sakkara in Egypt. Animals were extremely important in Egyptian religion and most of the Egyptian gods were shown in animal forms

sorcerers have jaguar familiars and African witches are believed to ride on hyenas at night.

Behind all this is an outlook which does not clearly differentiate between men, animals, spirits and gods. Primitive man does not draw our accustomed distinction between human beings and animals at all. They share the world with him, on his own level, and he admires them, fears them, respects them, in a way which is foreign to us in

Gerald Cubitt

Above Stone horse guarding imperial tombs at Nanking, China **Right** The prehistoric White Horse of Uffington, cut into the Berkshire downs, possibly a representation of the Celtic goddess Epona, 'divine horse'

cities or in our long-domesticated countryside. They are creatures of the same kind as himself, though differently shaped and in some ways better equipped. So they can turn into men, and vice versa. If a man wants to acquire the speed of the deer, the strength of the bear, the cunning of the fox, the night sight of the cat, he imitates the animal. He dresses up in its skin, mimics its cries, dances out its movements. He ruts as a stag, as a leopard he sinks his fangs into flesh. By concentratedly imagining himself as an animal, he can induce a state of mind in which he feels he has become it.

The line between man and animal is easily crossed, man being an animal himself. So is the line between animals and the spirit world, because in primitive thought everything that exists has a spirit as well as a body (see ANIMISM). Men have souls which survive death: so do animals, and like the ghosts of men their spirits may be good or evil. The gods, like the animals, have powers which surpass those of men. A god may be seen in an animal which shares some quality with him. And the magical mimicry by which a man turns himself into a beast may also be the magic by which he transforms himself into a god.

Man-Wallaby

Totemism is a type of social organization in which groups of people associate themselves closely with an animal (or a plant or an object — see TOTEM) as wolf-men, bear-men or whatever it may be. They use the totem as a badge of identification, much as a feudal knight was identifiable by the emblems on his armour, and the system may have originated from resemblances between a man and a particular animal. But it was evidently not merely a matter of saying of someone, 'he looks or behaves like a bear' but of implying, 'he *is* a bear'. In Australia, 'even today, when an aborigine says he is, for example, wallaby, he means what he says. He and the wallaby species are "one flesh". . .' (see AUSTRALIA). Except in special circumstances he does not kill or eat

a wallaby, and he and his group are responsible for carrying out the rituals which ensure a plentiful supply of wallabies for everyone else. This is because he and the wallabies are descended from the same ancestor, a hero of long ago who was both a man and a wallaby.

Sacred Cat and Crocodile

Whether totemism lies behind the animal cults of Egypt is disputed, as there is no certain evidence of any totemic stage in Egyptian history, but the importance of animals in Egyptian religion astonished Greek, Roman and early Christian authors and embarrasses Egyptologists. Most, though not all, of the Egyptian gods were portrayed as animals, or as human beings

with animals' heads, or in other mixed human and animal shapes. The sky goddess Hathor could be shown as a cow or as a woman's face with the horns and ears of a cow. The goddess Taurt, 'the great one', had the head of a hippo, the back and tail of a crocodile, a woman's breasts and the claws of a lioness.

Some animals were sacred in particular localities: the people of Bubastis in the Nile delta, home of the cat goddess Bast, would never kill a cat; in the Faiyum, where Sebek the crocodile god was worshipped, there was a pool of sacred crocodiles. Huge cemeteries have been discovered containing the mummified bodies of dogs, cats, crocodiles, falcons and bulls. Recent excavations at Sakkara have found

The mimicry by which a man turns himself into a beast may also be the magic by which he transforms himself into a god

races of a cemetery of mummified baboons, who were given names and apparently venerated as gods.

All cats were divine in Bubastis but in other instances only one animal of a species embodied a god. At Memphis the Apis bull lived in splendour as 'the herald of Ptah', a god who was not himself represented as a bull but always in human form. When the bull died, a calf with the special markings which identified it as the successor had to be found. For 40 days the calf was attended by women, who at intervals displayed their sexual organs to him. Then he was brought by boat to Memphis, his cabin lined with gold.

The prominence of animals in Egyptian religion was not merely a tolerated survival from more primitive times. Their cults aroused genuine devotion and were costly of time, trouble and money. In the late 4th century BC the funeral of one Apis bull was so expensive that the funds set aside for it were used up and it was necessary to borrow an extra amount equivalent to £25,000 in modern money. Henri Frankfort has commented that 'there is something altogether peculiar about the meaning which animals possessed for the Egyptians. Elsewhere, in Africa or North America, for example, it seems that either the terror of animal strength or the strong bond, the mutual dependence of man and beast (in the case of cattle cults, for instance), explains animal worship. But in Egypt *the animal as such*, irrespective of its specific nature, seems to possess religious significance; and the significance was so great that even the mature speculation of later times rarely dispensed with animal forms in plastic or literary images referring to the gods.'

Animal and God

One theory of animal gods is that the god first worshipped as an animal and later acquires human characteristics. His human nature grows gradually more important until he becomes fully human, though the animal often retains a connection with him and is sacred to him. But in many cases no such evolutionary pattern can be demonstrated; for Egyptian deities, for instance, or for Celtic gods. For example, the Celtic god Cernunnos, 'the horned one', who was closely connected with the stag and also

---

with a peculiar ram-horned serpent, appears as part stag or serpent and part human in both the earliest and the latest representations of him.

Again, although the symbolism of an animal and its connection with a particular god naturally tend to be based on its own most striking characteristics, the symbolism and the origin of the connection are not always clear. Wolves, as fierce predators, are associated with war gods, like the Roman Mars or the Teutonic Tyr, but also with the Greek god Apollo, who was not a war god. The inquisitive and chattering baboon seems well suited to Thoth, the Egyptian god of intelligent inquiry who invented speech. But whether this is the correct explanation and whether, if it is, the ape was connected with the god because it embodied part of his nature or, the other way round, its connection with him for

---

some other reason influenced later ideas of his nature, is uncertain.

Immortal Snake

One beast which has taken a firm grip on the human imagination is the serpent. It was thought to have found the secret of avoiding death, because it sloughs its old skin and appears rejuvenated in a new one, and so in myths like the Babylonian epic of Gilgamesh it steals the immortality which the gods had meant for man. This may have been its original role in the story of Adam and Eve (see FIRST MAN). The Eden story later gave the serpent its connection with the Devil, a connection assisted by the snake's phallic shape which linked it with lust, and also with fertility.

Some snakes were seen to live in holes in the ground or to appear from crannies in rocks, which connected them with the earth, with fertility again, and with the underworld and the dead. In Mesopotamia the Sumerian and Babylonian goddesses of the underworld were identified as serpents. In Greece sacred snakes were one of the marks of an underground god or spirit; honey-cakes were offered to them. The Fijian god Ndengei is a giant snake who lives in a cave and when he moves the earth quakes.

The cult of the house snake, offered milk and breadcrumbs, and addressed as 'master of the house', is not entirely dead in Greece even yet. There are many shrines of snake gods in India and python gods were common in Africa until this century. The plumed serpent appears in ancient Mexican religions and snakes, especially rattlesnakes, in the myths and rituals of North American Indians.

Bull and Boar

The bull is another important beast in the history of religions, impressive for its strength, its pawing hoof and fierce charge, and its formidable sexual powers. Enlil, the great Babylonian god of fertility and storm, was addressed as 'overpowering ox, exalted overpowering ox'. Gods of thunder, storm and rain, which fertilizes the earth, were often pictured as bulls. In India the Aryan sky god Dyaus, the red bull who smiles through the clouds, 'bellows downwards', which evidently means 'thunders', and later several Hindu gods have bull forms. Mithras, the Persian god of light whose cult

Michael Holford

rivalled Christianity in the early centuries AD, was connected with the bull. In Crete the spectacular and lethal sport of bull-leaping was a religious ritual. The first Minos, or bull king of Crete, had been begotten by Zeus in the form of a bull, and the bull was also connected with the noise and destruction of earthquakes. The horns of the bull, as of other horned animals like the stag, were widely regarded as peculiarly sacred and powerful (see HORNS).

Celtic mythology abounds with sacred boars, magic pigs which reappear whole after being killed and eaten, and fearsome supernatural boars which are hunted by heroes. In Welsh legend, King Arthur and his men hunted Twrch Trwyth, a king who had been turned into a boar, for the treasures, a comb and shears, which he carried between his ears. Pork was the meat on which chieftains feasted in northern Europe, as did warriors after death in Valhalla, and the Celts buried pigs' bones and joints of pork with the dead. But elsewhere, as among Jews and Mohammedans, pig's flesh has been considered 'unclean' and forbidden.

Sun Chariot

The horse-taming nomads of southern Russia, who spread into northern Europe, Greece, the Middle East and India in successive waves over a period of hundreds of years after c 2000 BC, connected their swift and powerful stallions with the sun, and imagined the sun crossing the sky in a horse-drawn chariot. The Celtic war god was closely associated with horses, perhaps

because of the use of horse chariots in battle, and in France and Britain the Celtic goddess Epona, 'divine horse', was popular with the cavalrymen of Roman armies. Freyr, the fertility god of the Vikings, was linked with both the boar and the horse.

The Animal in Man

The sacred horses of Freyr illustrate one of the reasons for sacrificing an animal to a god, which is simply to give him a good meal. In the 10th century AD a Christian king of Norway, Olaf Tryggvason, went to Thrandheim and seized a stallion which was about to be sacrificed 'for Freyr to eat'. But there is another and deeper motive, for the slaughtered animal may be believed to embody the god and the worshipper who eats its flesh eats the god; if only temporarily and partially, he becomes the god (see FOOD AND DRINK).

In the savagely orgiastic worship of Dionysus the lines between animal, man and god were spectacularly crossed. Dionysus was described as 'mad' and 'raving' (see DIONYSUS). His worshippers, who were predominantly women, went out to the mountainside dressed in the skins of fawns, some of them suckling young animals at the breast, baby deer perhaps or wolf cubs. As they sang and danced they felt a strange excitement. They began to run, finding in themselves superhuman energy and strength, until in frenzy they hunted down animals, wild or tame, and tore them to pieces alive, gnawing at the raw flesh. They behaved, in fact, as if they were animals in animals'

skins, suckling their young or tearing their prey. In the release of fierce animal passion their god possessed them: and it seems that the animals they hunted embodied Dionysus himself so that torn and devoured, he became one with his worshippers.

The same principle, that by imitating an animal and giving free rein to the animal elements in his nature, a man can reach a state of frenzied intoxication which breaks the chains that bind him to his human condition and makes him a sharer in the divine, appears in many other parts of the world. It lies behind the pagan European customs of dancing in animal costumes and masks which the Church tried to suppress and which have been preserved or revived in existing folk ceremonies. The *Liber Poenitentialis* of Theodore, Archbishop of Canterbury in the 7th century, forbids people to dress up as stags or bulls or to put on the heads of beasts on the first day of January.

All Creatures Great and Small

Medieval Christianity had its animal symbolism too. The lamb and the fish stood for Christ, the dove for the Holy Ghost, the sheep for the righteous, the goats for the wicked. Animals were carved in profusion in churches, not only as pleasing decoration but because God made them all and in each of them could be seen something of the mind of the Creator. The man, the lion, the ox and the eagle, which stood for the authors of the four gospels, also showed that the complete Christian must be a man for reason, a lion for courage, an ox for sacrifice

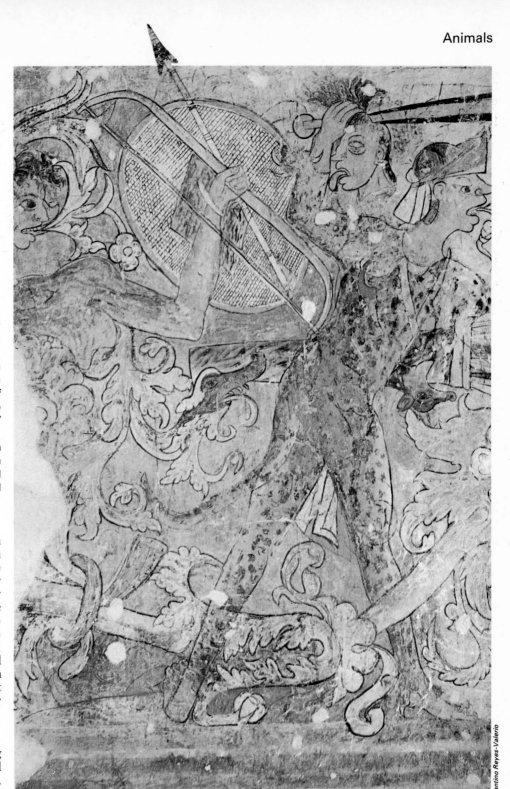

Far left Many Indian gods have animal incarnations: Vishnu as a boar, from a 17th century processional chariot
Left The Minotaur of ancient fable was a man with a bull's head who lurked in the Cretan labyrinth. 'There is a labyrinth in the heart of every man; and to each comes the day when he must reach the centre, and meet the Minotaur' (Mary Renault, *The Last of the Wine*)
Right Part of a mural showing the old Mexican myth of a battle between the gods Tezcatlipoca (the jaguar, standing for night and death) and Huitzilopochtli (the eagle, standing for day and life)

and an eagle for contemplation.

In the bestiaries fables of animals taken from pagan authors were given Christian interpretations, like the fable of the male elephant, an animal in its sagacity so totally uninterested in sex that he would mate only when the female gave him the aphrodisiac mandrake plant to eat. The elephants were interpreted as Adam and Eve in Eden, the mandrake as the forbidden fruit. Not until Eve gave Adam the fruit did he know sexual desire and the result was the expulsion from paradise. In the habits of the elephant God had painted the lesson of the Fall for men to see and understand.

Astrology and Magic

The European magical tradition, also seeing the universe as a logical design and interested in the underlying links connecting it together, makes much play with animal symbolism. Most of the signs of the zodiac are named for animals and traditional popular astrological lore is interestingly totemistic, in the sense that people are supposed to have the characteristics of their zodiac animal. Those born under Capricorn, the Goat, are told that they butt away obstacles and leap over difficulties like goats bounding from crag to crag. Those born under Leo, the Lion, are commanding and powerful like the king of beasts, and have fine heads of hair (manes) and large handwriting (paw marks).

In magic an animal is used for its own inherent occult qualities or because of its links with supernatural forces (see CORRESPONDENCES; RITUAL MAGIC). 'If we would call any evil Spirit to the Circle', says the *Fourth Book*, added to Agrippa's *Occult Philosophy* but probably not written by him, 'it first behoveth us to consider and to know

his nature, to which of the planets it agreeth . . .' It describes the forms in which the spirits may show themselves, including a she-goat, camel and dove for spirits connected with Venus, a horse or a stag for those of Mars, a cow or a goose for spirits of the moon. Other magical textbooks give similar descriptions, following the tradition which goes back to ancient Mesopotamia that demons appear in animal forms.

The purpose is to help the magician to understand the nature of the spirit or demon which he attempts to summon up and master. Its animal symbols and characteristics contribute to a vivid mental picture of it, on which the magician concentrates during the ceremony in which it is conjured up. Behind this is the old magical belief that to imagine

supernatural power, in its appropriate animal or other form, is to be possessed by it, to become it, to control it.
(See also BIRDS, FISH, INSECTS and articles on individual animals.)

FURTHER READING: There is much interesting material in J. G. Frazer, *The Golden Bough* (abridged edn. Macmillan, 1922) though not all Frazer's conclusions are now accepted, also in Mircea Eliade, *Patterns in Comparative Religion* (Sheed & Ward, 1957). For the Celts see Anne Ross, *Pagan Celtic Britain* (Columbia University Press, 1967); for Egypt, Henri Frankfort, *Ancient Egyptian Religion* (Harper Row, 1961); for the bull, J. R. Conrad, *The Horn and the Sword* (Dutton, 1957).

Animism is the belief that spirits inhabit everything in Nature; every hill, tree and stream, every breeze and cloud, every stone and pool, has its own spirit — a belief once seen as the origin of all religions

ANIMISM

DURING THE 19TH CENTURY various theories based on the scientific knowledge of the time were developed to explain the origin of religion. One of these theories was put forward by the Professor of Anthropology at Oxford, Sir Edward Tylor, who suggested in his book *Primitive Culture,* published in 1871, that Animism was the 'minimum' definition of religion and the explanation of its origin.

Tylor described animism as 'the doctrine of souls and other spiritual beings in general.' The name is derived from the Latin words *animus* and *anima,* which could mean 'life, soul, spirit', and were essentially connected with the 'life-breath'. Tylor argued that animism was the earliest stage in the evolution of religion.

It seems as though thinking men, as yet at a low level of culture, were deeply impressed by two groups of biological problems. In the first place, what is it that makes the difference between a living body and a dead one; what causes waking, sleep, trance, disease, death? In the second place, what are those human shapes which appear in dreams and visions? Looking at these two groups of phenomena, the ancient savage philosophers probably made their first step by the obvious inference that every man has two things belonging to him, namely, a life and a phantom. These two are evidently in close connexion with the body, the life as enabling it to feel and think and act, the phantom as being its image or second self; both, also, are perceived to be things separable from the body, the life as being able to go away and leave it insensible or dead, the phantom as appearing to people at a distance from it.

Above Animism is the belief that everything in Nature has a soul as well as a body: Indian tree spirit
Below Sir Edward Tylor, who put forward the theory of animism to explain the origin of religion

Mansell Collection

Michael Holford

A Multitude of Spirits

Tylor went on to argue that primitive man assumed that the 'life' and the 'phantom' were 'manifestations of the same soul'. From this combination emerged the idea of the soul as an apparition or a ghost. In turn, this idea produced the conception of the personal soul or spirit. Tylor graphically described this *anima* or soul.

It is a thin unsubstantial human image, in its nature a sort of vapour, film, or shadow; the cause of life and thought in the individual it animates; independently possessing the personal consciousness and volition of its corporeal owner, past or present; capable of leaving the body far behind, to flash swiftly from place to place; mostly impalpable and invisible, yet also manifesting physical power, and especially appearing to men waking or asleep as a phantasm separate from the body of which it bears the likeness; continuing to exist and appear to men after the death of that body; able to enter into, possess, and act in the bodies of other men, of animals, and even of things.'

Having argued that primitive man, from his experience of dreams and other related phenomena, conceived of a soul as the conscious animating entity within its own body, Tylor made a further deduction. He argued that from his conception of a personal soul, primitive man would have concluded that all natural phenomena, such as trees, streams, clouds, sun, moon and stars, also possessed souls that animated them, giving them life and movement.

This idea was vividly presented by Sir James Frazer, the famous disciple of Tylor and the author of one of the most influential studies of religion, *The Golden Bough*.

After men had peopled with a multitude of individual spirits every rock and hill, every tree and flower, every brook and river, every breeze that blew, and every cloud that flecked with silvery white the blue expanse of heaven, they began, in virtue of what we may call the economy of thought, to limit the number of the spiritual beings of whom their imagination at first had been so prodigal. Instead of a separate spirit for every individual tree, they came to conceive of a god of the woods in general, a Silvanus or what not; instead of personifying all the winds as gods, each with his distinct character and features, they imagined a single god of the winds, an Aeolus for example . . . To put it otherwise, the innumerable multitude of spirits and demons were generalized and reduced to a comparatively small number of deities; animism was replaced by polytheism.

It was believed that from this stage of the worship of many gods (polytheism), certain more enlightened peoples advanced to the idea of one solitary deity (monotheism), as among the Jews and Christians.

The Modern Attitude

The theory of animism as an explanation of the original nature of religion did not go unchallenged. A later Professor of Anthropology at Oxford, R. R. Marett, criticized Tylor's theory on the ground that it presupposed a consciousness of personality that was unlikely to have existed in the earliest stages of culture. Marett pointed out that supernaturalism, the attitude of the mind dictated by awe of the mysterious, which provided religion with its raw material, could exist apart from animism and might be the basis on which animism was founded.

Although animism long exercised a strong formative influence on speculation about the nature and origin of religion, more recent study approaches the problem along different lines. The earliest written records of religion, the Egyptian *Pyramid Texts* (c 2400 BC) reveal that in ancient Egypt there existed no idea of a clear-cut division between soul and body in human nature. On the contrary, a human being was regarded as a compound of physical body and various psychic elements of which the soul was only one. Similar, though less elaborate, conceptions were held by many other ancient peoples, including the Mesopotamians, Hebrews and Homeric Greeks. Tylor's dualistic idea of the soul as the inner essential self, independent of the body, first emerged comparatively late in India (c 700 BC) and Greece (c 600 BC).

The origin of the idea of deity is also far more complicated than Tylor thought. The evidence of archeology indicates that the earliest form of deity was that of the Mother Goddess, the deification of the female principle, which expressed man's desire for fertility and new life.
(See also ASTRAL BODY; BREATH; GHOSTS ORIGINS OF RELIGION; SOUL.)

S. G. F. BRANDON

St Anthony of Egypt is best known for the attacks made on him by demons. It has been suggested that these experiences were caused by the acid from which L.S.D. is derived

ST ANTHONY

A CHRISTIAN ASCETIC, noted for his victorious struggles against demons, St Anthony was born in Egypt, c 250 AD. St Athanasius, in the following century, wrote a biography of him, which says that he was brought up as a Christian by his wealthy parents. He was extremely devout as a boy and was too sensitive to be sent to school, so that he never learned to read or write. His parents died before he was 20 and he lived alone; 'he took no care for anything whatsoever except his soul, and he began to train himself in the habits of the strictest abstinence and self-denial.'

He lived on bread, salt and water, fasting for three or four days at a time and going without sleep for long periods. The Devil tempted him with anxieties over worldly matters, by sending him 'filthy and maddening thoughts' and by appearing to him as a woman, but the saint was able to resist these assaults and concentrate on God.

When he went to live in a tomb near his village, he was attacked by multitudes of demons, which raged at him and pummelled him into unconsciousness, but he defied them. They also appeared to him in frightening animal forms, a famous episode because

St Anthony and the Demons

From a biography of the Saint, written in the 4th century AD:

Now it is very easy for the Enemy to create apparitions and appearances of such a character that they shall be deemed real and actual objects, and phantasms of this kind caused a phantom earthquake, and they rent asunder the four corners of the house and entered therein in a body from all sides. One had the form of a lion and another had the appearance of a wolf and another was like unto a panther and all the others were in the forms and similitudes of serpents and vipers and scorpions. The lion was roaring as a lion roars when he is about to slay; the bull was ready to gore with his horns; the panther was prepared to spring; and the snakes and the vipers were hissing, and they appeared to be in the act of hurling themselves upon him; and the sounds which they made and the forms in which they showed themselves were terrible.

Now the blessed man ANTHONY was not disturbed by their commotion, and his mind remained wholly undisturbed. And as he was lying down he laughed at these phantoms . . .

St Athanasius
The Life of Saint Anthony

The bizarre and nightmare visions of St Anthony have fired the imagination of many artists. *The Temptation of St Anthony* by the Dutch painter Hieronymous Bosch

it was portrayed by painters of later generations. These demonic visitations may have been a natural result of the privations which the saint imposed on himself, and St Athanasius called them 'phantasms' or hallucinations but did not doubt that they were sent by the Enemy. 'The whole race of devils,' he said, 'is beyond measure an envious one and it is altogether jealous of all mankind and particularly of the monks, for they cannot bear to see . . . heavenly lives led upon the earth.'

More recently, it has been suggested that the saint may have eaten bread infected with the fungus *Claviceps purpurea*, which contains lysergic acid, from which the drug L.S.D. is derived.

When he was 31, St Anthony withdrew from human company altogether, shutting himself away in an old fort where he spent the next 20 years. Food was thrown in to him over the wall. He continued his ascetic self-denials 'and to the day of his death,' according to St Athanasius, 'he never touched his body with water . . . and he never dipped his feet in water without the sternest necessity.' A colony of disciples gathered round him, living in caves and huts, and vainly begging him for spiritual guidance. In the end he agreed to help them and spent several years teaching them and organizing them into a community. He is regarded as the founder of Christian monasticism.

The saint retreated from mankind again and spent the rest of his life as a solitary in the desert, though he received occasional visitors and went to Alexandria twice.

ANTICHRIST

THE FEAR OF A MESSIAH of evil, who would come with war, plague, famine and destruction to enslave the world, haunted men for hundreds of years in Europe, rather as the fear of nuclear war makes an ominous background to our lives now; though with a consolation we lack, the belief that Antichrist would eventually be overthrown by God. As Christ's opposite, Antichrist would claim to be God and would work miracles, raising the dead, walking on water, healing the sick, turning stones into bread, but his miracles would be shams. The Jews also expected the coming of the evil power and it was said that he would be bald, with one eye bigger than the other, his left arm longer than his right, and deaf in his right ear; right being traditionally the side of good.

The early Christians adopted the Jewish belief in a coming titanic battle between God and an evil adversary. The first human model for the adversary was the Syrian king Antiochus IV Epiphanes, who captured Jerusalem in the 2nd century BC and used the temple for the worship of pagan gods.

In the New Testament 2 Thessalonians (chapter 2) predicts the coming of 'the man of lawlessness, the son of perdition', who will claim to be God. Revelation (chapter 13) predicts the appearance of the Great Beast 666, supported by a second beast, who was later identified as Antichrist. The first and second letters of John describe rebels inside the Christian flock itself as 'antichrists', which set a precedent for the later employment of the word as a term of abuse, used by Christians for other Christians who failed to agree with them.

Opponents of Popes Boniface VIII and John XXII labelled each of them as Antichrist and many Protestants later regarded all Popes as Antichrist, an idea which lingers on among a few extreme Protestants. In this century the Kaiser and Hitler were both described as Antichrist.
(See also GREAT BEAST.)

In this 15th century fresco by Signorelli the Antichrist is shown working false miracles and deluding the people, but is overthrown by an angel in the sky

Antisemitism
Hostility to Jews, based partly on Jewish religious exclusiveness and partly on beliefs about supposed Jewish racial characteristics: common in Europe since the establishment of Christianity, and one of the ugliest principles of the Nazi programme in Germany.
See RACE MYTHS.

Anubis
Egyptian god of the dead, 'lord of the mummy wrappings' and inventor of embalming, who led the dead to the place of judgement after death and supervised the weighing of the heart; shown as a black jackal or a dog, both of which roamed the cemeteries in the Egyptian desert.
See JUDGEMENT OF THE DEAD.

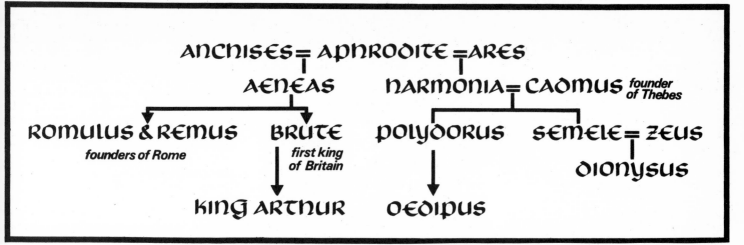

ANCHISES = APHRODITE = ARES
AENEAS   HARMONIA = CADMUS *founder of Thebes*
ROMULUS & REMUS   BRUTE   POLYDORUS   SEMELE = ZEUS
founders of Rome   *first king of Britain*   DIONYSUS
KING ARTHUR   OEDIPUS

Golden Aphrodite, lover of laughter, born of the sea-foam, was the Greek goddess of love and beauty. Homer refers to 'the beauty of her neck and her lovely breasts and sparkling eyes'

APHRODITE

APHRODITE WAS THE ancient Greek goddess of love, beauty, generation and fertility. She was, naturally, a popular goddess and her cult was widespread throughout almost all of the Greek world. The Romans identified her with their goddess Venus. She had famous sanctuaries at Corinth and on the island of Cythera, at Paphos and Amathus in Cyprus, and at Eryx in the west of Sicily. She figures prominently in Greek mythology, beginning with the *Iliad* and *Odyssey* of Homer (8th century BC) and the poetry of Hesiod (c 700 BC).

Despite her great popularity and important place in Greek religion and culture, Aphrodite was not in origin a native Greek goddess. Her cult came to Greece from Cyprus, where she was known as Kypris (Lady of Cyprus). Aphrodite was probably a local Cypriot version of the great mother goddess, whose worship under various names was almost universal throughout the Near and Middle East in ancient times, and was of great antiquity. The many primitive idols found in Cyprus, depicting a naked female figure with the sexual attributes grossly emphasized, are probably archaic representations of this mother goddess, to whom the ancient inhabitants of Cyprus gave the name of Aphrodite.

The Foam-Born
There has been much learned but inconclusive discussion about the original meaning of the goddess's name. The Greeks, from the time of Hesiod, tried to explain it as deriving from the word *aphros*, 'foam', in the sense that Aphrodite was 'foam-born'. Hesiod in his *Theogony* accounts for this 'foam-birth' in a strange way. Describing the origin of the universe, he tells how Earth gave birth to various beings through cohabiting with Uranus, the personification of Heaven. Uranus proved a tyrannous sire and imprisoned his offspring within the body of Earth, so that she groaned with the burden. Release came

finally when Cronus, one of the sons of Earth, with the connivance of his mother, castrated his father. Cronus threw the severed genitals into the sea, and a white foam gathered around them, from which a maiden emerged. According to Hesiod, 'first she drew near to holy Cythera, and from there, afterwards, she came to sea-girt Cyprus, and came forth an awful and lovely goddess, and grass grew up about her beneath her shapely feet.'

This idyllic scene has been immortalized by the Renaissance artist Botticelli in his painting, *The Birth of Venus*.

This strange tale, so shocking in conception and yet so poetic in its presentation of Aphrodite, may provide a clue to the origin of some of the Greek myths about the origin of the universe. On Hittite clay tablets there has been found an even stranger and more primitive myth of a primordial act of castration: the sky-god Alalus is emasculated by a divine hero Kumarbis, who swallows the genitals and becoming impregnated by them, gives birth to the storm god. Since it is known that the Achaeans (one of the earliest of the peoples we call Greeks), had dealings with the Hittites of Asia Minor, it is possible that

Bronze head, 2nd century BC, of Aphrodite, goddess of love and the supreme embodiment of feminine beauty, originally a Cypriot mother goddess

Michael Holford

Hesiod drew on some tradition that derived ultimately from this region.

The Hittite myth does not deal with the origin of a goddess like Aphrodite. But the similarity of the theme of generation resulting from the severed genitals of a god is remarkable, especially since Aphrodite personified the principle of generation. According to Hesiod's *Theogony*, Aphrodite was also called Philommedes (member-loving) because she 'sprang from the genitals'. The Christian scholar Clement of Alexandria, writing in the early 3rd century against pagan religion, asserts with reference to the name Philommedes that in the rites of Aphrodite, her birth from the sea-foam was symbolized by the presentation of a cake of salt and a phallus.

Desire as a Universal Force
In his account of the origin of things, Hesiod still further emphasizes the fundamental sexual significance of Aphrodite by associating her with Eros: 'And with her went Eros, and comely Himeros (Desire) followed her at her birth.' The Eros of Hesiod is not the young god of love or the mischievous Cupid of later mythology. He is a powerful creative force, described by Hesiod as one who 'unnerves the limbs and overcomes the mind and wise counsels of all gods and all men'.

It is evident that Hesiod regarded the traditional gods as deifications of basic universal forces. Seeing the creation of the universe in sexual terms, as the product of the intercourse of various pairs of cosmic beings, he felt the need for some factor that would unite and make fruitful the unions of the various pairs. In Eros he saw such a factor but he probably also drew on a primitive folk-tradition, where this view already existed. For the Athenian dramatist Aeschylus, in the 5th century BC, gives eloquent expression to the idea in some lines that have survived from his lost play of the *Danaids*. 'Love moves the pure Heaven to wed the Earth; and Love (*eros*) takes hold on Earth to join in marriage. And the rain, dropping from the husband Heaven, impregnates Earth, and she brings forth for men pasture for flocks and corn, the life of man.'

It would seem that the ancient Greeks had already made a god of sexual potency an agent in the creation of the universe, under the name of Eros, long before Aphrodite

entered their religion. Mindful of this, Hesiod evidently seeks to account for the later appearance of Aphrodite as the goddess of sexual love by using the strange and probably foreign myth of the castration of a primordial deity. By so doing he also manages to explain her non-Greek name of Aphrodite and to associate her with Eros, the older deification of the mysterious force that prompted the union of the sexes for the purpose of procreation. (See also EROS.)

Love and War

Hesiod's account of Aphrodite is especially important because, though somewhat later in date than Homer, he is aware of Aphrodite as a newcomer among the Greek deities; in the *Iliad* and *Odyssey* she has already been included in the company of the Olympian gods. Homer makes her the daughter of the supreme god Zeus and Dione, an obscure goddess. However, two small facts may preserve some tradition of Aphrodite's eastern origin. In Homer she is the wife of Hephaestus, the lame fire-god and divine craftsman, who was certainly of oriental origin. And her love affair with the war god Ares recalls the fact that some eastern goddesses, including Ishtar of Mesopotamia and Anat-Astarte of Canaan and Phoenicia, combined the roles of goddess of fertility and goddess of war.

In the Homeric poems, Aphrodite is often portrayed in a rather undignified manner, although she is 'golden Aphrodite', the daughter of Zeus. In the *Iliad* the goddess Hera is depicted as consulting her when she wanted to beguile her husband Zeus. The goddess asks Aphrodite to give her 'love and desire, wherewith thou art wont to subdue all immortals and mortal men.' Aphrodite helps by lending Hera the embroidered girdle that adorned her breast, 'wherein are fashioned all manner of allurements'. Such a service was probably deemed proper to the goddess of love, even though it assisted in the deception of the supreme god Zeus.

But more surprising, and contrary to our ideas of the status of a goddess, are two other episodes in which Aphrodite is involved. The first occurs in the *Iliad* in a lively account of the fighting before the walls of Troy. The Greek hero Diomedes severely wounds Aeneas, a Trojan leader who was the son of Aphrodite by Anchises, a mortal man. Aphrodite, seeing her human son in danger of death, intervenes to save him. When Diomedes recognizes the goddess he is not deterred but lunges at her with his spear. Aphrodite is wounded in the wrist, and the immortal *ichor*, which the Greek deities have instead of mortal blood, pours out. Aphrodite gives a piercing scream, drops the wounded Aeneas and flees, while Diomedes derides her.

The idea that a goddess could be wounded by the weapon of a mortal man is certainly strange, and we can only wonder why the Homeric poet depicted the goddess of love as suffering so humiliating and painful an experience. He seems, while recognizing

Detail from Botticelli's *Birth of Venus*: the goddess riding on a shell, an emblem of woman, over the sea from whose foam she was born

…er divinity, to mock the idea that she should …articipate in war. It may be that in this …manner he rebuts some older tradition of a …varlike aspect which the Greek Aphrodite …ad inherited from her eastern origins.

Under the Net

…ven more degrading is the episode recorded …n the *Odyssey*, where a minstrel sings of the …llicit love of Ares and Aphrodite. He tells …ow Helius, the sun god, reported their …iaison to Hephaestus, the lame and deformed …usband of Aphrodite. Furious at the news, …he craftsman god plans the punishment of …he guilty pair. He forges a net too fine to be …een but too strong to be broken, and spreads …t about the bed in his house. Giving out that …e is leaving to visit his favourite sanctuary, …e sets the trap for the lovers. Ares seizes …he opportunity of the husband's departure …o visit Aphrodite. Warned by Helius, …Hephaestus turns back and discovers the …overs together in his bed, where they are …enmeshed by the invisible but imprisoning …onds. Hephaestus calls the other gods to …vitness the shameful spectacle. The gods …gather in ribald mirth but the goddesses …keep demurely away. Hephaestus demands …that Zeus pay back the bridal gifts before he …releases his shameless daughter and her …paramour. The sea god Poseidon finally …persuades the angry Hephaestus to let the …guilty couple go, by guaranteeing the pay-…ment of damages by Ares. The extraordinary …episode ends by describing the 'laughter-…loving' Aphrodite's retreat to Paphos in …Cyprus, 'where is her demesne and fragrant

---

Aphrodite Beautiful

Idalian Aphrodite beautiful,
Fresh as the foam, new-bathed in Paphian wells,
With rosy slender fingers backward drew
From her warm brows and bosom her deep hair
Ambrosial, golden round her lucid throat
And shoulder; from the violets her light foot
Shone rosy-white, and o'er her rounded form
Between the shadows of the vine-bunches
Floated the glowing sunlights as she moved.

Tennyson *Oenone*

---

altar. There the Graces anointed her with immortal oil . . . and clothed her in a lovely raiment, a wonder to behold.'

Little, unfortunately, is known of the nature and form of the rites which were performed in the various temples of Aphrodite. At Corinth and in Cyprus she was served by sacred prostitutes; and at Abydos there was a temple of Aphrodite Porne (Aphrodite the Harlot). This connection with ritual prostitution attests Aphrodite's eastern origin; for the custom prevailed at the cult-centres of many eastern goddesses.

Aphrodite, however, was also the divine patron of marriage. At Athens, under the title of Pandemos (of all the people), her cult was dignified and unobjectionable. She had, in fact, many sides to her nature: she was a sea goddess, a goddess of animals, of gardens, and even of death — there was

a small statue at Delphi called 'Aphrodite by the Tomb'. This last association is not surprising, for the great mother goddess was also a subterranean deity concerned with the dead.

In mythology Aphrodite was also associated with the three Graces or *Charites* (personifications of charm, grace and beauty) and with the Hours (*Horae*), goddesses of the seasons. Various animals were connected with her (including doves, sparrows, swans, dolphins and mussels) and forms of vegetation (roses, myrtle, cypress and pomegranates).

Anemones for Adonis

Aphrodite's connection with Adonis (well known through Shakespeare's poem *Venus and Adonis*) reveals most clearly her original association with the Great Goddess of the ancient Near East. The story of Adonis appears in its most complete form in the *Metamorphoses* of the Latin poet Ovid (17 AD). Adonis is the incestuous offspring of Cinyras, King of Cyprus, and his daughter Myrrha who, in consequence of her sin, is transformed into a myrrh tree (the myrrh, exuded from the bark, is explained as the tears of Myrrha). This metamorphosis of his mother occurs before Adonis is born and his subsequent birth from the myrrh tree is

Paul Delvaux's *Venus Asleep*, 1944, a study in erotic frenzy. The skeleton is a reminder that the love goddess was also the bringer of death, 'the manslayer' and 'she of the tombs': Tate Gallery

Brompton Studios

Aphrodite is here seen in frivolous mood gambling with the god Pan, the amorous goat god whose task it was to make the flocks fertile: 4th century BC

significant of his origin as a vegetation god.

Grown to a beautiful youth, Adonis attracts the attention of Aphrodite, who falls passionately in love with him. Despite her warnings of the risks of hunting, Adonis is killed by a wild boar. Aphrodite is distraught with grief at his death and to commemorate the tragedy, she causes the anemone to spring from his blood.

An alternative Greek version of the Adonis myth is that when Adonis is born of the myrrh tree, Aphrodite, admiring his beauty, hides him in a chest and entrusts him to Persephone, the queen of the underworld. Persephone also falls in love with him and refuses to give him back, and Zeus has to decide between the two goddesses. He ordains that Adonis should stay for one third of the year with him, one third with Aphrodite, and the remaining third with Persephone.

The origin of Adonis is revealed by his name, which comes from a Semitic title 'Adoni', meaning 'my Lord'. The title signified a vegetation deity, whose annual death and resurrection commemorated the life-cycle of the corn. His death was lamented by a fertility goddess, he being her son or young lover. The relationship occurs in the cults of Anat and Astarte, goddesses of Canaan and Phoenicia, and finds its earliest expression in the relations of the Mesopotamian goddess Ishtar with Tammuz, the god of vegetation.

The death and resurrection of Adonis was celebrated annually in a ritual lamentation by women over an effigy of the dead god in many places, including Athens. In the Greek city of Alexandria in Egypt the sacred marriage of Aphrodite and Adonis was celebrated, followed next day by lamentation as an effigy of the dead god was taken out and cast into the sea. 'Gardens of Adonis' were also made, in which the forced growth of seedlings symbolized the resurrection of Adonis. The cult and myth of Adonis doubtless came to Greece from Cyprus with the cult of Aphrodite.

The Goddess in Art

The portrayal of Aphrodite in art deserves special notice. Greek classical art of the 5th century presents the goddess as a dignified figure, robed in contemporary costume, as in the Parthenon frieze, now in the British Museum. A notable but delicate exception is the representation of Aphrodite rising from the sea on the Ludovisi throne, where the body of the goddess is depicted as only lightly veiled.

The first notable figure of a nude Aphrodite was made in the 4th century BC by Praxiteles. The work was commissioned by the people of Cos, who rejected it for the traditional draped figure. It was accepted by the citizens of Cnidos, and became one of the most famous statues of the ancient world. The goddess was shown laying aside her robe, preparing for the bath; the original statue is known only through later Roman copies. The Cnidian Aphrodite inspired many later Hellenistic and Roman statues of which the Venus de Milo, now in the Louvre at Paris, is the most celebrated.

S. G. F. BRANDON

FURTHER READING: H. J. Rose, *A Handbook of Greek Mythology* (Dutton, 1959); J. Harrison, *Prolegomena to the Study of Greek Religion* (World Publishing, 1955); E. O. James, *The Cult of the Mother Goddess* (Barnes and Noble, 1961); S. G. F. Brandon, *Creation Legends of the Ancient Near East* (Verry, Lawrence, 1963); H. Licht, *Sexual Life in Ancient Greece* (Barnes and Noble, 1932); and for the goddess in art, K. Clark, *The Nude* (Doubleday, 1959).

Apis

Sacred bull of Memphis in Egypt, connected with the gods Ptah and Osiris, who later became the Graeco-Egyptian deity Serapis, a god of the underworld: Serapis appears on Roman Imperial coins and the famous library of Alexandria was attached to his temple there.
See ANIMALS; BULL.

Roger Wood London

Apocalypse

Alternative name for the last book of the Bible, the Revelation of St John: in a broader sense, 'apocalyptic' writings describe an approaching and usually catastrophic end of the world, involving a conflict between good and evil in which God intervenes to secure the victory of the good; besides Revelation, the books of Daniel and Enoch are examples.
See DANIEL; END OF THE WORLD; REVELATION.

LUCK AND FATE

Camera Press London

Beliefs about luck, fate and the future are human weapons against chance, accident and the menace of chaos which threatens the order of the universe: this introductory article paints a backcloth for future articles on fate, luck and many methods of fortune telling

TO DIE OF OLD AGE is not remarkable but when a man dies young, is it fate, ill luck, the will of God or mere chance which has taken him before his time? In different moods we may give different answers, for we have inherited a whole set of contradictory notions: the belief that the course of our lives is decided by fate or the gods; the conviction that our own actions affect what happens to us; the suspicion that things occur largely by accident; and the persistent

feeling that some people, things or periods of time are lucky and others unlucky, that 'there is a tide in the affairs of men' and 'we must take the current when it serves, or lose our ventures', the gambler's faith in a winning streak.

Contradictory beliefs about fate, luck and chance are not so strange if they are seen against the background of Nature. People observed long ago that there is order in Nature. The sun rises and sets, the seasons follow each other, the tides rise and fall, the stars wheel in their courses, and all men die. But people also saw disorder in Nature. They saw drought, earthquakes, eclipses, unexpected and disruptive events of all kinds, and they saw that some men prosper for no apparent reason while others

fail equally unreasonably.

In societies directly dependent on agriculture and stock-raising, it was a matter of the most immediate importance for the rain to fall and the sun to shine in due season. The ever-present enemy was a failure of order, the coming of chaos, and many ancient myths and rites, as well as all political institutions, were human weapons in the battle against chaos. But sometimes chaos came, and so men combined an uneasy awareness of chance and accident with a belief in the essential orderliness of the universe.

Of the two, the belief in order has been much the more important. Human life depends on the order of Nature and without it there would be no hope of making sense of the world: hence magic, philosophy,

All sorts of apparently random events, from the fall of playing cards to the patterns of tea leaves left in a cup, have been and still are taken as signs of the future

Syndication International

Previous page Mirrors and crystals are used to foresee the patterns of fate, the 'scryer' hoping to see the future in the glass *Above left* Symbols of the golden sun and the horned moon, in astrology the principal arbiters of a man's fate *Above right* A fairground palmist

science and the modern rise of probability theory, the subjection of chance itself to mathematical rules. The belief in order and the corresponding dislike of chance, the disinclination to allow chaos an important role in events, are the basis of ideas about luck and fate, and all methods of predicting the future, whether from the planets, from lines in the hand, from a Bible opened with your eyes shut or from a stray sneeze in the night, depend on the belief that the universe is an ordered design and that even the most trivial and outwardly random events have a place in the design, and therefore contain clues to the direction in which other events in the universe are moving.

The Design of the Future

Michael Scot, astrologer to the Emperor Frederick II in the 13th century, said that sneezing twice in the night for three successive nights is a warning of death in the house. Long before that, the Greeks believed that when you sneezed it meant that what you were thinking about at that moment would take place.

A sneeze was an important omen because it is an expulsion of breath, which was thought to be the soul and life of man. That is why we say 'bless you' when somebody sneezes but all sorts of other apparently random events, from the fall of playing cards to the patterns of tea leaves left in a cup, have been and still are taken as signs of the future because they are part of the design of the universe.

Fortune telling again involves contradictory beliefs. The many modern believers in astrology, palmistry and other ways of predicting the future, which imply that the future is already mapped out ahead of us, do not usually accept that they have no power to alter their own destinies. Astrologers who claim to predict the future accurately as much as 80% of the time will go on, in practically the same breath, to maintain that we can assert ourselves against our

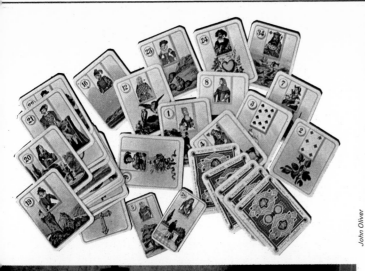

John Oliver

Transworld Feature Syndicate

Camera Press London

Giraudon

Refusal to believe in chance, random events is the basis of many methods of fortune-telling. Every event is part of a pattern and shows the direction in which other events in the universe are moving. The apparently random fall of playing cards *(above left)* or Tarot cards *(below left)* is believed to indicate the future. The gambler's wheel *(above right)* and the wheel of fortune *(below right)* are both concerned with 'runs' of luck, the ups and downs of life, in a pattern defying statistical probability

stars and that the astrologer's most important function is to help us to do so.

The Infernal Machine

Our beliefs about fate come to us from the old pagan world, especially from the Greeks, almost untouched by Christian influence. The Greeks took it that the universe is orderly and obeys laws, a belief which runs all through Greek literature.

The famous tale of Oedipus, for instance, which makes so profound an impact that Freud thought it expressed the unconscious desires of every man, can be seen as the story of a man who murders his father and sleeps with his mother because he is in the grip of a malignant and inexorable fate, an infernal machine as Jean Cocteau called it in his play of that name, an apparatus 'constructed by the infernal gods for the mathematical destruction of a mortal'. Or, in the hands of Sophocles, the story is used to suggest that behind the events of a man's life there is a pattern, a design. And that

the design is there, whatever the agonies it inflicts on us, is better than its not being there, which would mean that we lived in an intolerable chaos.

This sense of a divine order is cruelly but magnificently expressed in the last lines of *The Women of Trachis* by Sophocles, another play in which the characters are caught in an inexorable process which carries them to their doom. In E. F. Watling's translation:

You have seen strange things,
The awful hand of death, new shapes of woe,
Uncounted sufferings;
And all that you have seen
Is God.

R. B. Onians has shown (in *The Origins of*

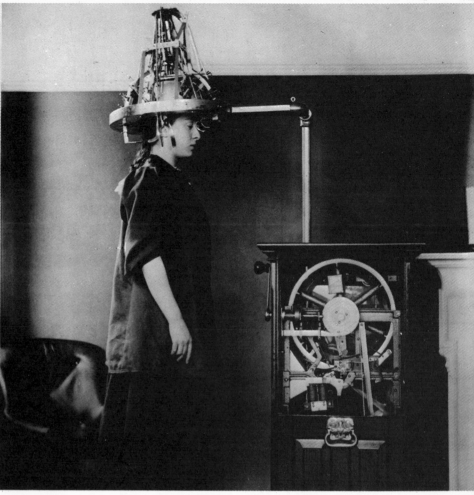

European Thought) the great importance in early Greek ideas of fate of the notion of bonds and binding, not as a symbol but as a factual account of what was thought to happen. Fate or the gods bind a man with invisible cords, which are also the threads spun by the Fates: Clotho who spins the thread, Lachesis who measures or apportions it, and the inflexible Atropos who severs it at death. The Fates (*Moirai* in Greek) became in Latin *Fata*, meaning 'things spoken', what is decreed. From the Latin come our words, fate, fay and fairy, including the fairy who visits the cradle of a newborn child to bring him good or evil gifts, which may have been the original function of the Greek Fates themselves.

The Spinners of Fate

The motifs of binding and of fate spinning the thread or weaving the pattern of our lives are not confined to Greece. In northern Europe the Norns were the spinners of destiny, in Anglo-Saxon literature fate is 'woven', and we still say of a man who is certain to do something that he is *bound* to do it. The idea of fate as a decree, 'what has been spoken', also reappears, in our use of the word doom, which originally meant a decree, a judgement.

Also not confined to Greece is the tendency to think of fate as something essentially evil, partly because the common fate of all men is death and partly because fate is the antagonist of human freedom. Some men, like Napoleon, have felt that they were destined to greatness, and the conviction has

given them strength, but more often fate is thought of in terms of misfortune. Mimnermos of Colophon in the 7th century BC, taking a figure of speech from Homer before him, struck a note re-echoed by countless poets since. We are like the leaves of springtime which grow strong in the sun and for a while we enjoy the 'flowering of youth. 'But the black Fates stand by, and one holds in her hand the goal of bitter old age, the other that of death.'

At its noblest, this pessimism has been expressed in a proud defiance, a refusal to be broken by fate's blows. Others have found serenity in bowing to the decrees of destiny. In the 2nd century AD the Roman Emperor Marcus Aurelius said that it was 'the characteristic of the good man to delight in and to welcome what befalls and what is being spun for him by destiny' and some 650 years earlier in China Confucius remarked that, 'If the wise man achieves something it is well; if he achieves nothing, it is also well; he recognizes destiny.'

Fate and Providence

An extreme view of fate, and a total disbelief in chance, is to suppose that everything we do is determined by destiny, but this picture of man as a fly in a spider's web has not appealed to many. More common is the belief that fate determines only the most important matters in a man's life, or the general direction of the path his life takes. The obvious example of a fate which awaits everyone is death, and sometimes fate is merely another word for death, as in our

expressions 'fatality' and 'fatal accident'. Sometimes fate is thought of mainly in terms of what happens after death, as in the doctrine of some Christian thinkers that each of us is predestined to be saved or damned in the next world, regardless of our actions in this one.

Fate is also commonly thought of in 'if . . . then' terms. '*If* you do this, *then* that will happen', not as a logical consequence of your action but because fate has so ruled. Nowadays we do not usually name fate itself in this connection but we use phrases which mean the same thing. 'I feel in my bones' that if I do this, things will go right or wrong, or 'something tells me' or even 'a little bird tells me', which is a reminiscence of one of the principal functions of birds in folklore, to deliver warnings of the future. That fate is not something inexorably fixed in advance but a power which may change its mind is implied in the fear of 'tempting fate', of attracting the attention of an unseen power which will punish you if you presume to express optimism about your future.

The doubtful morality of a power which acts in this way again recalls early Greek ideas. In the last book of the *Iliad* Achilles

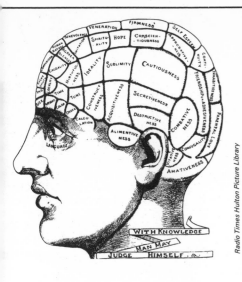

Luck might almost be defined as the poor man's substitute for fate

describes how Zeus deals out good and evil fortune to men. Morality is not involved: the man who is fortunate deserves no credit and the man who is unfortunate no blame. It is all in the lap of the gods, as we should say, or 'on the knees of the gods' as Homer said (spinning involved drawing the thread across the knees or the lap). It was the lack of morality of the Homeric gods that was criticized later in Greece, where some came to see fate as a moral power which punishes a man's crimes, an idea for which we and the Greeks use the term 'nemesis'. But in Homer evils which afflict a man are misfortunes, not punishments for sin.

This is a very different view from the Indian belief that your actions decide your fate in your future lives in the endless cycle of rebirths from which, in any case, you can escape. It also sees man's relationship to the divine in a way very different from the Jewish and Christian traditions. There is no word for 'love of God' in Homer, and no word for 'god-fearing' either.

In Judaism and Christianity what matters is the beneficent providence of God. The Old Testament is the record of the unfolding of God's plan for the world, a theme adopted by the Christians. Similarly in Moham-medanism, for the theologians at least, *kismet* is the providence of Allah, the divine plan (though in popular belief Allah behaves more like the Homeric Zeus, distributing good fortune and bad to men, from which there is no escape).

Here again is the belief in a divine order but in spite of centuries of Christian teach-ing, something nearer to the Homeric out-look seems deeply implanted in Western man. For many, it is not easy to feel, and perhaps it never has been, that 'God is work-ing his purpose out as year succeeds to year.'

Patterns of Luck
When a gambler calculates the odds against him, he is concerned with probability. When he is irrationally convinced that he is going to win, regardless of probability, he is con-cerned with luck. Luck might almost be defined as the poor man's substitute for fate. Kings, heroes and important people, who rise to great heights from which they can be dashed down, have fates; everyone else has good or bad luck. The bandy-legged Egyptian god of good luck, the dwarf Bes, has been called 'the poor man's god' and the Roman goddess of luck, Fortuna, was originally a rustic deity of fertility.

Presumably, the fertility goddess turned into a divinity of luck because successful farming depends so heavily on factors out-side the farmer's control. Luck is another human weapon against chaos and, like fate, it implies belief in an order, an order which has nothing to do with probability, normal cause and effect, human effort or human morality. If you get what you deserve, that is justice: if you get more or less, that is good or ill luck.

But unlike fate, luck is often thought of in a favourable light. To be lucky is to be fortunate, to be fated is generally ominous, which follows from the fact that luck operates in the short term, affecting events for a limited time only. This comes out in the very old belief in lucky and unlucky days, surviving in some people's reluctance to do anything important on a Friday, or in the belief which has lasted since Roman times that May is an unlucky month for a mar-riage. In the long run, which is the province of fate, there is misery in store for us, old age or death or both, but luck which works from day to day may have good or bad con-sequences.

The same idea lies behind the common use of magic, especially the wearing or carrying of charms, to ensure good luck. Only a magician of extraordinary powers could avoid death or the other grim gifts of fate, but anybody can try to attract fortu-nate influences or ward off unfortunate ones in the short run, and many people still do. J. D. Rockefeller Sr carried a lucky stone in his pocket to protect him against illness, shipwreck and other misfortunes. Others set great store by a rabbit's foot, a lump of coal, a car mascot or some other fortunate talis-man, and the sales of lucky charms support a sizeable industry.

It is in fact a common observation that there are runs of good and bad luck, and that some people are consistently luckier than others. C. G. Jung called this 'synchronicity' and suggested that there is a relationship between a man's psychological state and the events which are somehow attracted to him. Whatever the explanation, the belief in luck is part of the constant human determi-nation to see a pattern in the world around us and a design in our own lives.

The perfect embodiment of the Greek spirit, Apollo was perhaps the best-loved of all the Greek gods. Through his famous oracle at Delphi, he exercised a conciliatory influence on Greek politics, and he was believed to have founded many of the Greek colonies

APOLLO

APOLLO, brightest and best of the ancient Greek gods, was the god of music, archery, prophecy, healing, the care of animals and young growing creatures; and from the 5th century BC, at least, he was identified with the sun.

He was the only Greek god to have specific functions in each of the domains allotted separately to the three gods of the sky (Zeus), the sea (Poseidon), and the earth (Hades). His titles bear witness to these functions. He was, for example, Apollo Asgelatas – 'god of radiance'; Embasios – 'favouring embarkation'; and Arotrios – 'god of ploughing'. His titles, of which well over 300 have survived in ancient authors and inscriptions on stone, show that Apollo was a god much loved by people in all walks of life.

He was the inspiration of a great deal of ancient Greek painting, poetry and music. More than any other figure in Greek mythology or history, he embodied the spirit of Greek civilization. In art he was depicted as the ideal type of young, virile beauty.

In historical times Apollo was worshipped by all the Greeks. He plays a prominent part in the Homeric epics, and in the *Iliad* is the ally of the Trojans. In Homer, he is usually called Phoebus Apollo – 'bright Apollo'. Other epithets associated with him refer to his deadly aim as an archer, or to his silver bow.

But this most typically Greek of gods, if he did not come originally from Asia Minor, certainly incorporated many of the features of a prehistoric non-Greek deity. It is possible that the name Apollo is of Greek origin, although modern scholars are divided as to whether the root-meaning of the word is 'strength', 'sheep-fold' or 'assembly of voters'. But at an early date the original Greek god seems to have been identified with a Hittite god named Apulunas or Appaliunaas, and the Greeks themselves associated Apollo not only with a legendary northern people, the Hyperboreans, but also with Lycia, a country in what is now southwest Turkey. Apollo's mother's name, Leto, has often been connected by scholars with a Lycian word meaning 'woman'. The Greeks, however, were aware of an ambiguity in the title Lykeios (Lycian) often given to Apollo. Greek poets punned (and in ancient Greek puns had a serious, not a humorous significance) on the associations this title could have with Apollo's fame as a slayer of wolves – *lykos* being the Greek for 'wolf'.

Apollo's eastern connections partly account for an atmosphere of mystery which was another of his aspects. In time, he accumulated many exotic titles, some of them of undoubtedly non-Greek origin, and as the god of oracles he was known throughout the Greek world as Loxias – 'the ambiguous one'.

Apollo and his twin sister Armetis were the children of Zeus, king of the gods, and Leto, the Titaness. According to one version of the birth myth, Delos was the only land which would receive Leto as she felt her time to give birth drawing near. Other places feared the power of the god she would give birth to. In historic times, Apollo's birth at Delos was celebrated by an important festival held in that tiny island each spring. According to the historian Herodotus, the Hyperboreans came every year with offerings which they brought all the way from their northern homeland. There was also an oracle of Apollo at Delos.

Apollo at Delphi

Apollo's most important oracular shrine, however, was at Delphi on the Greek mainland, a place which preserves to this day much of the extraordinary, religious atmosphere which it had in ancient times. The Homeric Hymn to Apollo describes how the god came to this place 'beneath snowy Parnassus' and performed – while still a child, according to some accounts – one of his greatest exploits:

> Nearby there was a fair stream, where the Prince, son of Zeus, killed with an arrow from his bow a dragoness, a fat great wild monster, who had done much harm to men on earth and to their long-shanked flocks, for she was a blood-reeking bane.

Later tradition embroidered this story, and the female dragon became a male snake, a python, from which derived Apollo's title of Pythian, often accorded him in his connection with the oracle at Delphi. It is often said – and the belief was already prevalent in antiquity – that the dragon or snake represented an earlier earth cult which was ousted by Apollo. But there is nothing in this original account, in the Homeric Hymn, to suggest that the dragoness was in any way oracular, or the guardian of an oracle, and the theory seems to spring from a later interpretation of what, in the first place, was a simple dragon story of a type common in Greece and elsewhere.

The ruins of Apollo's temple and the small *omphalos* or navel-stone which the Greeks regarded as marking the true centre of the earth can still be seen. Apollo was sometimes shown in Greek art as sitting on the stone.

The oracle was run in historical times by priests who interpreted the more or less incoherent mutterings of the Pythia, a middle-aged woman dressed by convention as a maiden, who sat on a tripod, inhaling the fumes of barley, hemp and chopped bay-leaves burned over an oil-flame; she was believed to be in direct communication with the god. For over a thousand years the oracle was regularly consulted by both Greeks and Romans (and by orientals as well), who were anxious to know the divine purpose in relation to future events. The oracle's replies were almost always obscure or ambiguous, and often wrong, but Socrates was a firm believer, perhaps because Apollo had declared him to be the wisest of all men.

The oracle was closed for three months in winter, and during this time Apollo was supposed to be absent, visiting his special people, the Hyperboreans, who danced, sang and feasted in his honour.

It was through the oracle at Delphi that Apollo exercised his chief political influence in the Greek world, which can be summed up as moderate, conciliatory and conservative. His advice was considered especially valuable by anyone intending to found a colony overseas. It was here, too, that Apollo chiefly operated as a moral force in Greek life. The three famous maxims, or 'programmes' as the ancients called them, were carved on a column in the fore-temple at Delphi: 'Know thyself', 'Nothing in excess' and 'Go surety, and ruin is at hand'. They – or the first two, at least – epitomized that awareness and moderation which are usually taken to have been the Greek ideal.

Apollo lasted at Delphi well into the Christian era. He delivered his last oracle in the year 362 AD, to the physician of the Emperor Julian, the Byzantine ruler who tried to restore paganism after Christianity had become the official religion of the Byzantine Empire. 'Tell the king,' said the oracle, 'that the curiously built temple has fallen to the ground, that bright Apollo no longer has a roof over his head, or prophetic laurel, or babbling spring. Yes, even the murmuring water has dried up.' (See also ORACLES.)

Wolf and Mouse God

The primitive deity who developed, partly by assimilating some of the characteristics of an eastern god, into the glorious figure of classical Greece was very probably a wolf god, worshipped by herdsmen for his power over wolves, which meant that he could keep wolves away from their flocks. In later times, Apollo's connection with flocks and herds was not emphasized as much as his more civilized attributes as the patron of medicine, music and prophecy. But the persistence of dozens of cult names alluding to the more earth-bound side of his character probably shows that to humble countryfolk he remained pre-eminently the god of fields or of pastures – Apollo Enagrios or Nomios.

Apollo was known as the god of leafage, the ripener, the nourisher, the grower of things, the protector of corn, the warder-off of blight and the averter of locusts. One of his oldest titles was Smintheus, which connected him either with the Asian town of Sminthe, or with mice, or with both. Here, as so often, a number of concepts merged into one cult name. Mice were associated with snakes, such as the one which, according to some versions of the story, Apollo destroyed at Delphi; they were also destroyers of the crops Apollo was believed to protect.

Many of Apollo's higher functions arose out of these primitive agricultural ones. It is easy to see the connection between his care

The laurel, *daphne* in Greek, was sacred to Apollo. He fell in love with the nymph Daphne who escaped from his amorous attentions by turning into a laurel tree, as in this painting by the brothers Pollaiuolo, 15th century: National Gallery, London

The inspiration of ancient Greek painting, poetry and music, Apollo was depicted as the ideal type of young, virile beauty. Head of Apollo in the Rhodes Museum

of flocks and his skill with the bow which drove away predators. Shepherds to this day are known for their singing, playing and dancing in Greece and in other Balkan countries, and Apollo's patronage of music probably has its origin in this. The shepherd, too, must be able to care for his flocks, and Apollo was not only a healer himself, both of body and soul, and a god who kept away plagues and pests, but he was the father of the god of medicine, Asclepios.

The oriental cults which were absorbed into the worship of Apollo were as likely as not introduced into the Greek world during the period of overseas colonization which began in the 8th century BC, and from an early period Apollo took up the role of divine founder of colonies. Intending colonizers usually consulted the oracle at Delphi, and Apollo was often accorded the honorary title of 'Founder' in acknowledgement of the usually enigmatic advice his oracle had given. It was believed by some that he guided emigrants to their new settlements in the form of a sea-bird. Perhaps this is the origin of one of his more mysterious cult names – Opsophagos, 'fish-eater'.

In most of his remarkably numerous love affairs, Apollo was curiously unlucky. Deceit and disdain are the constant themes of these myths, and most of Apollo's affairs had a fatal ending.

One very unlucky love of Apollo's was Cassandra, daughter of King Priam of Troy. She resisted the god's advances strenuously, and he wooed her with gifts, including the power of prophecy. When Apollo saw that she would not yield to him, he could not, as a god, recall his gifts, but he turned his blessing into a curse by making sure that while Cassandra always foretold truly what would happen, none of her prophecies would ever be believed by those they most concerned, her own people, the Trojans.

The Ears of Midas

Although Apollo was a god of protection and patronage, he was also, like all the Greek gods, a deadly enemy on occasion. The story of Niobe, told by Homer, illustrates this side of Apollo's character. She had seven sons and seven daughters, and in an ill-fated moment, boasted that she was superior to Leto, who had only two children. At this, Apollo and Artemis drew their bows, and Apollo slew the boys, while Artemis slew the girls. Niobe in her grief wept until she was turned into a pillar of stone, from which the tears still flowed, as visitors to Mount Sipylon could see for themselves.

In another cruel legend, Marsyas the satyr challenged Apollo to a contest on the flute. Apollo agreed, on condition that whoever won might have his will with the loser. Having won by his divine skill, he flayed Marsyas alive. In another contest, this time with the god Pan, King Midas of Phrygia, who judged it, decided against Apollo. Apollo then turned Midas's ears into those of an ass, and Midas had to wear a special head-covering, so that only his barber knew about the ears. The barber had to tell someone, and he dug a hole in the ground and whispered the story into it. Rushes grew up on the spot, and still whisper about Midas's asses ears to this day.

Apollo was adopted by the Romans as a god of healing, and later as a patron of oracles and prophecy, but although his cult was developed by the Emperor Augustus, who put up a great temple to him on the Palatine Hill, the Roman Apollo was not such a vivid figure as the great Greek god.

In the early centuries of our era, a number of new religions and cults, imported from the east, were rivals for the allegiance of the people in the Greek and Roman world. From this religious struggle Christianity, of course, eventually emerged victorious. But Apollo, the god so widely respected and adored, was throughout these centuries a force still to be reckoned with. The early Christian fathers had to make a special effort to dislodge him from his place in the imagination and regard of the pagan masses they were trying to convert. It is possible that some of the later and more scurrilous stories put about concerning the god owed their inspiration to this Christian religious campaign.

DAVID PHILLIPS

FURTHER READING: Robert Graves, *The Greek Myths* (Braziller, 1959); H. J. Rose, *A Handbook of Greek Mythology* (Dutton, 1959); Charles Seltman, *The Twelve Olympians: Gods and Goddesses of Greece* (Apollo Editions).

Rescuing a young man from a beautiful ghoul and saving a city from a plague demon were two of the miracles of Apollonius, a wandering sage who some pagan diehards tried to set up as a rival to Christ

APOLLONIUS

THIS APOLLONIUS (the name is not an uncommon one) was born at Tyana, a town in Cappadocia (now part of Turkey). The date of his birth is uncertain. His age at his death was probably exaggerated by his biographer. He may have been born in the time of the Emperor Tiberius (reigned 14–37 AD) or of Caligula (37–41 AD). He survived till the reign of Nerva (96–98 AD).

Almost all our information about Apollonius comes from a long, rhetorical, romantic and probably highly unreliable biography of him, written more than a hundred years after his death (it was probably begun about 215 AD) by Philostratus, a literary man whose patroness was the Empress Julia Domna, mother of the then reigning Emperor Caracalla. This pious and cultivated Syrian lady had acquired a document purporting to be the memoirs of Damis of Nineveh, a disciple and companion of Apollonius, which seems to have impressed her, and she gave this to her favourite author-in-waiting to write up.

This work of Philostratus was a brilliant literary success: he was the most elegant and accomplished Greek writer of his age. But we cannot be sure how much genuine information it gives us about the real Apollonius – possibly not very much. It does, however, give a very good idea of the literary and religious tastes and enthusiasms of the devout, educated upper-class world of the Greek-speaking East in the 3rd century AD, a period of enormous importance in the development of European religious thought.

Apollonius as portrayed by Philostratus was a wandering religious teacher and wonder-worker who travelled widely in the Roman Empire and beyond. A visit to India is recorded at length, and he is said to have met the Brahmins, whom the Greeks of the time thought of as perfect Pythagorean philosophers. Apollonius himself was a Pythagorean. The Pythagorean revival, which began in the 1st century BC, produced some quite serious philosophers, but for Apollonius Pythagoreanism meant principally vegetarianism, refusal to wear clothes made of animal fibre, condemnation of animal sacrifices, and in general a celibate and ascetic way of life.

Philostratus puts into his mouth a large number of well-composed but rather tedious discourses on this and other subjects, full of the religious and moral commonplaces of the period. He represents Apollonius as having had several encounters with kings to whom he always showed himself superior, as a sage should. The climax of these is a trial before the tyrannical Emperor Domitian (reigned 81–96 AD) which came to an abrupt end when the sage miraculously disappeared from the court.

Philostratus describes a variety of

wonderful doings of Apollonius. There is the story of how he rescued a young man from an Empusa or Lamia, a ghoul in the form of a beautiful girl who was planning to marry her victim in order to eat him, which Keats re-tells in his poem *Lamia*. Another sensational, and very primitive, story tells how Apollonius delivered the people of Ephesus from the plague by making them stone the plague demon to death; it had conveniently appeared in the theatre in the form of an old beggar, but when the heap of stones was taken away the body of a monstrous dog was found. The whole book, and especially the account of the journey to India, is full of the most fantastic marvels. It is this combination of ascetic and high-minded, if not particularly original, religious and moral

teacher and spectacular wonder-worker which appealed so strongly to the Empress Julia Domna and her circle.

A Rival of Christ

There is no evidence that Philostratus or his patroness had any anti-Christian intention in producing the biography of Apollonius. But in the time of Diocletian, at the end of the 3rd and beginning of the 4th century, an attempt was made to set up Apollonius as a rival to Christ. Hierocles, a high imperial official who had a good deal to do with instigating the great persecution of the Christians under Diocletian, published in 303 AD an anti-Christian controversial work called *The Lover of Truth* which contained a comparison of Apollonius and

Christ, designed to show that Apollonius was superior to Christ as a teacher and miracle-worker. The Church historian Eusebius wrote an answer to this comparison. As so often happened with anti-Christian controversial works, for obvious reasons, the answer has been preserved and the original work has disappeared. The comparison of Apollonius with Christ does not seem to have been very successful, and Apollonius never received any widespread cult among pagans. He is occasionally referred to with veneration by later pagan writers, but the Emperor Julian, the greatest and most intelligent of the 4th century defenders of the old religion against Christianity, never even mentions him.

A. H. ARMSTRONG

Apotheosis

Recognition of a human being as a god: examples are the kings of Egypt, Peru, China and Japan, Alexander the Great, Julius Caesar and the Roman emperors, whose deification influenced the later European theory of the divine right of kings.
See KING.

Mansell Collection

Apparition

Appearance of the phantom of a person, living or dead, seen in the waking state or in a dream.
See ASTRAL BODY; GHOSTS; HAUNTED HOUSES; SPONTANEOUS PSI EXPERIENCES.

Michael Holford

APPLE

ORIGINALLY GROWING WILD in Europe and western Asia, and cultivated in Europe since Roman times, the apple is a particularly sacred tree in European mythology. A 7th century poem says that a man who cuts an apple to the axe must pay a fine of one cow, and the feeling that to cut one down is unlucky has persisted to the present day. So strong was this in Ireland, that an early Irish poem, the *Triads of Ireland*, calls for

the sacrifice of a living creature in payment for felling one.

Three unbreathing things paid for only with breathing things:
An apple tree, a hazel bush, a sacred grove.

Felling an apple tree is unlucky because the apple stands for immortality, for eternal youth and happiness in the life after death. The Scandinavian gods kept themselves forever young by eating the golden apples of Idun, goddess of youth and spring. In Welsh legends kings and heroes go after

earthly death to live happily in a paradise of apple trees called Avalon (the name possibly coming from the Welsh word for an apple, *afal*).

Today apples and good luck are still linked, as in the American belief that if the sun shines through the boughs of an apple tree on Christmas Day, the fruit will be abundant the next year. And gamblers will count an apple's seeds to find a lucky number for bets on, say, horse racing or the American 'numbers game'.

This link with the sun comes out strongly

Michael Holford

in the Greek story of the golden apples which were kept by the Hesperides or 'nymphs of the evening', the daughters of Night, in their garden in the farthest west, where the sun goes down to its death in the evening. A dragon with 100 heads guarded the apples but Hercules managed to kill the dragon and steal them. He took the apples to his master King Eurystheus, who gave them to the goddess Athene. She returned them to the Hesperides again, which makes this labour of Hercules seem singularly pointless. But it is likely that in the original story Hercules won immortality by stealing the apples.

The Apple of Desire

As an emblem of renewed life and youth, and because of its appearance when cut in half, the apple also stood for desire and belonged to love goddesses in Celtic and Greek mythology. This is its role in the story of the Judgement of Paris. A golden apple marked 'for the fairest' was thrown down at a wedding feast on Olympus, the home of the Greek gods. Three goddesses – Hera, Athene and Aphrodite – each claimed to be the most beautiful, and Zeus decided that the contest should be judged by Paris, one of the sons of the King of Troy and the handsomest man alive.

The goddesses stripped naked so that Paris could judge them properly and each of them tried to bribe him to give her the apple. Aphrodite, the goddess of desire, promised him the love of Helen, the most beautiful of mortal women. Paris gave the

apple to Aphrodite, which the other goddesses bitterly resented. She kept her promise and Helen ran away with Paris; which was the immediate cause of the Trojan War.

This story, intended to account for the origin of the war, appears only in the later legends about it and has an odd ring, as it explains no religious ritual or custom and does not seem to be connected with any particular religious belief, except that the apple belongs to Aphrodite as a love goddess. It may be an elaboration of a brief reference in Homer's *Iliad* to Paris humiliating Hera and Athene at a meeting in his shepherd's hut by his preference for Aphrodite, 'who offered him the pleasures and the penalties of love'.

It has also been suggested, by Robert Graves, that the story was a mistaken attempt to explain a sacred picture showing Hermes, three naked goddesses and a young man with an apple; which really represented the Mother Goddess in her triple aspect of maiden, mother and hag (see MOTHER GODDESS), giving the apple to the sacred king to assure him of immortality; while Hermes, who led dead souls down to the underworld stood by.

The apple still retains its connection with love – as in traditional American games played on Hallowe'en, designed to reveal whom the players will marry. Bobbing (or ducking) for apples floating in water was originally this kind of marriage divination: each apple was named for a player, and you would marry the one whose apple you managed to bite.

Above The judgement of Paris, in a painting by Rubens, the National Gallery, London
Previous page The apple's connection with the sun is shown in the story of the apples of the Hesperides, the nymphs who lived in the west where the sun sets. From a 19th century triptych by Hans von Marées

Eve and the Apple

Traditionally the fruit which the serpent of Eden maliciously persuaded Adam and Eve to eat was an apple, though the Bible does not say what type of fruit was involved but only that it was the fruit of the tree of the knowledge of good and evil. A more likely fruit than the apple would be the fig, which would connect neatly with the clothes that Adam and Eve made for themselves from figleaves after they had eaten the fruit. But what eating the fruit brought them was the guilty consciousness of desire, which the apple symbolizes.

Aquila of Pontus in Asia Minor, who was converted first to Christianity and then to Judaism, and translated the Old Testament into Greek in the 2nd century AD, is the first writer known to have identified the fruit as an apple. He translated Song of Solomon 8.5 'I raised thee up under the apple tree; there thy mother brought thee forth' – as 'I raised thee up under the apple tree; *there was thou corrupted*', evidently taking the verse as a reference to the tree of the knowledge of good and evil. St Jerome, translating the Old Testament into Latin, followed suit and the belief that the forbidden fruit was an apple has been generally accepted ever since.

The first of 12 articles on the signs of the zodiac describes the typical Aquarian, pre-eminently the scientist with a touch of the absent-minded professor

AQUARIUS

THE SIGN OF the zodiac occupied by the sun at the moment of your birth is one, though only one, of the most important factors in your horoscope, and is the factor on which astrology columns in newspapers and magazines are based. The zodiac signs are the 12 divisions of the circle in the sky through which the sun appears to pass.

Traditionally, your sign is Aquarius if you were born between 20 January and 18 February but, as explained later, in terms of the actual constellations in the sky your sign is Aquarius if you were born between 19 February and 20 March. The symbol of the sign is a man pouring out water from an urn, which has given Aquarius the traditional character of helpfulness and service to others. It is now often regarded as the ideal sign to be born under. This was not always the case, though the Roman author Manilius, who wrote an astrological poem in the 1st century AD, did say that:

The Good, the Pious and the Just are born
When first Aquarius pours out his urn.

In modern opinion Aquarius is pre-eminently the sign of the scientist, with a touch of the absent-minded professor. The Aquarian is quiet, gentle, not forceful, not inclined to insist or demand his own way. He speaks moderately and reasonably. He sees no point in taking a tough line, for truth will out in the end, and until it does there is nothing to be gained by saying anything at all.

The Amiable Aquarian

The Aquarian is frequently a little shy, perhaps because he is often physically large and rather slow. But although at times he may appear ponderous, he is not sluggish and he has more humour than people think. He just does not think it worthwhile to snatch at opportunities which will probably recur. Since Aquarius is traditionally 'ruled', or strongly influenced, by the planet Saturn, patience comes naturally to the Aquarian and less patient people may be irritated by his tolerance. He is said to be sensitive and easily moved to tears, and he hates being criticized.

His characteristic faults are few. The most tiresome is his inability to explain himself. Other people, left in uncertainty, will often put the worst construction on the Aquarian's actions and he will rely on the passage of time to vindicate him. This is not due to laziness, but often appears so. A similar fault of the Aquarian is that he cannot always convince people that he likes or admires them. He considers this is obvious and does not realize that others like to have unmistakable signs of his approval. The consequence may be that he will be considered not only lazy but cold and unfeeling, a reaction he will think is most unjust.

Two pleasing characteristics of the Aquarian are that he is not impressed by pomp and pretentiousness, nor does he attempt to pass himself off as being better than he is. He knows how necessary it is to be patient, and does not expect anything else from others. It is said that he is likely to exaggerate grievances, to think that things will take a long time to improve and are worse than they really are. He has little sympathy for prejudices of race or class but he will try to understand any point of view. A great reader, ideas interest him and he is not at all inclined to brush them aside because they are different from his own.

With this generally pleasing and amiable modern picture of the Aquarian can be contrasted the opinion of Vettius Valens, writing in the 2nd century AD, who described Aquarians as 'effeminate, inflexible, wicked, unfertile'. Though 'industrious and employed in public service', they were self-willed, misanthropic, atheistic and grudging.

The Age of Aquarius

It is important to bear in mind that the traditional 'tropical' zodiac, used for hundreds of years in Europe, is out of step with the 'sidereal' zodiac, the real constellations. When traditional astrology says that the sun is in Aquarius, it is really in the preceding constellation, Capricorn, and so on right round the zodiac circle. Since astrologers have begun to pay attention to this fact, in the last 20 years, people traditionally labelled as Pisceans have found themselves placed under Aquarius, traditional Aquarians under Capricorn, and so on. This confusing situation is caused by precession of equinoxes.

The equinoxes are the two periods of the year, in spring and autumn, when the days and nights are of equal length. At the spring equinox the Sun appears to cross over from the southern hemisphere to the northern, bringing the warmth of spring and summer. At the autumn equinox, it appears to cross back again, leaving the north to darkness.

The equinoxes are said to precess, or go backwards, because they move through the constellations in the direction that men have decided to call backwards, that is, against the direction of the planets. About four thousand years ago the Sun at the spring equinox was in the constellation Aries, but from the 3rd century AD until now the Sun at the spring equinox has actually been in the preceding constellation, Pisces, and from the 24th century it will be in the constellation Aquarius.

Precession of the equinoxes was discovered in the 2nd century BC but few people concerned themselves about the awkward consequences of the discovery, and astrologers have long gone on blandly saying that the zodiac must be very ancient although it was now clear that the equinox, from which they said that the zodiac had always been measured, was an invisible moving point. That early astronomers, who had no scientific instruments, should have chosen to measure their zodiac from an invisible moving point is not a probable suggestion.

The spring equinox precessed into the constellation Pisces, the Fishes, in the 3rd century AD. The fish was a well-known symbol of the early Christians, and so it was thought that this precession foreshadowed the coming Age of Christianity. Similarly the precession of the equinox, some four hundred years from now, into the constellation Aquarius is believed to herald the coming of an Aquarian Age of peace and harmony in a spirit of gentle moderation.

The only kind of Aquarius into which the equinox can precess is the constellation. This is worth emphasizing because astrologers used to insist that the constellations (as distinct from the signs) had no influence worth studying. And yet they attributed importance to the coming Aquarian Age which cannot exist except in terms of the constellation.

(See also ASTROLOGY; and articles on the other zodiac signs, and the planets.)

RUPERT GLEADOW

Traditional emblem of Aquarius, the water-carrier. The two-headed figure on the left symbolizes Janus, the god of beginnings, who gave his name to January. From a French 15th century manuscript, Bodleian Library

Bodleian Library Colour Filmstrip

Architecture

The shape and arrangement of churches, temples and other religious buildings frequently have symbolic significance.
See RELIGIOUS ARCHITECTURE.

Camera Press London

Ares

Greek god of war, equivalent to the Roman Mars: not a major deity, and an unpopular one, frequently described as a savage and bloodthirsty butcher.
See MARS.

ARIES

IN THE TRADITIONAL zodiac you are an Ariean if you were born between 21 March and 19 April, but in the sidereal zodiac which is increasingly used by modern astrologers (see AQUARIUS) Aries is the sign of those born between 20 April and 20 May.

The symbol of Aries is the ram, suggesting energy, initiative, aggression, and push. It should also be remembered that Aries means not only the ram as an animal but also the battering-ram, an instrument of aggression.

Aries owes its reputation for touchiness and dominance partly to the fact that it is the first of the signs and partly to the many political leaders born under it – including Hitler, Lenin and Jefferson. The sign also has a great military reputation, though in fact it has not produced as many successful military commanders as the sign of Scorpio.

Most of the famous people born under Aries – with a few exceptions, like Brahms, Chaplin and Freud – are men who have made their mark in politics. But though the ordinary Ariean is rarely the single-minded political and military genius that the lists of famous Arieans might suggest, he does tend to think of himself as the natural head of affairs. This at times leads to a certain self-centredness, with an apparent assumption that other people are not quite so real or so important as he is.

It was an Ariean, the Florentine Niccolo Machiavelli, who wrote the famous political textbook, *The Prince*, in which he advocated strong-minded and ruthless leadership of the state in the interests of the people.

The Ariean is said to be bad at early rising, but is very punctual and hates to be kept waiting. As one who inevitably considers himself the leader of any group, he naturally does not like people who try to take credit which he thinks should belong to him. In extreme cases he can degenerate into someone who is always grabbing for credit and honours.

A typical Ariean virtue is the combative one of not taking things lying down. He will assert his own point of view and is a useful leader for he is never afraid to make his

The sign of Aries, the ram, from a 15th century work on astrology by Leopold of Austria. Traditionally, those born under Aries have the aggressiveness of the ram

Victoria and Albert Museum

weight felt. Compromise does not readily occur to him as the easiest way out of a difficulty; he is more likely to think that if his position is stated clearly and emphatically, other people will probably give way.

He usually believes that he attained unaided the position he now holds: no one has ever perceptibly helped him. This often leads to egotism. As the Ariean considers himself number one and the only person who matters, he does not attach much importance to the feelings of others. As a result, he is not often an ideal partner in marriage.

In the old days Britain, Germany and ancient Rome – all political great powers – were said to be 'under' Aries. In the days when Britain had an empire, it seemed quite natural to British astrologers that their country should be under Aries, which was thought a noble and imperialistic sign. Now that it is less easy to justify or excuse the habit of telling other people how to run their lives or their countries, it has become more difficult to speak tactfully in praise of Aries, for if one is oneself number one this only implies that the rest are nowhere.

Aries is said to be the first of the signs but this was not always the case. In the first of his *Georgics*, the Roman poet Virgil mentions 'the white bull that with his golden horns opens the year', which suggests that Taurus, the Bull, was once considered the first sign. And the Babylonians did not recognize Aries at all, its place being taken by the constellation called the Hireling, the man who works for wages.

RUPERT GLEADOW

ARMIES

WAR IS SO MUCH a part of human life that it has invaded our dreams with nightmare visions which have turned into legends. On many battlefields the shades of forgotten fighting men, denied proper burial, have been believed to be condemned to re-enact their tragic fate until the end of time.

Near Glastonbury the phantom footsteps of marching knights in armour can still be heard at night, and at Woodmanton in Wiltshire, where Britons and Romans once fought, headless war-horses have been seen galloping wildly along the valley.

Other phantom armies have filled the skies. Of them all, none were more feared than the ferocious army of the restless dead, called the Wild Hunt. Led by the demon Wode of the broad-brimmed hat and the wide mantle, they ranged the night sky over Europe hunting human souls. An old legend of Normandy describes how a peasant, hearing them go by, dared to cry out to Wode, 'Share your spoils,' and afterwards found his own child dead in the hearth (see WILD HUNT).

In ancient Assyria armies of demons had been known to join forces with ghostly warriors in assaults on desert cities but in Christian Europe their organization took the form of cudgel-wielding guerilla bands who carried out sporadic attacks on defenceless hermits. In an early illustration a particularly well-equipped demon is shown mounted on a dragon, brandishing a lance, and glaring malevolently at the world through a pair of iron-rimmed spectacles.

The Roar of Phantom Cannon

For centuries an old house called 'Battlefield' which once stood on the site of the Battle of St Albans, resounded to the clash of sword on steel, harking back to the 15th century Wars of the Roses. When the English Civil War of the 17th century began to loom on the horizon, the air became filled with alarms and portents. As a psychic overture to the conflict, the roar of phantom cannon and the beating of unseen drums were heard at Echt near Aberdeen. Soon after the battle of Edgehill in 1642, when 4000 men lost their lives, there was a widespread rumour that the conflict had been re-enacted by an army of ghosts before the amazed eyes of many witnesses. The spirits of the newly-dead had risen from the earth to battle anew, to fill the air with the thunder of cannon, the throbbing of drums and the groans of the dying.

Perhaps the beginnings of psychical research can be traced to this event for, as related in Lord Nugent's *Memorials of John Hampden*, the hauntings caused such disquiet that King Charles I sent three officers and three private gentlemen to conduct an investigation on the spot. The Commission reported that not only was the story true but that they had personally witnessed the ghostly fight, recognizing among the contestants men whom they knew had been killed at Edgehill, including the King's standard bearer, Sir Edmund Verney.

For centuries there were persistent reports of restlessness among the spectres of Edgehill, but after the fencing of the area by the War Department the ghosts have been silent. Two years after Edgehill there were reports of a similar haunting on the night before the battle of Marston Moor, when a troop of horsemen was observed galloping through the sky over Helvellyn. Marston Moor produced its own ghosts as recently as 1932 when two motorists were startled to see cloaked men of Civil War vintage near the battlefield.

The Angels of Mons

Coming events cast their mournful shadows before the Jacobite rebellion of 1745 when, in 1735, a phantom army was observed in the sky over Souter Fell. Two years later, on Midsummer Eve 1737, a vast column of soldiers marched five abreast through the same sky, and in April 1744 a Scotsman named Forbes had a vision in which ghostly warriors began fighting on what was destined to be the field of Culloden. Then in June 1745 more than 26 witnesses reported seeing an armed host in the clouds, once again above Souter Fell. This appears to have been the last grand march of any phantom army in the British Isles.

The phantom armies made a brief but highly dramatic reappearance when the journalist Arthur Machen published an

Michael Holford

imaginary account of spectral bowmen in the British ranks during the retreat from Mons in 1914. Almost overnight this myth was accepted as factual by the British public and, when embellished with sword-brandishing saviours on horseback, became the famous story of the 'Angels of Mons', fighting on the British side.

The national anguish of the American Civil War left behind a number of haunted battlefields. At Cedar Creek in Virginia, for instance, ghostly squads of men march, bugles sound, and a church that was an army hospital echoes with the cries of the wounded – and a martial band. Also from the United States comes an odd tale of a colonial

The mythical warrior angels supposed to have fought in the retreat from Mons inspired popular songs. By kind permission of the Lawrence Wright Music Co., London

garrison, in 1692, that was inexplicably besieged by a phantom army. The attackers were lifelike, but unkillable. Finally the garrison decided to give up fighting and ignore their inhuman enemies – who then, bewilderingly, disappeared.

FURTHER READING: Christina Hole, *Haunted England* (British Books, 1951); Eric Maple, *The Realm of Ghosts* (American Book Co.), *The Domain of Devils* (A. S. Barnes, 1966).

ARROW

THE BOW was one of the earliest weapons invented by men, and the arrow's ability to kill at a distance has given it a place in magic and folklore all over the world. In Britain prehistoric flint arrowheads were called 'elf-bolts' and were believed to have been dropped by the 'little people'. The Aztec god Quetzalcoatl carries an arrow representing thunder, in his aspect as Wind God. And the Cheyenne Indians venerate four 'medicine arrows' as their main tribal totem object.

Almost every nation has a great bowman-hero of legend, a Robin Hood or William

Tell. The feats of a master archer were readily ascribable to magic and the 15th century *Malleus Maleficarum* (Hammer of Witches) accuses 'wizards who are archers', and whose skill comes from the Devil, of directing lethal arrows at an enemy by bending their whole will upon him.

The arrow can also be a symbol of virility and desire, as in central India, and anyone pierced by one of Cupid's arrows falls helplessly in love at once. The Kwakiutl Indians of Canada believed that an arrow under the bed of a woman in labour would ensure the birth of a male child.

Right **Cupid firing an arrow of desire, from a 15th century MS of the Romance of the Rose**

Bodleian Library Colour Filmstrip

ART

MAGIC OF THE MODERNS

A hundred years ago the artistic ideal was 'truth to Nature'; since then many artists have substituted 'truth to the supernatural', the attempt to express the mysterious, mystical and macabre

THE URGE to express a sense of the mysterious, the marvellous, the irrational — of all that is other than natural or normally to be seen — has produced many remarkable works of visual art since the later years of the last century. Reaction had grown by then against the prevailing realism in art and the materialist view of the world. The course of the Pre-Raphaelite movement in England shows this very clearly. The realistic aim of being 'true to Nature', which marked the movement's triumph in the 1850s, had lost its inspiring value 30 years after. The mystic and fanciful element later came uppermost in the work of Edward Burne-Jones and his followers.

On the continent of Europe the dominance of 'truth to Nature' was opposed in various ways. One contrast was the ideal conceived by Puvis de Chavannes in his serene and timeless mural paintings. But there were other artists who valued the diabolic and the macabre. Gustave Moreau was praised for the Satanic beauty of his *The Apparition*, a painting in which the head of John the Baptist appears in a blaze of ghostly light to Salome as she dances lasciviously before Herod.

Literature and painting found kinship in this pursuit of strange sensation. Moreau's painting inspired Oscar Wilde to write his dramatic prose-poem *Salome*. The Satanic and erotic character that Félicien Rops gave to his etchings had admirers in Baudelaire and Huysmans. The strange visions, inspired by Edgar Allan Poe and Baudelaire's *Fleurs du Mal*, in the lithographs of Odilon Redon are described with gusto by Huysmans in that 'decadent' masterpiece, his novel *A Rebours*, as being 'beyond anything imaginable' and showing 'a fantasy that was unique'. The influential graphic art of Aubrey Beardsley added a wittily Satanic twist to a style originally based on Burne-Jones's chaste designs.

All these artists contributed to what may be called the spirit of the 1890s. The search for new sensations, the fascination found in the 'lilies and languors of vice', a leaning towards the mystic and occult as well as

purely technical departures were ingredients to be found in varied proportion. The Salons of the Rose + Croix, which ran from 1892 to 1897, under the directorship of the critic and novelist, Joséphin Peladan (whose aim was 'to ruin realism') were full of mystically religious works in imitation of Burne-Jones, Moreau and Puvis.

The Painter as Magus

Symbolism was a key word of the period in France. It was an idea evolved in the circle of Paul Gauguin at Pont-Aven in Brittany. The purpose was to give visual form to ideas instead of an objective view of natural appearances. A more active theorist than Gauguin was Emile Bernard who besides working with him in Brittany exhibited religious works in the Rosicrucian Salon. A separate group, the Nabis, included artists who worked in the mood created in Brittany, of special note being Paul Sérusier and Maurice Denis.

In each of these related groups there was the thought that the artist had an inspired role. It was the function of the painter in the view of Peladan to be a 'magus', one not merely wise but entrusted with a special mission. The Nabis, who took their name from the Hebrew word *Naabiim*, meaning 'divinely inspired', invented titles and orders for themselves like an occult sect.

Gauguin can be viewed, like the other great post-Impressionists Paul Cézanne and Vincent van Gogh, as one who enriched the language of form and colour. But he was distinct from them as one who dreamed of a golden age, a fabulous primeval world to which he longed to return. All things primitive, as in some way giving evidence of this mythic past, stirred him. The peasant life and costume of Brittany, the rough religious carvings and crucifixes of the region, gave hints of what he sought. The colonial section of the Paris Exhibition of 1889 opened his eyes to the existence of more exotic and mysterious lands; in the glowing text of a handbook on Tahiti he found the promise of an earthly paradise.

It is possible to regard the pictures painted by Gauguin in Tahiti and the Marquesas Islands simply as superb renderings of native types in tropical landscapes and to relate them aesthetically to the classic and decorative manner of Puvis de Chavannes. Yet many of them also show his interest in

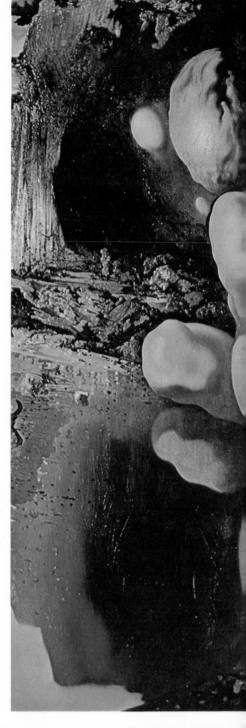

native religion and mythology, and how he introduced symbols of his own to represent them. He found fragmentary accounts of Tahitian lore in writings by earlier French travellers. In the absence of Tahitian representations of their gods he made up images to personify them.

His description of how he came to paint the famous *Manao Tupapau* is enlightening. A young girl lies on a couch in fear. He imagines she is frightened of the Tupapau (Spirit of the Dead), 'the constant dread of the Tahitians'. 'What', asks Gauguin, 'can be a Tahitian's idea of a ghost?' 'Naturally', he answers, 'she thinks of someone she has already seen. Therefore my ghost, my spirit, must be some sort of an old woman.' The flowers in the background, he adds, are

'upapau's flowers, 'phosphorescences and sign that the spirit has you in mind.'

It is true that the Cubists and other artists in the first decade of the 20th century were attracted by the ceremonial masks, carved idols and fetish figures of Africa but they separated their qualities as sculpture from the notions of the supernatural which they stood for. What the European artist studied was the directness of technique, the sharply-cut planes and concentration of the essentials of plastic form.

The Delirium of Dada

There was a reasoned sequence in the development of means in modern art until during the 1914–18 war there came the extraordinary revolt against all reason of the

Salvador Dali's *Metamorphosis of Narcissus*, the beautiful youth of Greek mythology who fell in love with his own reflection in a pool. He turned into the narcissus flower, which is hatching from the egg in the painting: in the Tate Gallery. By permission of the Edward James Foundation

movement called Dada. It started with a group of poets and painters who took refuge in the quiet centre of the hurricane of European conflict, at Zurich in neutral Switzerland. In these individuals the 1914–18 war was the cause of extraordinary behaviour bordering on frenzy. Bitterly opposed to the deadly struggle, they dissociated themselves from organized society and all its works and beliefs and conventions.

They were complete anarchists. They were anti-everything including art itself, which they linked with other expressions of society as a repository of false beliefs and conventions. The name Dada is said to have been the result of opening a German-French dictionary at random and lighting upon the word meaning 'hobby horse'. It has been suggested alternatively that it was taken from 'Da', the Russian for 'yes' of the Slav refugees in Zurich. Either way it was meaningless and as such delighted the wild poets and artists who took a prominent part in the movement; the Rumanian Tristan Tzara, the Germans Hugo Ball and Richard Huelsenbeck, the Alsatian Hans (Jean) Arp. 'What we call Dada is foolery, foolery extracted from the emptiness in which all the higher problems are wrapped, a gladiator's gesture . . . a public execution of false morality,' said Hugo Ball.

Dada in action stemmed from performances at the Cabaret Voltaire in Zurich which included the chanting of nonsense poems, accompanied by 'noise-music' made by drums, cowbells and whistles, interspersed with screams. It was found that the negro types of mask devised by a Rumanian artist, Marcel Janco, created in the wearer an irresistible desire for outlandish movement. They represented not human beings but 'characters and emotions that are larger than life.' 'The paralysing horror which is the backcloth of our age is here made visible,' said Hugo Ball.

Dada's defiant manifesto, mechanical noise, freakish typography, the simultaneous presentation of unlike images involved with one another, derived from Futurism. *Collage*, works fashioned out of all sorts of different materials stuck together, came from Cubism. But what element of the supernatural was there in all this? It might be said that the Dadaists in their public demonstrations whipped up something that approximated to the delirium of primitive tribal ceremonies. Did they envisage anything beyond?

The answer may be found, and was found by exponents of Dada, in Chance. Chance was their magic. When Jean Arp tore up a drawing and let the pieces flutter to the ground, he discovered that they fell into an arrangement that seemed to have a strange 'rightness' of its own. It could be imagined that some unknown law operated, 'as unfathomable to us', he said, 'as the depths from which all life arises'.

Exploration of the Unconscious

The unconscious mind, the mysterious inner presence that Freud had discovered, was an operative factor on which Dada relied. Release from consciously directed and rational processes produced a kind of ecstatic activity, a self-hypnotism in which anything was possible.

The 'found object' and the 'ready-made' were discoveries initiated by the French intellectual Marcel Duchamp. The implication was that any object, whether natural (a twisted tree-root or oddly shaped stone, for instance) or some commonplace man-made article, became magically invested with

significance if the observer chose to look at it in that way. He might be said to have 'invented' it.

Duchamp was uncompromisingly and contemptuously 'anti-art'. This was expressed in the notorious 'ready-made' called the 'Fountain' (a urinal) which he signed R. Mutt (the name of a firm of sanitary engineers) and sent to a New York exhibition to shock an art-worshipping public. It is a comment on the public's capacity for reverence that when the shock had worn off the 'Fountain' was many times a feature of exhibitions and that replicas of such 'ready-mades' as a bicycle-wheel mounted on a stool have been sold in art galleries in limited editions as modern masterpieces!

On Duchamp's part it was an ironic jest. He took trouble to disclaim any aesthetic pleasure in his choice. Yet it was a gesture that made a deep impression. For others it was a way of seeing that once again filled the world with wonders. Perhaps some memory even stirred of the spirit in which primitive men attributed superstitious meaning and powers to things seen. The 'found object' was not a passing fancy or joke quickly forgotten but an active ingredient in the movement that superseded but also came out of Dada — Surrealism.

The Surrealist Shock

The word 'surrealist' was first used by the poet and propagandist of Cubism, Guillaume Apollinaire, in 1917. He described his burlesque play *Les Mamelles de Tirésias*, as a 'surrealist drama'. Earlier the word

'surnaturalism' had been used by Baudelaire to suggest that the aim of art should be 'to create a suggestive magic', an 'enchantment'. 'Supernaturalism' was another term used by poets; Heinrich Heine had declared himself a 'supernaturalist' in art, believing that 'the artist cannot find all his types in Nature but that the most remarkable ones are revealed to him in his soul.' For Victor Hugo the 'surnatural' and 'supernatural' were ideas comprised in Nature referring to 'that part of Nature we do not perceive!'

These trains of thought do not necessarily conflict with one another or with the surrealism that began to emerge in the 1920s. The unconscious mind was 'the part of Nature we do not perceive', which poets and painters set themselves to explore. Surrealism in the definition of André Breton in 1924 was 'pure psychic automatism . . . Thought dictated in the absence of all control exerted by reason and outside all aesthetic or moral preoccupations.' The supernatural had a new and fascinating psychological location.

The relation with Dada is close. The Surrealists used similar shock tactics, were equally against 'art', that is, against works which they considered failed to express truth of feeling. Some of the same artists, Arp and Max Ernst for instance, figure in the history of both movements. But Surrealism was a more organized revolt and a more constructive effort to exploit the workings of instinct, intuition and states of being as in dreams, when the conscious reason is temporarily suspended.

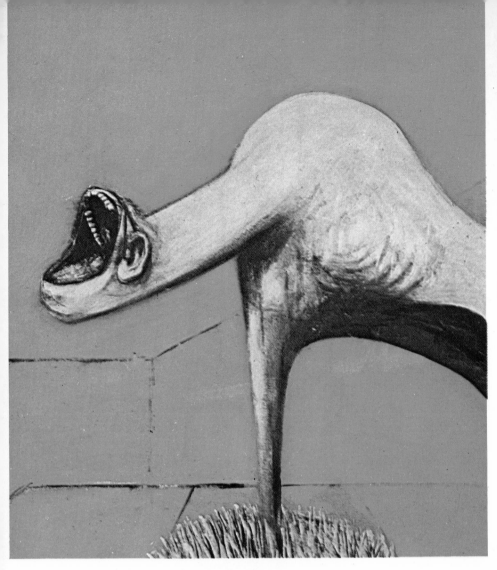

'Artists have been more conscious of the malign than the beneficent', as in the demonic forms painted by Francis Bacon: *Studies for figures at the base of a crucifixion*, in the Tate Gallery

Release from consciously directed and rational processes produced a kind of ecstatic activity, a self-hypnotism in which anything was possible

Artists in Wonderland

The importance attached to the operations of pure instinct and the unconscious mind, the outbursts of an untrammelled imagination and the creation of something equivalent to a dream, placed the history of both literature and painting in an altered perspective. For the French there was a literary foreshadowing of this in the poets Baudelaire, Rimbaud, Mallarmé, and Gérard de Nerval. But in the wider view such products of the Romantic period of the 18th and 19th centuries as the English 'Gothic novel' with all its terrors, spectres and fantasies could be seen in a new light. Edward Lear's *Book of Nonsense*, Lewis Carroll's transmuted Wonderland could be regarded as classic anticipations of Surrealism, and

there came a time when a French Surrealist set himself the task of translating *The Hunting of the Snark* into French!

Similarly a new value was attached in visual art to such works of the past as the stupendous fantasy of hell conceived by Hieronymus Bosch, the sinister *Colossus* of Goya, the *Nightmare* of Fuseli, the visions of Blake and the works of Moreau and Redon. The dream world of the 'modern primitive' was a spontaneous expression unaffected by ideas of technical correctness and an instance of the strange power of instinct that reinforced the opposition to professionalism in painting. In the same way the art of children up to early adolescence seemed to be automatically produced by the impulsion of a racial memory, recreating for

a time a type of primitive artist. From the study of child art and 'art in the raw', the French painter Jean Dubuffet has evolved apparitions of the unconscious.

The Surrealist painters of the 1920s and onwards were never a group closely knit together by ideas of style and technique, but only in imaginative freedom that took individual form. As they found affinities in the past, so also they found them in contemporaries who had little or no concern with the promotion of the movement. Thus the German-Swiss painter, Paul Klee was in the surrealist current of thought with his aim 'not to render the visible but to make visible'. The Italian painter Giorgio de Chirico was able to create an atmosphere of dreamlike reverie and suspense. The

Left A painting in the Tate Gallery, *Of this men shall know nothing*, by Max Ernst, a member of both the Dada and Surrealist movements, which sought to explore the workings of instinct, intuition and dream-like states of mind, in which the conscious reason is temporarily suspended
Right The Italian painter Giorgio de Chirico evoked a sinister atmosphere of suspense: *Melancholia*

The Estorick Collection

Russian-born painter Marc Chagall brought into art the fantasies and the defiance of all laws of nature found in Russian fairy tale and folklore. The Belgian painter, James Ensor, created sinister assemblies of masked and skeleton figures. Pablo Picasso was hailed by André Breton as the initiator of Surrealism and his destruction of surface appearances was suggestive to others, though much of his huge and protean output eludes the classification. His *Minotaur*, a powerfully modernized figure of myth, is an example of the way in which his work takes on a surrealist character.

New Nightmares for Old

Marcel Duchamp, independent of and yet inseparable from the histories of Futurism, Dada and Surrealism, produced the most enigmatic of works *The Bride Stripped Bare by Her Bachelors*, a combination of glass, engraving and petrified accumulation of dust that Breton called 'the trophy of a fabulous hunt over virgin lands.'

The elements of surrealist 'magic' in the work of those closely associated with the movement consist in the wonders of surprise, in the sensation produced by objects in incongruous relation, in sex symbolism — a reflection of Freudian influence — and the fantastic in many different forms. Max Ernst has imagined the landscape of another world; Yves Tanguy sets amoeba-like objects floating over endless plains; André Masson seems to have looked for a message from some mysterious eternal force in his automatic writing; Salvador Dali has conveyed the disquieting thrill of strange juxtapositions; Joan Miró filled abstract shapes with dynamic life; Alberto Giacometti gave a superhuman intensity to his elongated sculptured figures.

The disturbance set up or represented by Dada and Surrealism has not ceased to agitate the visual arts down to the present time. Mixed with the humorously 'frightening' and the juggling with media has been a sense of deep disquiet. The disquieting nature of Surrealism in the 1930s was sometimes like a premonition of war: consider *The Three Fates* of 1939 by Edward Burra.

Imaginative art in this century has gained little content from religious faith. The peace and joy of *The Resurrection* by Stanley Spencer is exceptional. Artists have been more conscious of the malign than the beneficent, as in the demonic forms that Francis Bacon painted in a *Crucifixion*. They have shared the uncertainties of science and a mechanical civilization, sometimes fascinated and yet repelled by the machine as a dictatorial monster, sometimes pointing to the mysteries that still lie beyond the frontiers of science's material gains and explanations. Modern painting and sculpture grapple with enigmas. Artists have gone beyond old limits in new confrontations of the material by the spiritual. They may be said, as a modern dramatist has said of his work, to reveal what they do not know.

WILLIAM GAUNT

Sonia Halliday

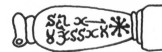

Artemis

Greek goddess of the hunt and wild animals, 'lady of wild things', sister of Apollo: probably of Cretan origin; later identified with the Roman Diana.
See DIANA.

Arthame

Or athame, the magic knife described in the *Key of Solomon* and other magical textbooks, used for drawing the magic circle; as used by modern witches, it has a black handle and magic symbols on its blade.

ARTHUR
The Once and Future King

'Arthur, the good King of Britain, whose prowess teaches us that we too should be brave and courteous . . .' In the medieval stories, Arthur and his knights became patterns of chivalry, and their typical sport the tournament, in which the knights fought to show their strength and skill, in honour of the watching ladies of the Court

121

Little is known of the real Arthur — probably a British war-chief of the 6th century AD — but the stories which clustered round his memory grew into one of the most romantic, exciting and beautiful of all legends

THE HERO of a famous cycle of legends and romances, Arthur was said to have been born at Tintagel in Cornwall. He became King of Britain and held court at Camelot as the leader of a band of noble warriors, the Knights of the Round Table. The knights rode out to seek adventure and great deeds, notably in the quest of the Grail — in Christian legend the holy cup used by Christ at the Last Supper. Arthur was betrayed by his wife Guinevere and his nephew, or son, Mordred. Wounded in battle against Mordred, he was carried away by three fairy queens to Avalon, the land of immortal heroes, from which he will return to lead his countrymen in the time of their greatest peril.

The Real Arthur

Most scholars think it likely that there was a real Arthur. The name is Roman (Artorius) and the original Arthur was probably a leader of the Romanized Britons against the Saxon war-bands which invaded and plundered Britain from c 450 AD onwards, after the Roman armies had been withdrawn. If so, ironically enough, the great British hero fought against the ancestors of the majority of modern Englishmen. It has been suggested that he may have trained and commanded a force of heavy cavalry, and that this was the origin of the mounted knights of the later stories.

The real Arthur probably lived about 500 AD. A gloomy author named Gildas, who wrote a *Book of Complaints* c 540, says that the Saxons were defeated in a great battle at Mount Badon in about the year 500. Gildas does not mention Arthur but there is some slight evidence that he disliked Arthur and left him out of his history on purpose. However, Nennius in his *History of the Britons*, written in the early 9th century, says that Arthur was *dux bellorum* of the Britons — 'war-chief' or general, not king — at the battle of Mount Badon.

The 10th century *Cambrian Annals* say that Arthur defeated the Saxons at Mount Badon in 516, and also mention in 537 'the battle of Camlann, in which Arthur and Medraut (Mordred) fell.'

The Celtic Hero

The rest of our information about Arthur comes from romantic stories which may or may not be founded partly on fact. In Celtic legend he became a great hero, violent and boisterous, who rid the land of giants, monsters and witches. He seems to have resembled the Greek hero Hercules in performing superhuman feats or 'labours'. He slaughtered the Demon Cat of Losanne, he hunted the fabulous boar Twrch Trwyth and drove him into the sea. A Welsh poem

Left King Arthur, from a late 14th century French tapestry. The real Arthur was probably a war-chief who fought against the Saxons invading Britain c 500 AD

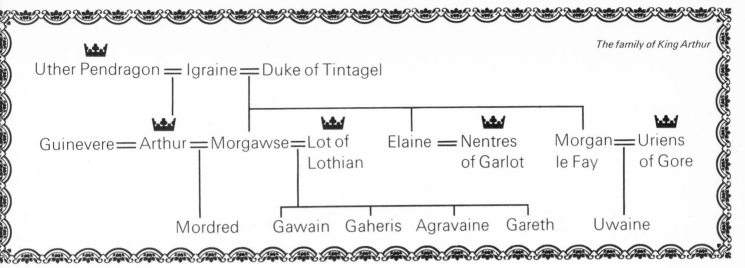

The family of King Arthur

Uther Pendragon = Igraine = Duke of Tintagel

Guinevere = Arthur = Morgawse = Lot of Lothian — Elaine = Nentres of Garlot — Morgan le Fay = Uriens of Gore

Mordred — Gawain — Gaheris — Agravaine — Gareth — Uwaine

called *The Spoils of Annwn*, probably written in the 10th century, refers to Arthur's raid on the land of the dead, the isle of Annwn. He sailed there in his ship Prydwen and although he took three times Prydwen's normal complement with him, only seven men returned from the expedition alive. In Robert Graves's translation:

> I will not allow praise to the lords of literature.
> Beyond Caer Wydr they beheld not the prowess of Arthur.
> Three times twenty hundred men stood on the wall.
> It was difficult to converse with their sentinel.
> Three times the fullness of Prydwen, we went with Arthur.
> Except seven, none returned from Caer Colur.

The object of the raid was to seize the magic cauldron of Annwn, from which only the brave and the true could eat — 'It will not boil the food of a coward or one forsworn.' This cauldron may be the original Grail and if it supplied the food of immortal heroes, Arthur may have gained immortality by seizing it.

Arthur was generous and open-handed as befits a hero. In *Culhwch and Olwen*, a Welsh story which was written down about 1100, a visitor to his court is offered 'Meat for thy dogs and corn for thy horse, and hot peppered chops for thyself, and wine brimming over, and delectable songs before thee. Food for fifty men shall come to thee in the hospice . . . It will be no worse for thee there than for Arthur in the court: a woman to sleep with thee and delectable songs before thee.'

In the early Celtic stories Arthur has a large band of heroic comrades, including Cei Wynn (who became Sir Kay in the later romances), Bedwyr (Sir Bedivere), Gereint (Sir Gareth), Gwalchmai (Sir Gawain), Llenlleawc (Sir Lancelot) and Drwst Iron-Fist (probably Tristan). His wife is Gwenhwyfar (Guinevere). Some of the old Celtic gods are with him, now turned into men — Manawydan, Teyrnon and Gwynn son of Nudd, the master of hell. Also in his retinue are personifications of superhuman qualities, like Drem son of Dremidydd (Sight son of Seer) who could see a fly in Scotland from as far away as Cornwall, and Clust son of Clustfeinad (Ear son of Hearer) who could hear an ant getting up in the morning 50 miles off.

The Breton Tales

Before 1100 there were evidently various stories about Arthur and his exploits, which were popular in Wales and Cornwall. They were also well known in Brittany. Wandering Breton poets and story-tellers translated the stories about Arthur into French, embroidering them and adding to them in the process, and spread them all over France. One of the popular pastimes of the day was listening to the tales of a travelling bard, who moved on from court to castle to manor house and lived on what he could collect from his audiences.

Each bard's stories might differ in detail. One of them, for instance, said that Arthur had not really killed the Demon Cat; the truth was that the Demon Cat had defeated him and carried him off, but it was not safe to tell that version of the story to a British audience. The bards also tended to make the stories more real for their hearers by bringing the historical setting up to date, so that the Arthur who fought the Saxons turned into a medieval baron and his British troops became feudal knights.

By 1100 tales of Arthur had spread as far as Italy. There is a sculpture over one of the doors of Modena Cathedral which shows Arthur, Gawain and Kay rescuing Guinevere from a moated castle defended by enemy knights.

Geoffrey of Monmouth

An English chronicler named William of Malmesbury, writing in 1125, said that the Britons (or possibly Bretons) told many fables about Arthur, though he was 'a man worthy to be celebrated, not by idle fictions but by authentic history'; and that in 1087 the tomb of Walwin (Gawain) had been discovered in Wales on the sea coast, but no one knew where Arthur was buried and so 'ancient ballads fable that he will return'.

William's implied call for an authentic history of Arthur was never answered but a few years later, c 1135, the first full and connected account of the hero appeared in Geoffrey of Monmouth's *History of the Kings of Britain*. This brilliant and compelling work, which masqueraded as history, has been described as 'the most successful work of fiction ever composed.' It has also been condemned by some slightly humourless modern scholars as an impertinent forgery and an outrage upon historical truth,

but it still makes good reading today, eight centuries after it was written.

Geoffrey was born in Wales and was apparently of Breton descent. His father's name was Arthur, which may be significant. He drew on earlier histories and on traditions and legends for his *History* but seems to have drawn far more heavily on his own imagination. To account for the mass of previously unknown material in his book, he said he had used 'a certain most ancient book in the British language', though whether this book really existed is uncertain.

Geoffrey's book begins with the supposed first King of Britain — Brute (Brutus), great-grandson of Aeneas, who was one of the survivors of the Trojan War and the hero of Virgil's *Aeneid*. Brute and his Trojan retinue came to Albion (Britain), which was inhabited only by a few giants, and founded the city of New Troy (London). The island came to be called Britain, from Brute, and subsequent British kings were descended from him, down to Uther Pendragon, who succeeded to the throne when the Britons were hard pressed by the Saxons. Uther Pendragon does not seem to have ever existed in reality, and his name may come from a mistranslation of the Welsh phrase *Arthur mab Uthr*, 'Arthur the terrible', as Arthur son of Uther.

According to Geoffrey, Uther Pendragon fell violently in love with Igerna, the beautiful wife of the Duke of Cornwall. Her husband snatched her away from court and shut her up in Tintagel castle while he went to gather troops. Uther was furious and led an army into Cornwall to punish the duke. He also appealed to Merlin, the great magician, who by magic art made Uther look exactly like the duke. Disguised as Igerna's husband, Uther had no difficulty in entering both Tintagel castle and Igerna's bed, and Arthur was conceived at Tintagel.

Arthur was 15 when Uther Pendragon died and was buried at Stonehenge. He was crowned king at Silchester. He defeated and harried the Saxons, plundering them of much treasure with which he rewarded his fighting men. He won a great victory in Somerset, in a battle probably intended to be Mount Badon though Geoffrey does not say so. Arthur wore 'a helm of gold graven with the semblance of a dragon.' His shield was called Pridwen (formerly his ship in *The Spoils of Annwn*). His sword was called

Caliburn (later Excalibur) and had been forged in Avalon.

Arthur went on to subdue the Scots and to marry the beautiful Guinevere. His sister married Loth, Duke of Lothian, and by him had two sons, Gawain and Mordred. Kay and Bedivere were also prominent among Arthur's knights.

After Arthur had conquered both Ireland and Iceland, 'he invited unto him all soever of most prowess from far-off kingdoms and began to multiply his household retinue, and to hold such courtly fashion in his household as begat rivalry amongst peoples at a distance, insomuch as the noblest in the land, fain to vie with him, would hold himself as naught, save in the cut of his clothes and the manner of his arms he followed the pattern of Arthur's knights.' This is a foretaste of the Arthurian court of the later legends, attended by those 'of most prowess' and a centre of 'courtly fashion'.

Arthur's Conquests

Foreign rulers were alarmed by Arthur's successes and when he discovered this, 'his heart was uplifted for that he was a terror unto them all, and he set his desire upon subduing the whole of Europe unto himself.' He conquered Norway and Denmark, and then descended on France.

It took Arthur nine years to subdue all France. He then recrossed the Channel and held a great court at Caerleon in Wales. All his vassals came to pay him homage and there were tournaments and contests of strength and skill, including archery, chess and putting the weight. Geoffrey again provides an early trace of the later Arthurian court of chivalry, for the ladies 'would deign have the love of none save he had thrice approved him in the wars' (and as a result, he adds sardonically, 'did dames wax chaste') and the knights would fight mock battles, cheered on by 'the dames and damsels looking on from the top of the walls, for whose sake the courtly knights make believe to be fighting.'

Annoyed by a demand for tribute from the Roman Emperor, Arthur and his barons led an army to the continent, leaving Guinevere and Mordred, Arthur's nephew, to govern Britain. The Roman Emperor, Lucius Hiberius, brought levies from Byzantium, Africa, Spain, Persia, Egypt, Syria and Babylon in an army of over 40,000

men against Arthur. The armies met in France and Arthur was victorious in a tremendous battle of 'thrust of spear and stroke of swords and fling of javelin.' Bedivere was killed and Kay died of the wounds he received. After 'a most unconscionable slaughter', the Romans were driven from the field and Lucius himself was killed.

The Treachery of Mordred

Arthur intended to march on Rome but meanwhile in Britain Mordred 'had tyrannously and traitorously set the crown of the kingdom upon his own head, and had linked him in unhallowed union with Guinevere the Queen.'

Arthur returned at once to Britain with his army. The gallant Gawain was killed in battle against his evil brother Mordred, who was driven back to the river Camel in Cornwall, while Guinevere fled to a nunnery. In a final battle at the Camel (Geoffrey's interpretation of the *Cambrian Annals'* battle of Camlann), the traitor Mordred fell 'and many thousands along with him'. But 'the renowned King Arthur himself was wounded deadly and was borne thence unto the Isle of Avalon for the healing of his wounds, where he gave up the crown of Britain unto his kinsman Constantine . . . in the year of the Incarnation of Our Lord five hundred and forty-two.'

Like other histories written in the same period, Geoffrey's book includes marvels, superhuman feats and supernatural monsters. Arthur is conceived as a result of Merlin's magic spell, he kills 470 of the enemy single-handed in one battle, and Geoffrey records that he slaughtered the giant of Mount St Michael who had been terrorizing the neighbourhood. But in the main Geoffrey's account of Arthur is realistic and is far less concerned with the supernatural than the earlier Celtic stories. Arthur is an ideal but not impossibly romanticized feudal leader. He is generous to his followers, a faithful but not tiresomely pious son of the Church, a fierce fighter and an excellent general, and he keeps a splendid and glittering court. When tragedy comes upon him, it is the result of ambition and treachery in his own family – an accustomed reality in the lives of real medieval kings. Even when he is carried away wounded to Avalon, there is no suggestion that fairies

Above left Part of a mosaic pavement in Otranto Cathedral, dated 1166, showing Arthur with crown and sceptre. Tales of Arthur had spread to Italy by 1100. This part of the pavement has been heavily restored and it is not certain that Arthur was originally meant to be riding a goat. If he was, the artist's intentions were presumably satirical
Above right Sculpture at Modena Cathedral, c 1100, showing Arthur, Gawain and Kay rescuing Guinevere from a moated castle

took him there, and though Geoffrey does not say that Arthur died, he also does not tell us that the hero will return again.

Geoffrey's *History* was accepted, quoted and followed by most later historians. Even towards the end of the 15th century, Henry VII based his claim to the throne of England on a genealogy taken from Geoffrey and going right back through Arthur to Brute.

The book was also a great popular success. It appealed to Welshmen, Cornishmen and Bretons as the story of a successful native British warrior. It appealed to the Norman aristocracy of England, to whom fighting was the one occupation supremely worthy of a gentleman; an attitude which Geoffrey puts into the mouth of one of Arthur's barons. 'For where use of arms is none, and naught is there to do but to toy with women and play at the dice and suchlike follies, none need doubt but that cowardice will tarnish all they once had of valour and honour and hardihood and renown.' To men who thought like this, Geoffrey's Arthur was an attractive figure and the belief that he had conquered half Europe appealed to Norman barons, whose own fathers and grandfathers had conquered England, Sicily and southern Italy, ruled large areas of France, and fought against Byzantines and Arabs.

In the year of Geoffrey's death, 1155, Robert Wace translated Geoffrey's *History* from Latin into French under the title of *Roman de Brut* (The Story of Brute). He remarked that the Bretons of his day told many stories of the Round Table, and this is the first reference to the Round Table which has survived. By 1200 an English cleric named Layamon had turned Wace's *Brut* into English, adding to it the story that after the final battle with Mordred, the fairy queen Morgan took Arthur in a boat to Avalon. He also said that Arthur had the Round Table specially built so as to avoid

Chèze-Brown

disputes about precedence among his knights; it seated 1600 men.

Meanwhile in France, another able writer, Chrétien de Troyes, had turned his attention to the Arthurian legends.

Arthur and Chivalry

The poems of the Frenchman Chrétien de Troyes had an even greater influence on the later legends of Arthur than the prose of the British Geoffrey of Monmouth. It was Chrétien who firmly established Arthur's court as the centre of a company of gallant knights and beautiful women, engaged in dangerous adventures and amorous intrigues. Very little is known about his life but in the 1160s – about 30 years after Geoffrey had written his *History* – Chrétien

lived at the court of the Countess of Champagne in Troyes. He based his poems, or said he did, on earlier written texts which have not survived and on the tales of travelling bards.

In Geoffrey of Monmouth Arthur is the central figure and hero; in Chrétien and the later French legends Arthur recedes into the background. Chrétien's poems are about the adventures of individual knights of Arthur's court. Gawain, Yvain, Erec, Lancelot and Perceval. Geoffrey as an Englishman was pleased to imagine Arthur conquering most of western Europe, including France; Chrétien and other Frenchmen imagined no such thing and their Arthur is not a great conqueror. Geoffrey placed Arthur and his court in real surroundings;

Tintagel Castle in Cornwall where, according to the legends, Arthur was magically conceived, with the aid of Merlin the wizard

in the French legends, though a few names of real places are used, Arthur and his knights live in a country that never was, a timeless fairyland beyond reality. Geoffrey never mentions the Grail; Chrétien began a poem about the Grail but did not live to finish it. Geoffrey has comparatively little to offer in the way of marvels and magic; Chrétien and his successors have far more. This element of the marvellous and the supernatural probably came to French writers from the travelling story-tellers, and originally from Celtic sources.

Chrétien portrayed Arthur's court in a

The Welsh Arthur

Said Arthur, 'Is there any of the marvels still unobtained?' Said one of the men, 'There is: the blood of the Black Witch, daughter of the White Witch, from the head of the Valley of Grief in the uplands of Hell.' Arthur set out for the North and came to where the hag's cave was. And it was the counsel of Gwyn son of Greidawl that Cacamwri and Hygwydd his brother be sent to fight with the hag. And as they came inside the cave the hag grabbed at them, and caught Hygwydd by the hair of his head and flung him to the floor beneath her. And Cacamwri seized her by the hair of her head, and dragged her to the ground off Hygwydd, but she then turned on Cacamwri and dressed them down both and disarmed them, and drove them out squealing and squalling. And Arthur was angered to see his two servants well nigh slain, and he sought to seize the cave. And then Gwyn and Gwythyr told him, 'It is neither seemly nor pleasant for us to see thee scuffling with a hag. Send Long Amren and Long Eiddil into the cave.' And they went. But if ill was the plight of the first two, the plight of those two was worse, so that God knows not one of the whole four could have stirred from the place, but for the way they were all four loaded on Llamrei, Arthur's mare. And then Arthur seized the entrance to the cave, and from the entrance he took aim at the hag with Carwennan his knife, and struck her across the middle until she was as two tubs. And Cadw of Prydein took the witch's blood and kept it with him.

Culhwch and Olwen
(trans. G. & T. Jones)

---

way which suited his own surroundings and his own ideals. He was heavily influenced by the code of chivalry which affected the polite society of courts and castles in France in his time. His descriptions of the way in which Arthur's knights behaved are object-lessons in the proper conduct befitting chivalrous gentlemen. As he says at the beginning of his *Yvain*, 'Arthur, the good King of Britain, whose prowess teaches us that we too should be brave and courteous...'

The Contest of the Hawk
The opening scenes of Chrétien's first Arthurian poem, *Erec et Enide*, set the tone of bravery and courtesy. The hero Erec rides off from Arthur's court at Cardigan to chastise a stranger knight who has insulted one of Queen Guinevere's ladies-in-waiting. He follows the knight, whose name eventually turns out to be Yder (for some reason Chrétien hated to reveal the names of his characters until the last possible moment) to a town where he meets a surpassingly beautiful girl named Enide. 'Nature herself had marvelled more than five hundred times how upon this one occasion she had succeeded in creating such a perfect thing.' Erec discovers that next day there will be a contest, which Yder the stranger knight is expected to win, 'for in the presence of all the people there will be set upon a silver perch a sparrow-hawk of five or six moult-ings – the best you can imagine. Whoever wishes to gain the hawk must have a mistress who is fair, prudent and courteous. And if there be a knight so bold as to wish to defend the worth and the name of the fairest in his eyes, he will cause his mistress to step forward and lift the hawk from the perch, if no one dares to interfere.'

Next day, the prize is claimed for his lady by Yder, of whom everyone else is terrified, but Erec challenges him and demands the hawk for the lovely Enide. The crowd quickly clear a space and the two knights fight a long-drawn duel – 'they reach for each other with the tips of their lances' as they charge together on horseback, 'and strike each other so hard that the shields are pierced and broken; the lances split and crack . . .' The two knights fight on until they are both exhausted and bleeding. Both are ashamed to be striking such faint blows and they agree to rest. Yder says, 'Let us withdraw and rest a little; for too weak are these blows we deal. We must deal better blows than these; for now it draws near evening. It is shameful and highly dis-creditable that this battle should last so long . . . Surely we should do our best with blades of steel for the sake of our lady-loves.'

Presently the combat is renewed. Erec hacks through Yder's armour into his shoulder and then 'deals him such a tre-mendous blow upon the helmet that it quite stuns him.' Erec drags off the fallen Yder's helmet to kill him but to do so would be a breach of the code of chivalry, as Yder is quick to point out. 'Mercy now, and do not kill me after having overcome me and taken me prisoner: that would never bring thee praise or glory.' Erec relents and orders Yder to go to Arthur's court and surrender himself to Guinevere.

The story emphasizes the chivalrous virtues of courage, strength and skill in fighting, showing mercy to a defeated foe, keeping one's word, refusing to tolerate an insult to a woman. The contest of the hawk is a typical institution of chivalry which occurs again and again in different forms in the later Arthurian stories – a romantic beauty contest which automatically leads to violent knightly combat, but a combat which is supposed to be fought in a fair and sporting spirit. Not that Chrétien and his successors were unduly starry-eyed about their heroes. The knights have the defects of their qualities. They can be reckless, haughty, stubborn, and in the heat of battle or rage, savage and bloodthirsty. They feel fear and do not always manage to overcome it. Their sexual morals are often decidedly loose (and did not appeal to Victorian critics). A knight worsted in combat may willingly admire the prowess of his opponent, or he may simply sulk.

The Knightly Quest
Quests are the principal feature of Chrétien's stories and of the later romances. A knight rides out to seek adventure and to preserve, or re-establish, his honour and reputation as a ferocious but courteous fighting man. During the quest he does battle against enemy knights, who may be chivalrous warriors like himself or evil, crafty and treacherous oppressors of the poor and weak. He rescues beautiful women from wicked knights and wizards. He is often captured and escapes death or dishonour by a hair's breadth at the last moment. He encounters savage beasts and monsters, glamorous seducers and witches, enchanted castles and spell-bound forests.

The extent to which Arthur himself has shrunk in stature in Chrétien is shown in his *Lancelot*. The court is at Camelot. A stranger knight appears before the king and announces that he holds prisoner many knights and ladies of Arthur's household. But he has no intention of returning them to Arthur's court. 'Rather do I wish to proclaim and serve thee notice that thou hast not the strength or the resources to enable thee to secure them again.' Geoffrey's Arthur would have replied to this insult by leading an army to rescue the captives. Chrétien's Arthur merely replies meekly that 'he must needs endure what he has not the power to change.'

In the same poem Chrétien tells the story of the love affair of Lancelot and Guinevere, Arthur's wife, in which Arthur is cuckolded and which became a stock feature of the later legends.

Chrétien's successors also added details which became accepted episodes of the

Right **Arthur's knights, renowned for their chivalry and courage, constantly set out in search of adventure and to perform deeds of valour. The supreme quest was that of the Holy Grail – in Christian legend the holy cup used by Christ at the Last Supper.** *The Knights Swear the Quest for the Grail,* **from the Bibliothèque Nationale, Paris**
Below **When Arthur lay dying, Sir Bedivere took the sword Excalibur and threw it into the water, from which a hand rose and caught it. Early 14th century manuscript**

British Museum

'Whoso pulleth out the sword of this stone and anvil, is rightwise king born of all England'

legends. Robert de Borron's *Merlin,* written soon after 1200, follows Geoffrey of Monmouth's story of Arthur's conception and birth, and adds that he was brought up by Kay's father and won the crown of Britain by drawing a sword from a stone. The *Mort Artu* (Death of Arthur) brings in the disappearance of Arthur's sword Excalibur into a magic lake when Arthur is carried away to Avalon.

From the 13th century onwards the stories of the Round Table continued to be told, with additions and alterations, to generations of audiences. The stories had the same appeal as the popular romantic escape-literature of our own day, for which they largely created the pattern, with many of the same ingredients: heroes and villains

considerably larger than life, sex and violence, feats of strength and last-minute escapes, misunderstandings and mistaken identities, the thwarting of evil designs and the triumph of courage and honour.

The Legend in Full Flower

In the 15th century the Arthurian legend reached its finest expression in Sir Thomas Malory's *Morte D'Arthur* (written in English despite its French title). The book is a reworking of much of the earlier Arthurian and Grail material and although there are inconsistencies and confusions because so many different tales are combined together, the result glows with the charm and splendour of Malory's style.

According to Malory' Arthur was the son

of Uther Pendragon and Igraine of Cornwall, conceived at Tintagel after Merlin had magically transformed Uther into the likeness of Igraine's husband. Ignorant of his true parentage, Arthur was brought up by Sir Ector, the father of Kay.

When Uther Pendragon died, there was no one to succeed him and various great barons struggled for the throne. Eventually, at Merlin's instigation, the Archbishop of Canterbury summoned all the barons to London where Merlin had provided 'a great stone four square, like unto a marble stone; and in midst thereof was like an anvil of steel a foot on high, and therein stuck a fair sword naked by the point, and letters there were written in gold about the sword, that said thus: Whoso pulleth out the sword of

The Passing of Arthur

Then Sir Bedivere departed and went to the sword, and lightly took it up, and went to the water side; and there he bound the girdle about the hilts, and then he threw the sword as far into the water as he might; and there came an arm and an hand above the water and met it, and caught it, and so shook it thrice and brandished, and then vanished away the hand with the sword in the water. So Sir Bedivere came again to the king, and told him what he saw. Alas, said the king, help me hence, for I dread me I have tarried over long. Then Sir Bedivere took the king upon his back, and so went with

him to that water side. And when they were at the water side, even fast by the bank hoved a little barge with many fair ladies on it, and among them all was a queen, and all they had black hoods, and all they wept and shrieked when they saw King Arthur. Now put me into the barge, said the king. And so he did softly; and there received him three queens with great mourning; and so they set them down, and in one of their laps King Arthur laid his head. And then that queen said: Ah, dear brother, why have ye tarried so long from me? Alas, this wound on your head hath caught over-much cold.

And so then they rowed from land, and Sir Bedivere beheld all those ladies go from him. Then Sir Bedivere cried: Ah my lord Arthur, what shall become of me, now ye go from me and leave me here alone among mine enemies? Comfort thyself, said the king, and do as well as thou mayst, for in me is no trust for to trust in; for I will into the vale of Avilion to heal me of my grievous wound: and if thou hear never more of me, pray for my soul.

Sir Thomas Malory
Le Morte D'Arthur

---

this stone and anvil, is rightwise king born of all England.'

No one succeeded in pulling out the sword, though many tried, until the young Arthur came by and casually took it to give to his foster-brother Kay. When this was discovered, Arthur was crowned king and defeated all rivals in a series of battles.

Not realizing that she was his own half-sister, Arthur made love to King Lot's wife when she came to the court, and she gave birth to the traitor Mordred, who was thus both the son and nephew of Arthur. It was this unwitting incest which brought Arthur and the Round Table to destruction, as Merlin prophesied. 'But ye have done a thing late that God is displeased with you, for ye have lain by your sister, and on her ye have gotten a child that shall destroy you and all the knights of your realm.'

The Round Table

Merlin and Arthur went to a lake, from the middle of which an arm protruded holding a sword. The sword, Excalibur, belonged to the Lady of the Lake, who gave it to Arthur. When Arthur married Guinevere, his father-in-law gave him the Round Table as a wedding present. It seated 150 knights.

In the later books, Arthur recedes into the background, as in the French legends. The bulk of the *Morte D'Arthur* is concerned with the chivalrous quests of the knights: Lancelot, Gawain, Gareth, Galahad, Uwaine (Chrétien's Yvain), Perceval, Tristram of Lyonesse (Tristan) and many more. The story of Lancelot's love for Guinevere is told, and the adventures of the knights who go in search of the Grail.

Malory's tales are full of supernatural marvels and beings – giants, goblins, fairies, invisible warriors, wizards and enchanters. Arthur was enticed into the Forest Perilous in North Wales by a great sorceress but was rescued by his knights and cut off the witch's head. Sir Bors came to a castle of beautiful women but when he crossed himself, the castle and the ladies vanished and 'he heard a great noise and a great cry, as though all the fiends of hell had been about him.'

The Road to Avalon

In the last book of the *Morte D'Arthur* Arthur himself emerges again as the central figure. Realizing that Lancelot and Guine-

vere were in love, he refused to admit it to himself or anyone else, because of his affection for Lancelot. But Mordred and Agravaine, who hated Lancelot, insisted on accusing him to the king's face, in spite of the opposition of Gawain and Gareth, who saw that it would mean the end of the fellowship of the Round Table. Their misgivings were justified, for when the accusation of adultery and treason was made in public, Arthur gave Mordred and Agravaine leave to seize Lancelot. Lancelot escaped them, killing Agravaine, and fled to France. Some of the knights went with him, others remained loyal to Arthur and when Arthur and Gawain took an army to France against Lancelot, good knights were killed on both sides, Gawain himself dying of wounds received in combat with Lancelot.

Mordred, left behind to rule England, seized the crown and tried also to seize Guinevere but she resisted him. Arthur returned to England and in a great battle sought out Mordred and killed him with a spearthrust, but the dying Mordred struck Arthur a terrible blow with his sword. Sir Bedivere helped Arthur away to the waterside and, on Arthur's instructions, threw the sword Excalibur far out into the water; an arm came up from the water and caught it

An oak table in Winchester Castle, once believed to be the original Round Table. Henry VIII showed it proudly to royal visitors. It has the Tudor rose in the middle because the Tudors based their claim to the English throne partly on their supposed descent from Arthur

and vanished away again. Then the wounded king was taken into a fairy barge and carried away to Avalon, the land of immortal heroes.

This last, magnificently written scene is set in Glastonbury. There was a tradition that Glastonbury was the Isle of Avalon, and much of the area round Glastonbury was water-logged and marshy. Long before, in 1191, the monks of Glastonbury had unearthed an oak coffin from 16 feet underground, which they claimed to be Arthur's. They showed an inscription, 'Here lies buried the renowned King Arthur with Guineveré his second wife in the Isle of Avalon', on a lead cross which they said had been found inside the coffin. Malory says that it was still a popular belief that Arthur would return again one day, and it was said that on his tomb was written *Hic jacet Arthurus rex quondam rexque futurus*, 'Here lies Arthur, the once and future king.'

The story of Arthur has attracted many writers and artists since Malory, including Spenser, Tennyson, the Pre-Raphaelites and Masefield. Whether Arthur was originally a sacred king has been hotly disputed. An old Welsh poem says that he had three wives, all named Guinevere, which might suggest that he was regarded as a sacred king married to the Triple Goddess. Mordred's attempt to seize both the throne and Guinevere suggests the combat between the sacred king and his rival and attempted successor, who tries to oust him as consort of the Goddess. The evidence is inadequate to prove the theory but it may be that this ancient theme, lying beneath the surface of the legend, has helped to give it a deep and timeless appeal.

RICHARD CAVENDISH

(For the Grail legends, see GRAIL: and see also CAMELOT AND ARTHURIAN BRITAIN; GALAHAD; GAWAIN; LANCELOT; MERLIN; MORGAN LE FAY; PARSIFAL; TRISTAN.)

FURTHER READING: Malory's *Morte D'Arthur* is available in numerous editions; there are Penguin and Everyman editions of Geoffrey of Monmouth, and an Everyman edition of Chrétien de Troyes; for the origin and growth of the legend, see R. W. Barber, *Arthur of Albion* (Barnes & Noble, 1961); for the real Arthur, see Geoffrey Ashe, *From Caesar to Arthur* (Collins, London, 1960).

Michael Holford

POSSESSION AND TRANCE

The medium in trance, the person possessed by a spirit, the speaker in tongues, the mystic in ecstasy, the art-lover entranced . . . are they in touch with a reality beyond the normal world? A psychiatrist's view of a complicated human mechanism

STATES OF TRANCE and so-called possession form the core of many experiences which seem spiritual, mysterious and supernatural. All through history men have thought that in trance contact could be made with an order of reality lying behind the everyday world, an order of reality with which we are not in touch in our everyday condition of mind and body.

A dictionary definition of the word trance is 'a morbid sleep, differing from natural repose in duration, in profound sensibility, etc. — the concomitant or symptom of diseases of the nervous system, particularly hysteria: catalepsy'. This definition points us straight to the connection between the 'morbid sleep' of trance, in which contact with supernatural truth is thought to be made, and disorders of the human mental and physical system.

In many trance states the subject is mentally absorbed, apparently unaware of the external world around him, perhaps in a condition of exultation or ecstasy; but he may continue to talk and behave in ways which make sense, though afterwards he cannot remember what he said and did. It is this combination of a frightening and abnormal state of mind with comprehensible speech and behaviour that has impressed men with the notion that someone in trance is the mouthpiece of the gods.

The same thing can happen to someone who is kicked on the head while playing

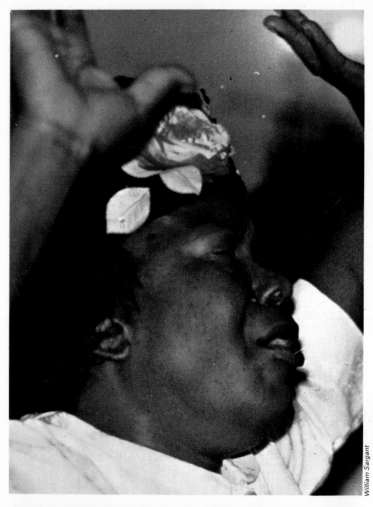
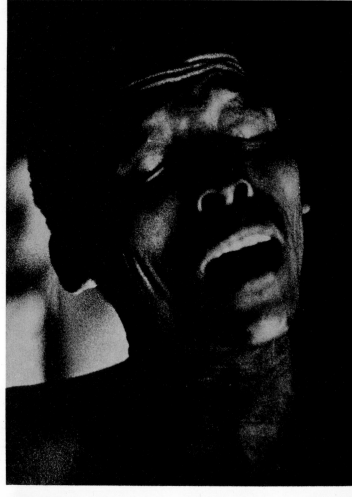

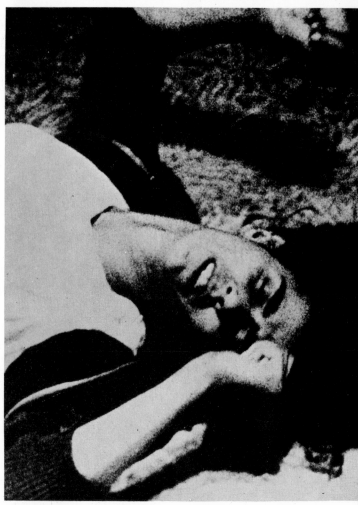

William Sargant

Popperfoto

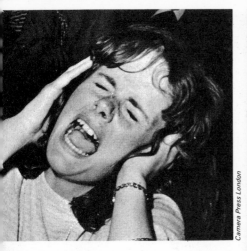

Camera Press London

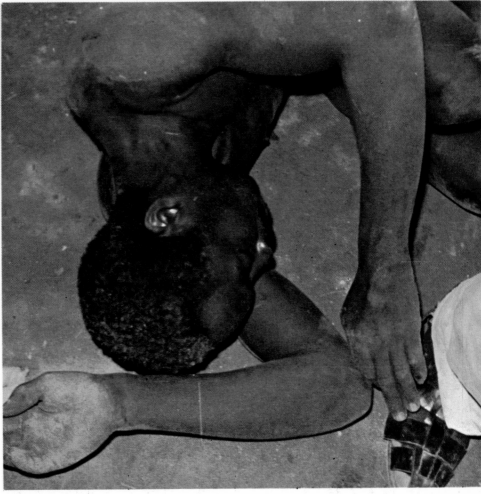

William Sargant

All over the world it is believed that people in trances are controlled by gods and spirits

1 Woman being 'sent' during a church ceremony in Watts, Los Angeles. Fundamentalist services often produce trance and semi-trance states among the congregation

2 African dancer in trance. African medicine-men frequently put a patient into trance to expel the spirit which has possessed him

3 Priest making the first gesture in the Voodoo greeting ritual

4 Member of a fundamentalist sect in Kentucky, believing herself possessed by the Holy Ghost

5 Rhythmic music and dancing can induce trance and semi-trance states; a scene from a concert by the Rolling Stones

6 Lying in a state of collapse, a West Indian possessed during a Voodoo ceremony

football or who suffers from loss of memory after a violent shock. Some drugs, hashish, L.S.D., mescaline and the like, induce a trance state or ecstatic state, not necessarily involving loss of memory. Trance states can also occur as a result of tumours of the brain or other brain injuries.

But there are also trances which are not induced by a sudden blow or shock, and although it is perfectly possible to fake a trance, and people have done so, there is no doubt that genuine trance states of this sort do occur. They occur in the ecstasies of mystics or magicians, when the mind is concentrated on a powerful idea or image, of a god perhaps, and the link between the mind and the normal world seems to snap. They occur in clairvoyants and fortune tellers, and quite frequently in mediums.

Speaking in Tongues

There is also the phenomenon called possession, in which a god or spirit, which may be good or evil, is thought to have taken control of the person in trance, to speak through his mouth and act through his limbs; the person afterwards remembering nothing of what happened during the trance. The words and actions of someone possessed by a god or a spirit naturally carry considerable weight with an audience which believes them to be the words and actions of the god or spirit itself.

All over the world and at all times, including the present day, trances have served to inculcate or fortify a variety of beliefs. In Tibet, before the coming of the Communists,

important decisions of policy were generally taken by the Dalai Lama and his advisers only after they had consulted the state oracle. The oracle was a young man who went into a trance and spoke strange words, which the priests interpreted. Hundreds of years before, the oracle of the temple of Apollo at Delphi was a woman who went into trance. Through her mouth, it was believed, the god himself answered the questions put to him. Although the answers were famous for being riddling, obscure and frequently misleading, many important decisions were made by Greek politicians only after consulting the oracle and in an attempt to follow its advice.

Some of the early Christians, including St Paul, experienced ecstatic trance states and the Church festival of Pentecost (Whitsun) still commemorates the descent of the Holy Ghost to the apostles. There was the sound of a great rushing wind, they saw what appeared to be cloven tongues of fire and they began to speak in foreign languages which they had never learned. This 'speaking in tongues' is a valued experience today among some groups of Christians who believe that it is a sign of contact with God.

Trance states are seen very commonly in Africa. During initiation ceremonies at puberty, states of trance are induced in boys and girls who experience a collapse or 'little death' after being exposed to rhythmic drumming, exhausting dancing, the pain of circumcision and the display to them of masks of the supposed tribal spirits. These spirits may talk to them through the mouths

of witch-doctors who are themselves in states of trance and who wear the grotesque and frightening masks of the spirits they represent.

Real Healing Value

It is an old belief, still prevalent in some parts of the world, that illness is caused by possession. Either the disease is itself an evil spirit which has seized the unfortunate patient in its grip, or it has been brought by an evil being which has taken hold of him. To cure him, the evil spirit must be cast out. The patient is often put into a trance, again through rhythmic dancing and singing, and the healer may also go into trance. Unknown to the patient, the evil spirit talks through his mouth telling the medicine-man why it has possessed the patient — perhaps because of some moral lapse on his part or as the result of a spell which an enemy has put on him. The medicine-man then tries to expel the spirit from the patient and, if he is successful, the patient emerges from his trance mentally or physically healed.

Cures of this type do work in practice. From a psychiatrist's point of view, what happens is that in trance the patient is able to confess his sins and pour out his anxieties and problems in the same way as a patient on a Western psychotherapist's couch, though because he is in trance the African patient is not conscious of what he is saying and does not remember it afterwards. This process has real healing value for a variety of reasons, one of which is the patient's responding to suggestion and fully believing

that the spirit which possessed him has been driven out.

Most of us in the West do not experience full-scale trance or possession at first-hand but we sometimes come close to it. Many people who went to hear Hitler speak – the effects of his hypnotic ranting reinforced by music, ceremonial, the response of a great crowd – were carried out of themselves into an uncritical state of mind in which they felt that he was almost a divine being. Enthusiastic listeners to the Beatles have been known to go into states akin to trance, with or without temporary loss of consciousness, when the music seems to take on a richness of significance of which the listener is powerfully aware though he cannot describe it in words. Lovers of classical music are not

immune from the same effect. The state which we commonly call being 'entranced', held in the grip of an experience of immeasurable beauty, immeasurable meaning, induced by works of art or by splendours of landscape, is the nearest approach to the true trance state which most of us ever make.

The Validity of Trance

There will always be arguments about trance. Some people believe that the medium in trance, the person possessed by a spirit, the speaker in tongues, the mystic in ecstasy, the art-lover entranced, may be truly in touch with a reality beyond the normal world. Others believe that trance is a splitting of the field of consciousness and that the subject is not in touch with any mysterious

or greater reality but is expressing beliefs, ideas, hopes or fears which he himself unconsciously holds or which are part of the general currency of his society.

The person in trance generally retains some vague awareness of his surroundings. He rarely falls and hurts himself and he generally talks of things which he knows about. He may in fact exhibit a sharper perception and awareness of what is going on around him than in his normal conscious state, so that in trance he gives the impression of having an enhanced power to read other men's minds, to analyse their present actions and prophesy their future ones. Strange tongues are spoken in trance but there is no completely proven instance of a language being spoken in trance by someone

Left Frenzies and trances were also part of the religious experience of the ancient Greeks: amphora of c 500 BC showing two maenads, worshippers of Dionysus, in ecstasy, dancing to the music of a satyr
Right At a service of a snake-handling sect in Tennessee the worshippers often go into ecstatic states, in which they believe that the intensity of their faith will keep them from harm
Below To the rhythmic sound of drums, a voodoo dancer works herself into a state of sexual frenzy, which is an aspect of ceremonies leading to states of possession

who was totally unacquainted with it beforehand. Subconscious, forgotten memories can rise to the surface in trance: facts once known and languages once learned can be brought back by an individual who has little or no recollection of them in his normal state.

I do not myself believe that in states of trance gods ever speak to men. Trance is usually a state of self-hypnosis, through which all sorts of dubious beliefs can be implanted and maintained. Fortunes are not made because the subject of a trance is able to predict something readily checkable and profitable, the movements of prices on the Stock Exchange or the winners of horse-races. But trance states have been used through the ages, and will continue to be used, to prop up belief in a great variety of gods, spirits, ghosts and the rest. Those who have experienced trance themselves can rarely be convinced that something supernatural has not happened to them, because autosuggestibility tends to become so greatly enhanced in the trance state.

We shall know much more about trance when we know better how the human brain really works. Readers of this encyclopedia will find states of trance mentioned in connection with gods, demons, ghosts, telepathy, witches, spirit possessions, and supernatural powers of all sorts. The reader is best left to his own final judgement as to whether man is deceived or elevated to high realms of the spirit by this fascinating but complicated mechanism of the human mind.

WILLIAM SARGANT

William Sargant

Transworld Feature Syndicate

Asafoetida

Evil-smelling gum, made by drying the juice of the plant *Ferula asafoetida* and used as a condiment: it is recommended in a magical textbook called the *Lemegeton* for calling up a demon, as its stench is suitable to the nature of demons, which stink of hell.

Asceticism

The practice of abstinence and austerity, based on the belief that the desires of the flesh are a spiritual hindrance, and intended to subdue the body or to make it holy. See SELF-DENIAL.

ASH

VARIOUS GREEK MYTHS link the birth of mankind with a universal ash tree. The poet Hesiod's fable of Zeus creating a race of brazen men from ashes accounts for the reference in Homer, when Penelope says to Ulysses, 'Tell me thy family from whence thou art; for thou art not sprung from the olden tree . . .'

Nordic myths also suggest that man was created from the wood of the ash by the god Odin; and the word itself derives from the Norse *aska*, meaning 'man'. In the *Edda*, a collection of old myths and legends, the ash becomes the World Tree, Yggdrasill. Its branches overspread the world and reached the heavens, while its roots penetrated the abyss known as Hel, from which our modern word 'hell' is derived. Halfway up the trunk was Midgard, the disc-shaped earth, surrounded by ocean, with the serpent of eternity and a final mountain boundary on its outer rim. Asgard, the mountain of the gods at the base of Valhalla, reared up around the trunk. The ash also figures in a creation myth of the Algonquin Indians of North America, in which the creator god shot an arrow into an ash tree and the first humans emerged from the wound.

The association of the ash and snakes is widespread. In the 1st century AD Pliny wrote on ash's magical efficacy against snakes, how a snake would rather perish in a fire than crawl over an ash twig, and that they even avoid the shade cast by an ash

Yggdrasill, the world tree in Nordic myth, was an ash-tree: its roots reached to hell and its uppermost branches touched heaven. It was also believed that the disc-shaped earth was situated half-way up the trunk.

tree. That belief lasted for centuries, in backwoods American lore and elsewhere. To carry an ash twig or wear ash leaves in your hat would protect you against being bitten by snakes; if you were, drinking ash sap would cure the bite.

Witches were also repelled by the ash, a

bunch of ash keys being considered particularly useful against them. Ash sap was fed to new-born babies to protect them from evil spirits, and a baby's first bath should be before a fire of ash wood. A bunch of ash leaves would guard a bed and its occupant; a house within an ash grove was secure from supernatural influences.

The Irish burnt ash to keep the Devil away, and it was the original Yule log, the burning faggot from which the old year's sacred flame was transmitted to the new. Ash is in fact a splendid wood for fires, burning even if green.

There are many minor bits of magic connected with this tree. It could be employed to cure warts by pressing a pin into the wart and then into the tree saying:

Ash tree, ash tree
Pray buy these warts off me.

Children could be cured of rupture by passing them naked through a cleft, made in an ash tree and held open by oaken wedges, which was then closed and bandaged. If the tree's wound healed satisfactorily, the rupture would do likewise. Gilbert White describes the rite in *The Natural History of Selborne*, where he also notes the even odder custom of the 'shrew-ash'. Shrews were believed to cause cramp and lameness if they ran over cattle. If a live shrew was sealed into a hole bored in an ash, the cattle could be cured by stroking them with a branch from this tree. Ash could in any case not injure animals, and was one of the trees recommended for making shepherds' crooks.

'Good morning to you, God, good morning.' The Supreme Being of the Ashanti is everywhere and sees everything; if you have something to say to him, you say it to the wind

ASHANTI

THE ASHANTI PEOPLE live in Ghana, in West Africa. Religious rites and ceremonies are important in traditional Ashanti society because it is believed that men interact not only with each other but also with their ancestors and with supernatural beings and spirits which inhabit the universe. This interaction is possible because man himself

is made of material and non-material elements. He has a body formed out of the blood of his mother, a spirit derived partly from his father and a soul given to him by the Supreme Being.

To the Ashanti, therefore, man's well-being depends on both physical and spiritual factors. When a person is sick, the cause of his illness may be spiritual as well as physical. When his affairs do not go right, he may have been thwarted not only by his fellow men but by supernatural forces and spirits invoked by evil men to their aid, or by spirits and beings which he has offended.

In a society which holds this view, religion cannot but dominate its way of life. Man

must worship and pray to the supernatural beings and spirits on whom he depends for his well-being. Religion is one of the means by which he lives his life on this earth, and recourse to methods of controlling supernatural forces and spirits for his own benefit becomes a matter of practical necessity.

Although the Ashanti believe in a hereafter, they are more concerned with the here-and-now. They do not hold the view that the fruits of man's toils and labours are reaped only after death. You do not do good in order to reap the benefits after death but in order to live a full life on earth. If a person does not fare well, he must do something about it. If he still does not succeed, he can only hope to have his destiny changed

in the other world before he returns to be born anew, if he so wishes. The hereafter only provides the consolation of continuity, of knowing that you can join your kinsmen after death or that you can hope for a better life to be relived on earth.

The Dependable God

To the Ashanti the universe is the work of a Creator, Odomankoma. It is he who created the heaven and the earth, men and all creatures of the earth, trees and rivers. As they say on their drums, things that owe their origin to the Creator must be clearly distinguished from the works of man who draws on Nature for his own benefit. The things of Nature are from long ago.

> The path has crossed the river,
> The river has crossed the path,
> Which is the elder?
> We made the path and found the river.
> The river is from long ago,
> From the Creator of the universe.

When Odomankoma the Creator created the world, he also created life and death. According to an Ashanti myth, Death became so powerful that he was able to kill the Creator himself. But when the Creator died, the universe continued to be controlled by a Supreme Being, called Nyame. At first this Supreme Being lived very close to earth and was within easy reach of man but he was obliged to move far out into the heavens because women hit the earth continually as they pounded grain in mortars.

From his abode on high Nyame is able to

see everything, for he sees even with his eyes turned away. He seems to be everywhere, for the Ashanti say, 'If you have something to say to the Supreme Being, say it to the wind'. He is the giver of rain and sunshine who controls the seasons. He offers protection and help to those who need it. As summarized in Ashanti proverbs: 'It is the Supreme Being that brushes off flies from the tailless animal.' 'It is the Supreme Being that pounds food for the one who has lost his arm.'

The Supreme Being is the source of morality. He does not like men to cheat one another. Man's destiny is in his hands: 'If the Supreme Being does not want you to die and a human being tries to kill you, you will not die.' Men can depend on him, for he is someone on whom one leans and does not fall. And so the drummer exhorts his listeners:

> The Dependable God bids us all
> Abide by his injunctions.
> Then shall we get whatever we want,
> Be it white or red.
> It is God, Creator of the firmament.
> Good morning to you, God, good morning.
> I am learning, let me succeed.

It is not only human beings who owe their lives to the Creator. The Ashanti believe that the supernatural beings which inhabit the universe also owe their existence and power to him.

Of these beings, those who wield the greatest power are the gods (*abosom*), who may be identified with particular features

At the birth of their nation the Ashanti believed that a golden stool descended from the heavens. The stool has always been a powerful symbol, 'the soul of the nation', and an insurrection resulted when the British tried to take possession of it in 1900

of Nature. They include river gods, tree gods and mountain gods, as well as gods without any clearly defined habitat. All of them rank below the Supreme Being and are sometimes described as his children. However, within the limits of the powers given to them, they act independently.

Gods Born of Woman

Gods may be given a temporary home in a special shrine, consisting of a brass pan and effigies or other objects to which sacrifices can be made. This makes it possible for gods identified with particular places to be worshipped wherever a shrine can be made for them; provided, of course, that they are served by priests appointed by them, or by priests familiar with their mode of worship.

Various human characteristics are attributed to the gods. They have sex, some being male, some being female and a few being both. They tend to specialize, to be more effective in some spheres than in others. There are gods of war and gods of victory. There are gods of peace and gods who are consulted about the causes of epidemics or other calamities.

The Ashanti believe that a god can enter into a woman's womb and be born into the world. Usually he does not come forth in the form of a human being but as a piece of stone, which is subsequently discovered to be a god. The gods can change their shapes, turning themselves into animals or birds when it suits them, or appearing in human form – in the guise of beautiful women or people who are insane.

The gods also have unlimited mobility. They can stay in and out of their shrines as they like. The fact that shrines are made for some of them in different localities suggests that their worshippers believe that the gods can be present in many places at the same time.

Ashanti religious practice allows freedom of movement and freedom of worship. Every god is available for consultation by anyone who needs help and people travel to the particular gods who can give them the kind of help they need. Sometimes the gods themselves direct those who come to them to other gods. Naturally, some gods become more renowned than others and attract people to their shrines from all over Ashanti, and indeed from other places.

Earth Spirit
As well as the gods, the Ashanti recognize the existence of Nature spirits, which find a permanent or temporary home in natural objects and may be beneficial to those who recognize them and harmful to those who ignore them. They are generally not the objects of organized cults. They have no priests, no set form of worship, even though they may occasionally be the focus of rituals.

The most important Nature spirit recognized by the Ashanti is the spirit of the Earth. This is a feminine spirit, for the Earth is like a mother to humanity. Her sacred day is Thursday and in the old days work on the farm was prohibited on this day.

The attitude of the Ashanti to the spirit of the Earth is expressed in drink-offerings and in the poetry of drums. The priest of a god acknowledges the Supreme Being and the spirit of the Earth before he starts the trance dance. In the poetry of drums, the drummer addresses the spirit of Earth, saying:

Earth when I am in life, I depend on you.
When I am about to die, I depend on you.
Earth that receives the body of the dead,
Good morning to you. Earth; good morning, great one. . . .

Apart from the Earth, no planets are recognized by the Ashanti as belonging to the world of spirits. Neither the sun nor the moon appears in prayers or rituals.

Dangers of the Forest
Other Nature spirits are associated with particular trees, especially those used for carving or building. These trees are not the objects of organized cults because they are not personified gods (and so are distinguished from tree gods proper). When an Ashanti wishes to cut down any of them for use, he performs a little ritual so that the spirit enshrined in it may not harm him.

There is a widespread belief that many spirits inhabit the forest and that it is dangerous for anyone to venture alone into the thick forest unless he knows the lore of

the forest. And it is not only Nature spirits that loiter there. Gods may also be met and some of those who become priests discover their gods through being possessed while in the forest. When they are possessed elsewhere, there is a tendency for them to run into the bush, to live there in seclusion so that they will be in constant touch with the god who has possessed them.

The rites performed during festivals set aside for some gods include bringing the god from the bush in a procession to the town.

The Living and the Dead
The position of man's soul and spirit in the universe of spirits is also of concern to the Ashanti. While on earth, man must keep his own soul pure and strong. He must also respond to the spiritual influences and powers around him, because he has no power of his own to determine the course of his own life. Although he has a spirit, it does not make him a member of the world of spirits. It is when he dies that he can join the world of spirits, and in this state he shares such attributes of the gods as unlimited mobility, shape-changing, the power to show himself visibly through some human being and the gift of invisible presence.

Because the dead have supernatural powers beyond the reach of living men, it is believed that they can be of help to the living when they are reached through prayers and ritual. The Ashanti pray to the dead in much the same way as they spoke to them while they were alive. They offer them food

Ancestor worship is an important element in Ashanti religion. Funerary urn of an ancestor: because the dead have supernatural powers, they can help or harm the living. They are prayed to, and offered food and drink

and drink, conscious of their human past. They slaughter a sheep for them and afterwards cut it up and share it, as it were, with them.

Though the Ashanti revere the dead and behave in their presence in a religious manner, they think of them not as gods but as persons in another world, as kinsmen who are no longer visible but who can help the living.

Magical Force
The Ashanti believe in the magico-religious power of witches and sorcerers and in the protective powers of charms and amulets, prepared by experts, and worn on the body or hung in a room. There are amulets believed to provide protection against being shot, or assaulted, charms against witchcraft and bad medicine. These provide additional security to that offered by the gods and may be prepared or prescribed by a priest for the use of a client.

Closely related to the belief in magico-religious power is the belief that there is vital force inherent in some material things. This belief shows itself in the choice of ritual materials – in the selection of herbs, liquids, and substances assumed to have spiritual power. Such materials are used to harness spirits, to act as a vehicle of communication with the unseen, and to act as agents of a person's desires.

Charms, amulets or other preparations of vital force can be used to influence not only gods and spirits but also man — to influence his mind or his heart, to weaken his body or destroy him completely. They are important bridges to the supernatural and may operate in the worship of supernatural beings as well as in magic designed to achieve its ends without the direct intervention of a supernatural being.

When they form part of the rituals of worship, they may be combined with actions and speech (in ritual formulae and prayers) or music and movement. When they are exploited for magical purposes, they may be combined with spells or incantations and prescribed actions.

The Axe of Nyame

Although there is evidence in the past of temples and priests of Nyame the Supreme Being, a distinctive organized cult of the Supreme Being has not survived. There are no set rituals for Nyame, no set occasions for worship exclusive to him. The central place which he occupied in Ashanti religious thought has continued to be expressed through the symbol of *nyamedua*. This is a forked branch of a tree (Alstonia congensis) named after Nyame the Supreme Being, which is fixed outside houses to serve as an altar for him.

A pot containing a neolithic axe is placed on this altar. The axe is called *Nyame akuma*, the axe of Nyame, for it is believed to come down from the heavens during thunderstorms. Offerings to the Supreme Being are placed in the pot.

On all ritual occasions focused primarily on the lesser gods, formal prayers and libations begin with a call to the Supreme Being. Apart from this, nothing else seems to be required for bringing people in touch with him, for he can always be reached through prayers.

The Worship of the Gods

Nature spirits similarly have no shrines or formal organized cults. Earth is mentioned in prayers and libations but there does not appear to be a distinctive organized form of worship for the spirit of the Earth. Similarly other Nature spirits become the focus of attention only when man is in need of objects with which they are associated. The rites that are performed for them are done privately: they do not call for general participation or the intensity of public worship.

It is the lesser gods and the ancestors who receive the greatest attention in Ashanti religious practice, for they are worshipped at fairly regular intervals. But there is a vast difference in the forms of worship devoted to the ancestors and those set aside for the gods.

The ancestors have no priests trained specially for the purpose of worship or the performance of rituals, for the ancestors are guardian spirits that may be approached by any of their kinsmen. Communication with them is established through prayers, pouring libations, offerings of food and blood sacrifice, usually of a sheep. In the case of ancestor chiefs, those who officiate on ritual occasions are the chief and his elders, the members of the tribe who are the keepers of the royal mausoleum and a selected number of officials and servants of the court.

The worship of the gods, on the other hand, requires trained priests. All those who assume this role undergo long periods of training, generally lasting not less than three years, during which they learn the music and dance of the gods, the particular songs of the gods they serve, the elements of drama embodied in public worship, the rites of the cult, methods of divination and healing, the use of herbs, the preparation of charms and amulets or how to counteract their powers, and methods of dealing with the personal problems of their clients.

In traditional Ashanti society then, religion provides an important means of dealing with the day-to-day problems of living that can be attributed to spiritual causes, as well as a focal point for rallying the members of a community and strengthening their solidarity.

Worship is regarded not just as an expression of faith in the unseen but as a service which gods and spirits demand. In this connection, the traditional religion of the Ashanti shows greater concern with the lesser beings and spirits than with the Supreme Being himself because it is believed that they are both more capricious and more directly involved in every day life.
(See also CULT OF THE DEAD.)

J. H. KWABENA NKETIA

Ashes have been used to promote fertility, to give strength or to bring rain: ashes of burned Bibles have been recommended for treating potato disease

ASHES

ASHES ARE the residue of fire, and just as fire is regarded in mythology and folklore as something which purifies and also regenerates, or brings new life, so the same properties are associated with ashes. Some primitive peoples regard ashes as the 'seeds' of fire, falling from it as it dies in the same way that the seeds of plants do, and so containing the life of the fire itself.

The ancient Jews sacrificed a red heifer by fire, the ashes being used to purify the unclean. The ancient Egyptians burned red-haired men, not as a purificatory rite but so that their ashes could be scattered on the fields to quicken the seed in the earth.

At the root of the custom of burning living creatures in sacred fires to fertilize the soil lies the conviction that ash is the soul of fire and so brings renewal. It was long a folk custom in Europe for the ashes of the Midsummer fires to be spread on the crops or

Ashes, like fire which creates them, are widely believed to carry new life and strength, as among the Nuba people of the southern Sudan whose wrestlers cover themselves with ashes for extra vigour

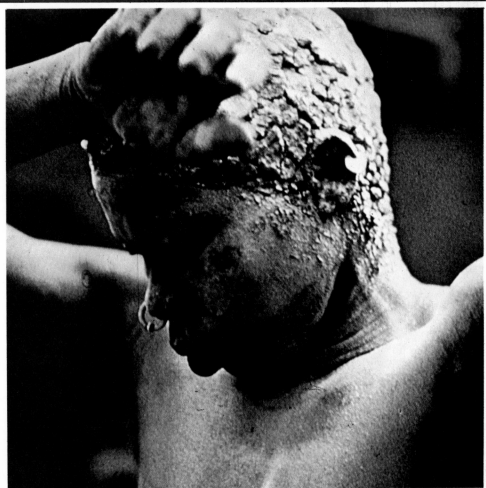

Leni Riefenstahl

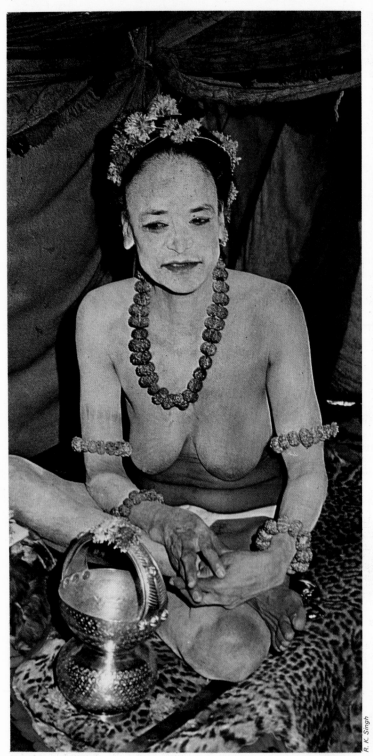

R. K. Singh

fed to farm animals. In modern Germany a flaming Easter wheel is rolled down the hillside and its ashes are then spread on the fields.

Ashes have also played their part in the rites of rainmakers and in control of the weather. South American tribes, particularly the Muyscas of Colombia, throw ashes into the sky to condense the clouds and induce rain, or scatter ashes on water as a charm to produce fair weather. In Central Europe ashes were spread on the fields to prevent hailstones, and in France as a defence against lightning.

Sometimes linked with the idea of ashes as renewers of life is the belief that when a creature has been burned, its ashes contain its qualities in concentrated form. In

Luther's *Martyr's Hymn*, the ashes of Christian martyrs are the seeds of faith.

Flung to the heedless winds
Or on the waters cast,
The martyr's ashes watched
Shall gathered be at last.
And from that scattered dust
Shall spring a plenteous seed
Of witnesses for God.

To ensure that the power of a witch was utterly extinguished, it was necessary that her body be burned and that her ashes be scattered to the winds. After the burning of Urbain Grandier at Loudun in 1634, his ashes were shovelled by the executioner towards each of the four points of the compass, while the mob searched among the

Above left Indian disciple of the god Shiva, whitened with ashes; the god was represented as a white or silver-coloured man
Above Nuba wrestler covered with ashes before fighting
Above right Indian child, during a festival of Shiva, covered in ashes believed to contain holy and curative properties
Below right Victorious Nuba wrestlers are awarded branches which are burnt; the wrestler covers himself with the ashes before the next fight

dead embers of the pyre for charred bones, which would serve as aphrodisiacs or as cures for constipation. (See GRANDIER.)

In New Guinea it was believed that the qualities associated with one living creature

R. K. Singh

Leni Riefenstahl

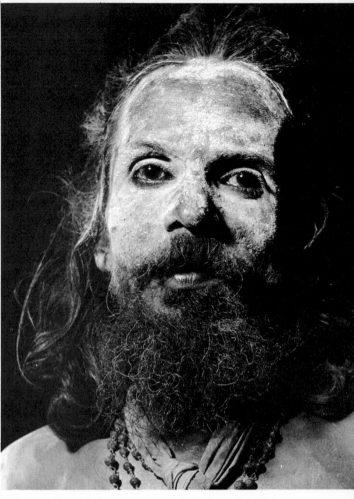

could be magically transferred to another by a ritual involving ashes. A snake was killed and its ashes smeared on the legs as a defence against snake-bite. Even today certain South American tribes mix the ashes of their loved ones with their food and drink in order to absorb the qualities of the dead.

In popular American superstition, ill luck will befall a home where ashes from the fireplace are taken up or swept out after 4 p.m., or during Christmas, or on any Friday. The Pueblo Indians and some other tribes use ashes as a protection against witches. And a curious old belief from North Carolina intermingles a little magic with some folk medicine of the veterinary kind. It advises sprinkling ashes on domestic animals, on Ash Wednesday, to

protect them not from witches but from lice.

Ashes were often used in divination, one of the strangest examples being in Yorkshire where, on the eve of St Mark's day (24 April) the ashes were riddled in the hearth and left overnight, and in the morning carefully examined for any mark resembling a footprint. Should this be found, the member of the family whose foot fitted the print was doomed to die within 12 months.

In Ireland, the Isle of Man and Lancashire divination by ashes was carried out at Hallowe'en, when a curious love ritual was sometimes performed by single men. The bachelor would sprinkle ashes or seeds along some quiet lane and then wait and watch. The first girl to pass along that way after him was destined to become his wife.

Left Ash-daubed Indian holy man
Right The Perchera, or tribal chief, of the sanctuary at Kataragama, Ceylon, has smeared his face with ashes, symbol of purification

An entirely different way of looking at ashes is found among medieval alchemists, who saw them as the dead body of a substance. If you burned a piece of wood, the smoke rising up was the 'soul' of the wood and the ashes left behind were its corpse.

A similar connection between ashes and death lies behind their widespread use as a badge of sorrow, bereavement and repentance. In Roman Catholic churches on Ash Wednesday, the ashes of the palms used on Palm Sunday the previous year are sprinkled on the heads of penitents.

Ashur

Chief god and war god of the Assyrians, often shown firing an arrow from his bow and enclosed in a winged disc; he replaced the god Marduk when the Assyrians dominated Mesopotamia.
See MARDUK; MESOPOTAMIA.

ASMODEUS

THIS DEMON OF LUST was probably originally the Persian 'fiend of the wounding spear', Aeshma Daeva, from a root *aesh*, meaning 'to rush forward' or 'violent movement'. He was a storm spirit and a personification of rage, who filled men's hearts with anger and desire for revenge. Anger was regarded in the ancient world as something pre-eminently evil, stirred up like the violence of thunder and lightning by powerful supernatural forces.

Imported from Persia into Palestine, Asmodeus or Ashmedai appears frequently in Jewish literature, where his original function was to cause frustration in marriage, probably in order to provoke rage and violence. In the book of Tobit, written c 250 BC, Tobias marries Sarah, who has had seven husbands before but all of them have been strangled by Asmodeus to prevent them from lying with her. On the advice of the angel Raphael, Tobias burns the heart and liver of a fish, and the smoke drives the demon away. No explanation of the effectiveness of the fish-smoke is given, though it was evidently an unusually fierce and voracious fish as it had earlier jumped at Tobias and attempted to devour him while he was washing himself in the river Tigris.

The Latin version of Tobit adds that Tobias and Sarah also defeated the demon by remaining chaste for the first three nights of their marriage, which was the foundation of the later custom of the 'Tobias nights'. Down to the 19th century in parts of France, Germany and the Balkans, it was the custom to follow the example of Tobias and Sarah. In medieval France husbands sometimes paid a fee to the Church for a licence to disregard the rule.

According to Jewish stories, Asmodeus was the son of a mortal woman, Naamah, either by one of the fallen angels or by Adam before the creation of Eve. In the *Testament of Solomon*, written between 100 and 400 AD, he says, 'I was born of angel's seed by a daughter of man.' Described as 'furious and shouting', he not only prevents intercourse between husband and wife but also encourages adultery. 'My business', he says, 'is to plot against the newly married, so that they may not know one another . . . I transport men into fits of madness and desire

when they have wives of their own, so that they leave them and go off by night and day to others that belong to other men with the result that they commit sin . . .'

In this way the demon's functions extended from frustrating desire to arousing it. He developed into a supernatural power of lechery and was said to have the feet of a cock, a bird noted for indiscriminate sexual vigour.

According to other Jewish tales, Asmodeus was the king of demons and lived on a mountain top. He liked to go up to heaven every day to take part in learned discussions there. The master magician King Solomon forced Asmodeus and the other devils to build the Temple at Jerusalem but Asmodeus took his revenge when Solomon foolishly

allowed him to seize the magic ring in which his power resided. Asmodeus promptly hurled the ring down to the bottom of the sea, sent Solomon into exile and reigned in his place. But Solomon miraculously recovered the ring from the belly of a fish and imprisoned Asmodeus and the other demons in a large jar.

A magical textbook called the *Lemegeton*, which gives a long list of demons, says that when Asmodeus shows himself to human eyes he rides a dragon, carries a spear and has three heads — of a ram, a bull and a man, all traditionally lecherous creatures. The magician must summon him bareheaded as a mark of respect. He can make the magician invisible and lead him to hidden treasure.

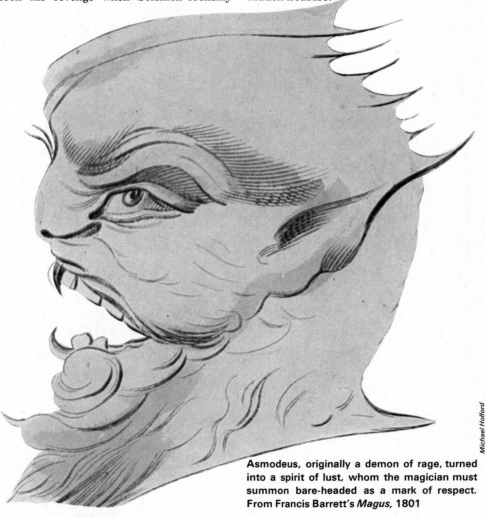

Michael Holford

Asmodeus, originally a demon of rage, turned into a spirit of lust, whom the magician must summon bare-headed as a mark of respect. From Francis Barrett's *Magus*, 1801

Jean Ribière

Ass

Often a symbol of stupidity, and sometimes of lust; in Christian symbolism it stands for humble patience and courage: some classical writers accused the Jews and the early Christians of worshipping an ass.

Mansell Collection

Assyria

Empire in northern Mesopotamia, which reached its peak of dominance in the Middle East in the 8th and 7th centuries BC; named from its chief town and god, Ashur. See MESOPOTAMIA.

*This Queen of Heaven, with crescent horns, was a
rival of the God of the Jews, noted for the sensuality of her worship*

ASTARTE

A GREAT MOTHER GODDESS was worshipped
under various names throughout the Middle
East, as Ishtar in Mesopotamia, as Ashtart
or Asherah by the Phoenicians and Canaanites. The Greeks called her Astarte and
equated her with their own love goddess
Aphrodite, who was originally one of her
many forms (see APHRODITE). Numerous
clay plaques representing her have been
found in Syria and Palestine, dating from
1700 to 1100 BC and probably worn as
charms to promote fertility. She is mentioned
frequently and with violent disapproval in the
Old Testament and eventually, like many
other deities who were rivals of the God of
Jews and Christians, she turned into a
demon and is one of the fallen angels in
Milton's *Paradise Lost*.

> . . . Astoreth, whom the Phoenicians called
> Astarte,
> Queen of Heaven, with crescent horns;
> To whose bright image nightly by the moon,
> Sidonian virgins paid their vows and songs.

W. F. Albright has remarked that, 'Goddesses of fertility play a much greater role
among the Canaanites than they do among
any other ancient people': evidently because
of their dread of drought and famine. Though
these goddesses had different names and
were independent personalities, they had
similar functions and were essentially the
same goddess. They ruled war as well as
fertility, motherhood and sex, and they
were frequently represented naked and with
the sexual organs emphasized.

The Bride of Heaven

Ashtart was the chief goddess of the Phoenicians at Tyre and Sidon, and wherever they
established colonies they took her with
them. She had a temple in their colony at
Memphis in Egypt, for instance, and temples
at Carthage. A Phoenician statuette of her in
alabaster has been found at Galera, near
Granada in Spain: she sits on a throne,
flanked by sphinxes and with a bowl under
her breasts. At some point in her ritual milk
was poured into the head of the statuette
and flowed into the bowl through holes
pierced in the goddess's breasts.

Asherah or Asherat, often called Asherat
of the Sea, was the wife of the Canaanite
supreme god El, whose name means simply
'the god', and by him was the mother of 70
deities. The same goddess was also worshipped in the south of Arabia and by the
Amorites, the Semitic nomads who by 2000
BC had spread northwards from Arabia into
Palestine, Syria and Mesopotamia. There is
an Amorite inscription to her of the 18th
century BC, in which she is called 'the bride
of heaven'.

In the Ugaritic texts, dating from c 1400
BC, found at Ras Shamra in northern Syria
since 1929, the goddess Anat plays a leading
role. The chief god El stays in the back-

ground and the most active god is Baal, the storm god who sends the rains which bring fertility to the earth. Anat is his sister and wife, and she plays the vital part in killing the god of drought and sterility or, in other words, in reviving the life of Nature (see BAAL).

Asherah, the wife of the old supreme god El and the mother of Baal, seems to have been hostile to Baal at first but later joined forces with Anat to help him. Apparently, the followers of both goddesses tried to attach them to the fertility god as the cult of Baal developed.

All these goddesses were imported into Egypt and in the 13th century BC Pharaoh Rameses II called himself 'the companion of Anat'. Ashtart or Asherah appears in an Egyptian sculpture where she is called Qodshu or Qedeshat, 'the sacred prostitute'. She is naked, stands on a lion, and holds a lotus flower, a symbol of life, in her right hand. In her left hand the goddess holds a pair of serpents, which are symbols of life renewed because snakes slough their old skins each year.

In Canaan the symbol of Asherah was a wooden pole, called an *asherah*. It might be a living tree but was more often a tree-trunk with the branches lopped off, standing in a socket on a stone base. The upright pole is again a symbol of life, generation and fertilizing power, and may be the 'tree of life' which appears frequently in Canaanite art.

The Abomination of the Sidonians

When the Israelites invaded Palestine they found numerous local fertility gods and goddesses established, Baals and Ashtarts or Asherahs. The Old Testament writers called the goddess Ashtoreth, combining her name with the Hebrew word for 'shame', *bosheth*, as a comment on the licentiousness of her rites. But many Jews worshipped her. '. . . They forsook the Lord, the God of their fathers, who had brought them out of the land of Egypt; they went after other gods, from among the gods of the peoples who were round about them, and bowed down to them.' When Gideon pulled down his father's altar of Baal and cut down the asherah which stood beside it, 'he was too afraid of his family and the men of the town to do it by day, and he did it by night,' (Judges, chapters 2 and 6).

It was natural to feel that the gods already established in the country were powerful there, and the worship of a fertility goddess appealed to Jewish farmers who were just as concerned for the increase of their herds, crops and families as the Canaanites were. In spite of the efforts of the prophets, many Jews continued to worship the mother. In the 10th century BC King Solomon built a 'high place' or sanctuary 'on the right hand of the mountain of corruption . . . for Ashtoreth, the abomination of the Sidonians' (2 Kings, chapter 23).

In the 9th century at Mizpeh, north of Jerusalem, temples of Yahweh and Asherah

The great Semitic goddess Astarte eventually turned into the male demon Astaroth, who was said to have very bad breath. From Collin de Plancy's *Dictionnaire Infernal*, 1863

stood side by side. King Ahab and his wife, the notorious Jezebel, were devoted to the Canaanite gods and maintained 450 prophets of Baal and 400 prophets of Asherah. It was against these priests that Elijah fought his great ritual battle on Mount Carmel (1 Kings, chapter 18). He succeeded in calling down fire from heaven when they could not, but the reaction against him was so strong that he fled for his life.

In the late 7th century BC the prophet Jeremiah still bewailed that 'the children gather wood, the fathers kindle fire, and the women knead dough, to make cakes for the queen of heaven' but those he reproached answered that they would continue to burn incense to the queen of heaven and pour libations to her, as they and their fathers had done, because attempts to suppress her worship had brought nothing but disaster (Jeremiah, chapters 7 and 44).

Priests and Prostitutes

As goddess of fertility, Astarte typified the reproductive powers of Nature and woman. She was associated with the moon, and often shown with the horns of the crescent moon, because the moon was believed to govern the growth, decay and rebirth of all things as it waxed and waned in the sky (see MOON). The dove, an amorous bird, belonged to her and at Ascalon in the 1st century AD a visitor saw 'an impossible number of doves' in the streets and houses, because they were sacred and no one ever killed them. Fishes were sacred to her also, perhaps for their numerous offspring.

The Jewish prophets condemned the worship of Astarte, not only because they believed that Yahweh was the one true god but also because of the sexual rituals of the goddess, who was served by sacred prostitutes. Their activities had a practical use, for their earnings financed the goddess's cult, but the sexuality of Astarte's worship was basically imitative magic, intended to sustain the fertility of Nature.

Greek and Roman writers were also repelled by the worship of the Middle Eastern goddesses whose rituals spread westwards, with their phallic symbols, sacred prostitutes and painted priests in women's clothes. In *The Golden Ass* Apuleius (born c 123 AD) describes the priests, 'their faces daubed with rouge and their eye sockets painted to bring out the brightness of their eyes', who carried the image of 'the Syrian goddess' about on an ass, dancing to the sound of castanets and cymbals, cutting themselves with knives and flagellating themselves for the edification of the spectators before going round with the collecting box. Earlier, in the biblical account of the contest between Elijah and the prophets of Baal, the Canaanite god's priests were said to 'cut themselves after their custom with swords and lances, until the blood gushed out upon them.'

Lake of Holy Fishes

The travelling lecturer and humorist Lucian, a contemporary of Apuleius, wrote an essay about the Astarte of Hierapolis, north-west of Aleppo in Syria. Tame bulls, bears, lions and eagles were kept in the

Michael Holford

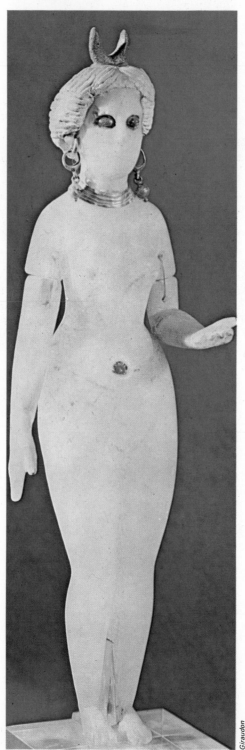

Giraudon

grounds of the temple and there was a lake full of holy fishes, some of which knew their names and came when called. In the early summer there was a great festival of the goddess, when trees were brought and erected outside the temple, with goats, sheep and objects of gold and silver hung on them. The sacred idols were carried about among the trees and then burned.

The temple attendants were eunuchs who wore white robes with pointed caps. They cut their arms till the blood ran, and beat each other. Sometimes a young man, carried away in the ecstasy of the goddess's worship, would devote himself to her service by castrating himself. He would then run through the city and the occupants of the house into which he threw his severed members would supply him with women's clothes.

Princes of Amity

As a result of the denunciations of Ashtoreth in the Old Testament as an 'abomination' and an enemy of God, Jews and Christians decided that she was a demon but for unknown reasons the goddess turned into a male demon, with very bad breath. If he is summoned up by a magician, he appears in human form, half black and half white. He reveals all events of the past, present and future, and knows all secrets.

In the magical textbooks the demon Astaroth has lost all connection with sex but in the early 17th century Astaroth and Asmodeus were among the devils who possessed Madeleine de Demandolx (see AIX-EN-PROVENCE NUNS). Under their influence, or so it was believed, she danced and sang lewd songs, writhed in indecent postures and told spine-chilling stories of orgies and cannibalism at witch-revels she had attended. In 1673 Madame de Montespan sacrificed children to Astaroth and Asmodeus, 'princes of amity', in her attempt to secure her hold on Louis XIV's affections by black magic (see BLACK MASS).

FURTHER READING: John Gray, *The Canaanites* (Praeger, 1964); Donald Harden, *The Phoenicians* (Praeger); E. O. James, *The Ancient Gods* (Putnam, 1964); W. F. Albright, *From the Stone Age to Christianity* (John Hopkins Press, 1957); Lucian's 'The Goddess of Syria' is in volume 4 of the Loeb edition of his works, though in an eccentric and tiresome translation.

Above The head and magical symbol of Astaroth from Francis Barrett's *Magus*. The goddess came to be considered a demon because the Old Testament prophets denounced the licentious rites with which she was worshipped
Left Astarte in alabaster, a Mesopotamian statue of the goddess of love c 2000 BC. The crescent or horn-shaped head-dress signifies her connection with the moon, and with sexuality

The experience of seeming to leave one's own body and look at it from outside is not uncommon. It usually happens briefly and involuntarily but some people have deliberately experimented with 'astral travel'

ASTRAL BODY

FOR CENTURIES it has been a common idea that man is made of two components – a soul or spirit which comes from God, and a material body of flesh and blood. But some philosophers and occult theorists have suggested that each man has a third component, an astral body, meaning literally 'starry body' and sometimes called 'the body of light'.

This astral body is an exact copy of the flesh and blood body but is made of a finer material and has a shining and luminous appearance. It is supposed to be capable of separating itself from the physical body and travelling about, passing through walls, ceilings and other solid obstructions. It is also said to survive death, when it leaves the physical body. It exists in what is called the astral plane, which includes the normal, everyday world but extends beyond it.

An amusing account of astral travel was given by the French Roman Catholic journalist and occultist Anne Osmont, who died in 1953. She described how on her first attempt at astral travel she succeeded in leaving behind physical evidence of what she had done. She was friendly with a husband and wife, both sculptors. The wife, who was called Annie, had one evening expressed her strong disbelief in the possibility of astral travel. Mlle Osmont resolved to prove her wrong the same night.

It took a full quarter of an hour of effort to project herself out of her physical body, and then passing through the wall, she went to her friends' flat. They were asleep in bed. She took note of the colour and style of their nightclothes, but thought that was poor evidence, and looked around for some object to topple. On the mantelpiece was a gilt liqueur glass, and she tried to move it. It seemed as difficult to move as a piano, but presently she noticed it had moved a little, and continuing her efforts she got it to the edge and over. It smashed on the floor.

The couple sat up in bed with a start, and she heard Annie say grumpily, 'I bet it's that imbecile Osmont!' On her next ordinary visit she first saw the husband and repeated Annie's words to him. He recognized the reference and told her that his wife was very angry as the goblet had been a family heirloom. Mlle Osmont records that she was desperately exhausted for several days as a result of this effort. Movement of physical objects while in the astral body is rare.

The Skinless Hag

Among the magicians of the West Indies the projection of the astral body is achieved by singing special charm songs. They speak of this accomplishment as 'hagging', and those of either sex who are feared as possessors of this power are 'hags'. The operation, collo-

The astral body departing after death, as seen in a clairvoyant vision. It is also said to be capable of leaving the physical body during life, and travelling independently through walls and ceilings. This and all subsequent illustrations are from *The Projection of the Astral Body* by S. Muldoon and H. C. Carrington (Rider, 1929)

quially called 'changing the skin' is generally supposed to be performed after nightfall in a cool and unfrequented place. The hag strips naked, settles in a comfortable position, and begins to sing a song. At the end of the song, the body is left unconscious.

The hag is said to be visible or invisible at will, or to take any appearance he or she chooses. According to the West Indians, the normal night-time appearance of a 'skin-less hag' is an egg-shaped mass of faint light or fire. This light is said to be similar to the glow of decaying fish or rotten wood, seen in the dark. If the hag is near enough, the light is seen as a transparent mist through which the features and shape of the hag are visible.

'It's not me, it's my double'

Dr Francis Lefébure, who at the time had been practising yoga breathing exercises for about seven years, describes an occasion when his astral body became visible. During World War Two he was the doctor at a prisoner-of-war camp near Guelma in Algeria. His ideas were well known in the officers' mess and he was the butt of many jokes. One morning, Lefébure was told to go and see the lieutenant.

Getting into the Astral Body

The proper method is as follows: Develop the body of Light until it is just as real to you as your other body . . . Ultimately, the relation of that body with your own must be exceedingly intimate; but before this harmonizing takes place, you should begin by a careful differentiation. The first thing to do, therefore, is to get the body outside your own. To avoid muddling the two, you begin by imagining a shape resembling yourself standing in front of you. Do not say: 'Oh, it's only imagination!' The time to test that is later on, when you have secured a fairly clear mental image of such a body. Try to imagine how your own body would look if you were standing in its place; try to transfer your consciousness to the Body of Light. Your own body has its eyes shut. Use the eyes of the Body of Light to describe the objects in the room behind you . . .

As soon as you feel more or less at home in the fine body, let it rise in the air. Keep on feeling the sense of rising: keep on looking about you as you rise until you see landscapes or beings of the astral plane. Such have a quality all their own. They are not like material things — they are not like mental pictures — they seem to lie between the two . . .

Now, however unsuccessful your getting out of the body may apparently have been, it is most necessary to use every effort to bring it properly back. Make the Body of Light coincide in space with the physical body . . . then recover the unity of consciousness. If you fail to do this properly you may find yourself in serious trouble. Your Body of Light may wander away uncontrolled, and be attacked and obsessed. You will become aware of this through the occurrence of headache, bad dreams, or even more serious signs such as hysteria, fainting fits, possibly madness or paralysis. Even the worst of these attacks will probably wear off, but it may leave you permanently damaged to a greater or less extent.

Aleister Crowley.
Magick in Theory and Practice

'I went to find him. He was in the barber's shop. Always the first to chaff me, and fearless under fire, he didn't seem quite happy in my presence. This is more or less the story he gave me: "Last night about midnight, having gone to the little station (about three kilometres from the camp), I suddenly saw you so clearly there could be no possible mistake. I said to you, Hallo, Lefébure, what are you doing here at this time of night? And you replied, It's not me, it's my double! and then you disappeared as if by magic. Then I ran all the way to the camp and verified that you were in your room. I questioned the orderlies and the sentries, and they all guaranteed that you hadn't gone out during the night."

'The lieutenant, who seemed very impressed, did not make fun of me any more. As investigation proved that he was not in the least drunk that day, and that in fact he never was, the rumour spread in Guelma that I did strange tricks. Some months later I discovered that the phrase "It's not me, it's my double" was still famous in the town.'

The Sensation of Astral Travel

From accounts given by people who have travelled astrally, the general sensation is at first indistinguishable from the ordinary physical waking state, except sometimes for a feeling of well-being and buoyancy.

Dr Lefébure cites instances where he found himself walking round his bedroom and could not tell whether he was sleepwalking in his normal body or travelling in his astral body — until he felt himself floating upwards. He compares the limbs of the double to the phantom limbs felt by an amputee. He describes using his phantom arms to lever up the top half of his phantom body; but he adds that the most satisfactory results followed when he withdrew upwards from feet to head, like drawing a sword from its sheath.

To project himself astrally, Dr Lefébure relied on an effort of will, but also used yoga exercises involving more and more extended intervals of suspension of breathing.

The most experienced of modern astral travellers, the American author Sylvan Muldoon, attaches importance first to the building into the subconscious of a strong desire to be conscious in the astral body, then to the practice of concentrating on one's own image in a mirror. Next, attention is to be centred on the rhythm of the heart-beats, and the attempt made to be conscious of the heart beating at any point in the body. Then by repeated mental suggestion the heart should be slowed down. Needless to say, no one with heart weakness or irregularity should use this method.

Muldoon's unique series of experiences probably hinged on his abnormally slow heart-beat and his general frail health. He emphasizes that it is the feeling of suspense in the mind, not the actual projection of the astral body, that is unpleasant. He says that a really intense study of, and desire for, astral projection will always bring results because the force built up in the subconscious will inevitably express itself.

Apparitions

The evidence points to the possibility that some apparitions, or immaterial appearances of persons living or dead, are due to the presence of an astral body. There is the phenomenon of an observed apparition where more than one person, differently situated, sees the figure from an angle appropriate to his position. An example is the case of Lady B. and her daughter, who in about 1892 claimed they had seen the ghostly figure of a woman looking at herself in a mirror in their bedroom. Hornell Hart writes of the occurrence in *The Enigma of Survival*. 'Lady B. saw the face in quarter profile, the head intercepting its own reflection in the mirror. Miss B. saw the back of the figure with its long dark hair; the face was not directly visible to her, but she saw it clearly reflected in the mirror.' The record shows that the aspects seen by the two ladies were just as if a physical person had stood there.

Envelope of the Soul

The idea of an astral body is very old. Ancient Indian writings describe the eight *siddhis* or supernormal powers which can be acquired through a type of yoga called *Pranayama*. The sixth of these is 'flying in the sky', apparently referring to what is now called astral projection.

E. R. Dodds has shown that the western idea of the astral body originated in classical Greek philosophy, apparently without any important influences from oriental ideas. In his *Laws* (book ten) Plato discusses the souls

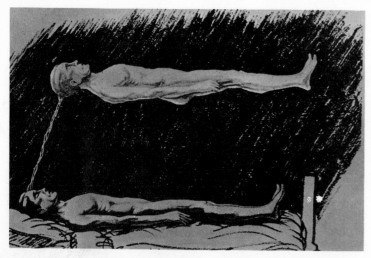

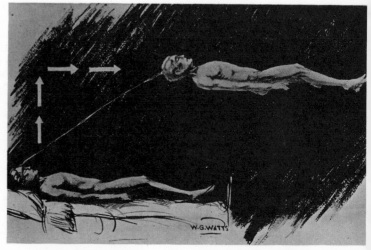

The most famous of modern astral travellers was the American author Sylvan Muldoon. He believed that an intense desire for astral projection would always bring results
Below The astral body lying in the air above the physical body, to which it is connected by an elastic 'cord'. Arrows show the route the phantom takes in projecting. The phantom then stands upright, though the push and pull of the 'cord' causes instability in the phantom. Finally the phantom interiorizes, or returns to the physical body

of the stars, which guide them in their courses. Some believe, he says, that these souls have bodies 'of fire, or it may be of air' in addition to the material bodies of the stars; though he also says that the human soul is not visible and 'enfolds us in a fashion utterly imperceptible to all bodily senses'. In the *Timaeus* the Creator is said to have made souls which he 'mounted' on the stars 'as it were on chariots'. These souls were later to be born as men and if they lived good lives, would return happily to the stars in the life after death.

Plato's pupil Aristotle developed a theory of *pneuma* (air or breath) as a constituent of the bodies of men and animals in which the sensitive soul resides and which is 'analogous to that element of which the stars are made'.

The linking together of the starry soul-chariots, the fiery or airy bodies of the souls of stars, and the Aristotelian starry soul-container, produced the idea of the astral body as a starry envelope of the soul.

The theory was taken up by the Neoplatonist philosophers. Porphyry, for instance, in the 3rd century AD, said that as the soul descends from heaven to earth, where it will acquire a physical body, its pneuma gradually thickens and darkens as it absorbs moisture from the air until it can be seen visibly. After death, the soul's efforts to climb back up to heaven again are hampered by this moist envelope, to such an extent that it may even be carried downwards, to a place of punishment. If it succeeds in rising, it gradually sheds the envelope. Some disembodied spirits have a misty pneuma which takes any shape they care to imagine, so that they appear to us in different guises, as gods perhaps or as souls of the dead.

The notion of the astral body has a continuous history in the West from classical times on. Dante's *Purgatorio* (canto 25), written in the 14th century, says that after death the soul 'around it beams its own creative power, like to its living form in shape and size . . . the circumambient air adopts the shape the soul imposes on it'. In the 16th century, Agrippa von Nettesheim seems to be referring to astral travel when he talks of 'vacation of the body, when the spirit is enabled to transcend its bounds, and as a light escaped from a lantern to spread over space'.

The Etheric Double
The terms 'astral body' and 'double' are used to cover several different types of phenomena. One of them is what is called the 'etheric double', identical with the Egyptian *Ka*, the vital force which gave the body life and which was represented in art as an exact replica of the physical body. The Hindus called it the *linga sharira* or 'vital form' which was, so to speak, the body's 'wiring system'.

The fact that Sylvan Muldoon placed so much emphasis on the 'cord', which he found linked his projected double to his physical body, suggests that his experiences involved the extrusion from the physical body of the etheric double as well as the astral body.

Another false trail occurs in the concept of the likeness of a person projected at some point in space by his intense thought or reverie. In Scotland they spoke of 'the forerunner', meaning some manifestation of a person's presence occurring at his destination before he arrived there. This is different from

the conception of an astral body, which contains the full functioning consciousness.

The true astral body also applies to the condition of some dream states, and to the experience of seeming to be dissociated from one's body during sleep or loss of physical consciousness. The dream-cures at the shrines of the Greek god of healing, Asclepios (see HEALING GODS), which apparently affected a ghostly counterpart of the physical body seem to have been concerned with the etheric double rather than the astral.

Fantasy or Reality?
Of modern authorities some, like D. J. West and Antony Flew, maintain an attitude of good-humoured scepticism towards astral bodies and projections. On the other side Professor Hart's conclusions are noteworthy. He has summarized with great fairness the evidence and contentions of the holders of all points of view, sceptical or convinced, in his *The Enigma of Survival*. He thinks that 'these diversities among the different descriptions of the astral world, and of the afterlife in general, cannot be explained by claiming that all such accounts are mere fantasies. The verified evidence of the reality of astral projection seems quite conclusive, and the evidence that apparitions of the dead may often be and usually are vehicles of surviving conscious personalities, seems also to be convincing'.
(See also DOUBLE; LIGHT; OUT OF THE BODY EXPERIENCES.)

C. NELSON STEWART

FURTHER READING: A. Flew, *A New Approach to Psychical Research* (Watts, 1953); H. Hart, *The Enigma of Survival* (Rider, 1959); D. J. West, *Psychical Research Today* (Hillary, 1954). For accounts of astral travel, see also two books by R. Crookall, *The Study and Practice of Astral Projection* (Wehman, 1961) and *The Techniques of Astral Projection* (Wehman, 1964); C. Green, *Out-of-the-Body Experiences* (Institute of Psychophysical Research, Oxford, 1968); F. Lefébure, *Expérientes Initiatiques* (Omnium Litteraire, Paris, 1956); S. J. Muldoon and H. Carrington, *The Projection of the Astral Body* (Weiser). For the Greek origins and the Neoplatonists, see E. R. Dodds ed. *Proclus: The Elements of Theology* (Clarendon Press, Oxford, 1923) appendix 2.

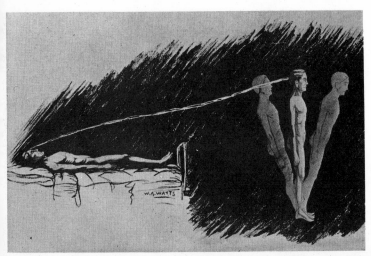

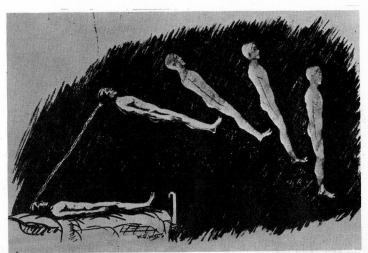

ASTROLOGY

Buried in the earth lies evidence of our past;
on its surface we live in the present;
and it has long been believed that in the sky
the stars predict our future

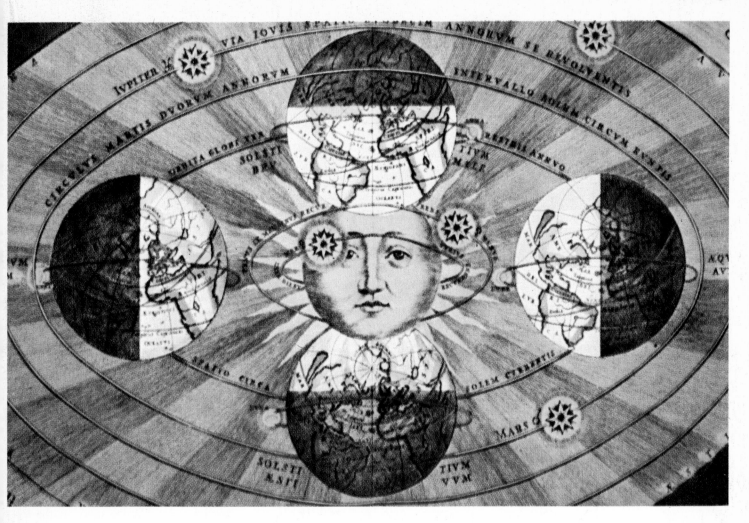

ASTROLOGY IS THE alleged art or science of judging the influence of the planets in the solar system upon human affairs. A horoscope is a diagram showing the geocentric positions of the Sun, Moon and planets: Mercury, Venus, Mars, Jupiter, Saturn, Uranus, Neptune and Pluto. Geocentric means seen as if the planet Earth were at the centre of the solar system. For the sake of convenience in astrology the Sun and Moon rank as planets. All the planetary positions must be calculated in relation to a given moment of time and a specific geographical co-ordinate, expressed in degrees and minutes of latitude (north or south of the equator) and longitude (east or west of the meridian of Greenwich).

The horoscope itself represents a simple statement of certain astronomical facts, and as such is an objective scientific document. In this context one must exclude the twelve so-called Houses, whose areas can be calculated according to any one of half a dozen

The zodiac is a circular band in the sky, through which the planets are seen to move. It is divided into 12 equal sections, known as the signs of the zodiac. In astrology, a planet's influence varies according to which part of the zodiac it is occupying. *Left* **The Planesphaerium Copernicus, a chart of the heavens, c 17th century, showing the zodiac signs in the outer ring** *Above* **The planets were also thought to influence the seasons: 17th century chart illustrating the earth's position in relation to the sun during the year shows planetary spheres of influence**

or more highly speculative mathematical procedures. The supposed significance of the Houses will be discussed later in this article.

While the horoscope itself can purport to be a scientific diagram, an essentially unscientific activity begins when the astrologer attempts to make deductions based on: the zodiacal positions of the planets; the presence of a planet or planets in one or other of the twelve Houses; and certain angular relationships between one or more planets.

Today almost everyone in Western Europe and the U.S.A. knows his zodiacal sign, meaning the sector of the zodiac through which the Sun was passing when he was born. The zodiac is a notional band of sky representing the Sun's annual path through the fixed stars. The concept of the zodiac was evolved during the Babylonian era. This ancient measuring device consists of twelve sectors each measuring thirty degrees. The 30° sectors are each named after fixed star constellations: Aries, Taurus, Gemini, Cancer, Leo, Virgo, Libra, Scorpio, Sagittarius, Capricorn, Aquarius and Pisces.

If a person says that he was born 'under Taurus' it means that his birth occurred between 21 April and 22 May, when the Sun would have been anywhere between 0°–29° Taurus. If, however, he states that he was born on 10 May 1950, the Sun's position was at about 19° Taurus, which is more specific. Finally, in the case of a birth at exactly noon (Greenwich Mean Time) on

that day, the Sun was at 19° 15′ 17″ Taurus, which is even more precise. The theories of scientific astrology require the horoscope to be calculated upon the basis of an *accurate* time and, as has been mentioned, an identifiable geographical location. These are the requirements for a strictly *individual* horoscope. The astrological 'information' published in newspapers and magazines does not refer to individual horoscopes.

Truth or Nonsense?

The fact that so many people know their birth sign is a product of the mass-circulation newspaper and periodical astrological journalism that began during the early 1930s. Those who have a detailed knowledge of the principles of astrology almost unanimously condemn this 'popular' astrology as childish nonsense. Nevertheless, the daily forecasts and the feature articles in magazines have persuaded countless thousands that 'the stars' may conceivably influence human destinies and that an individual personality in some way reflects the psychological qualities traditionally ascribed to his or her zodiacal sign.

As for the daily prognostications, it is obvious that by the law of averages a proportion of the readership will suppose that this or that prediction has been fulfilled. All the same, we are confronted with a system which divides humanity into types based on astrological symbolism, and this is perhaps astrology's most interesting feature.

Far left The zodiac as we know it is a combined invention of the Egyptians and Babylonians. An ancient Egyptian map of the sky, the 'Zodiac of Denderah'
Left Astrology originally developed in Mesopotamia and was more concerned with kings and peoples than with the destinies of individuals; a tablet giving astrological forecasts in cuneiform writing, derived from observations of the moon
Right The zodiac man from *Les Très Riches Heures* of the Duc de Berry shows the association between astrological signs and the parts of the human body. For example, people born under Leo, which controls the heart, are thought likely to suffer from heart trouble. Similarly Aquarians may suffer from weak ankles and Librans from kidney troubles

Despite all its unsatisfactory qualities, 'scientific' natal astrology, which means analyzing your personality from your horoscope – as opposed to predicting future events – raises a great many fascinating, although probably insoluble, problems. Logically the 'art' should be dismissed as the obstinate survival of very ancient superstitious beliefs. However, it is possible that fairly accurate, although limited deductions can, in fact, be made from a natal or birth horoscope.

What is surprising is the survival of a system of divination that was first developed in Babylon before the Christian era, and which eventually reached the West in the 12th century via Latin translations of Arabic texts (10th century), which were themselves based upon far earlier Hellenistic Greek texts (c150 BC to 350 AD).

The Modern Revival
The astrological tradition in the form that is encountered today consists of a huge collection of rules and procedures which have been transmitted through the centuries, although not without substantial alterations and reformulations. In the West the contemporary astrological idiom represents an up-to-date version of the one current at the time of the Renaissance, when there was a widespread interest in astrology in educated circles. The invention of printing (c1440) facilitated the circulation of material that had hitherto only existed in manuscript form and the publication of ephemerides – tables containing the daily noon positions of the Sun, Moon and planets. Astrology still ranked as astronomy's twin sister and enjoyed equal respectability.

Educated men began to lose interest in astrology towards the beginning of the 17th century, when the discoveries of the first of the modern astronomers, including Galileo, Copernicus and Kepler, were beginning to be understood. This increasing scepticism was evident in Europe, but not in England where there was a noticeably lively interest in astrology during the second half of the 17th century. This was reflected by the large domestic output of textbooks and predictive almanacs.

Astrology was already well underground in Europe during the 18th century and in England the appearance of new textbooks dwindled to a trickle between 1700 and c1790. But while astrology was practically forgotten in Europe until the end of the 19th century, there were minor astrological revivals in England during the 1790s and 1820s and an important one during the 1890s. The French did not rediscover the art until c1890 and the German revival only began shortly before the First World War. Indeed, if the British had not kept astrology alive when it was forgotten elsewhere, it might conceivably have disappeared altogether. The British and French revivals during the 1890s, and the somewhat later German one, were by-products of a new and widespread interest in occultism, magic, the Cabala and, above all, H. P. Blavatsky's Theosophical teachings (see BLAVATSKY; THEOSOPHY). Alan Leo (1860–1917), the first important modern astrological publicist and the author of a long series of popular textbooks, was above all a Theosophical astrologer. This meant, in effect, that for Leo and his followers astrology had a considerable esoteric or occult component. Even today the ranks of the astrologers contain many who claim to be occultists.

It was the Germans, in particular, who investigated and experimented with astrology with enormous energy and interest during the years between the two World Wars. Furthermore, many of these people were highly-educated men and women. During the early 1930s, for instance, at least 30 German medical men practised astrology and there were undoubtedly many more whose names are unrecorded. While the German astrological movement contained the expected quota of charlatans and mild lunatics, a cultured and intelligent minority worked on the development of a new kind of astrology based, as far as possible, upon current academic psychological and typological concepts.

Jung and Astrology
C. G. Jung, a Swiss-German, whose renown as a pioneer in the field of analytical psychology almost equals that of Sigmund Freud, had a deep personal interest in astrology. In 1931 he observed that 'the cultural philistines believed until recently that astrology had been disposed of long since and was something that could safely be laughed at. But today, rising out of the social deeps, it knocks at the doors of the universities, from which it was banished some

300 years ago'.

Elsewhere Jung wrote: 'For those of my readers who are unaware of these things and think that I am exaggerating, I can point to the easily verifiable fact that the heyday of astrology was not in the benighted Middle Ages but is in the middle of the 20th century, when even the newspapers do not hesitate to publish the week's horoscope. A thin layer of rootless rationalists reads with satisfaction that in the year 1723 Mr So-and-so had a horoscope cast for his children, and do not know that nowadays the horoscope has almost attained the rank of a visiting card.'

Jung's remarks should be read in the context of the contemporary German astrological scene. While the knocks at the doors of the universities were too faint to be heard, a surprising number of Germans had a superficial knowledge of astrology.

It is evident that Jung himself studied the horoscopes of some of his patients, not in order to predict their future, but because he believed that a natal horoscope could provide information of a purely psychological nature; for example, why an individual might be latently susceptible to a particular kind of neurosis.

Theoretically, then, if a medically trained psychologist can use astrology successfully for psycho-diagnostic purposes, it could also be employed for personnel selection, or to assess whether or not two people who intend to marry are temperamentally suited to one another. In Germany the present writer has met professional experts on handwriting who are engaged by large firms to sift written applications for jobs and to identify the most promising applicants. Some of them also take a look at the candidates' horoscopes as an additional check. On the Continent birth certificates are frequently required to be submitted in such cases, and on these the birth time is stated, at least within about 15 minutes. British and American birth certificates do not record the birth time. In the absence of the latter it is impossible to calculate a more or less accurate Ascendant and without the Ascendant the horoscope is incomplete. In the absence of a birth time one can only erect the horoscope on the basis of noon Greenwich Mean Time for the day of birth, and so it could equally well apply to everyone else born on that day.

ARIES ♈ 21 Mar.			LIBRA ♎ 23 Sept.	
TAURUS ♉ 20 Apr.			SCORPIO ♏ 24 Oct.	
GEMINI ♊ 21 May			SAGITTARIUS ♐ 23 Nov.	
CANCER ♋ 22 June			CAPRICORN ♑ 22 Dec.	
LEO ♌ 23 July			AQUARIUS ♒ 20 Jan.	
VIRGO ♍ 23 Aug.			PISCES ♓ 19 Feb.	

Drawing a Horoscope

The apprentice astrologer begins by learning the names of the twelve signs of the zodiac and the traditional 'qualities' ascribed to each of them. The signs are shown above (and Fig. 1) in their conventional order with the approximate date when the Sun 'enters' each sign.

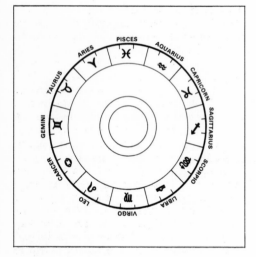

Diagramatically a horoscope expresses, among other things, the idea of the Sun rising in the East, that is, *ascending* above the eastern horizon at dawn; culminating or reaching its highest point in the sky at noon; setting in the west in the evening, and invisible below the horizon during the night.

Fig. 2 represents the Sun ascending at dawn, reaching the *Medium Coeli* (Midheaven) at noon, setting in the evening (Descendant), and below the horizon at midnight (*Immum Coeli*). It is particularly important to notice the Ascendant/Descendant – MC/IC axes, because these form the so-called 'angles' of a horoscope.

During the course of a 24-hour period every one of the 360 degrees of the zodiac successively 'rises' on the eastern celestial horizon. Roughly speaking, therefore, every two hours a new zodiacal sign is on the Ascendant. In order to discover the Ascendant (expressed for instance as '18° 27′ Leo rising') the astrologer must first calculate the MC (Midheaven). This is done with the help of an ephemeris and a few simple arithmetical computations. Once the MC has been identified the degree of the Ascendant can be found in the appropriate

tables. The astrologer then fills in the 'angles', mentioned above, on the horoscope chart.

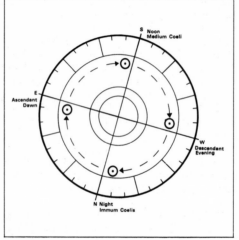

The horoscope of K. E. Krafft, the Swiss who was wrongly supposed to have been Hitler's personal astrologer, will serve as a typical example for an abbreviated account of the procedure for calculating a horoscope. He was born at Basle on 10 May 1900 at 12.45 p.m. Central European Time. His Sun was therefore in Taurus.

Since all the information in an ephemeris is based on noon Greenwich Mean Time, it is necessary to convert CET to GMT by subtracting one hour, giving a birth time of 11.45 a.m.

Basle is 47° 34′ north of the equator and 7° 40′ east of Greenwich. Having established the *sidereal* ('star-time', not clock time) for 11.45 a.m. GMT, and converted 7° 40′ E to minutes and seconds of time because Basle is east of the meridian of Greenwich, and we require to know the local sidereal time, a reference to a Table of Houses for latitude 47° North will show that Krafft's MC was 24° Taurus and the related Ascendant was 1° 43′ Virgo.

The next step is to establish the actual zodiacal positions of the planets at 11.45 a.m. on 10 May 1900. The birth time was so close to noon that with the exception of the Moon, for which a small adjustment (7′ 27″) is required, one could take the actual noon positions direct from the ephemeris. If the birth had occurred at, say, 7.45 p.m. some further simple arithmetical

calculations would be needed. At 11.45 a.m. on 10 May 1900 the planetary positions were as shown in Fig. 3.

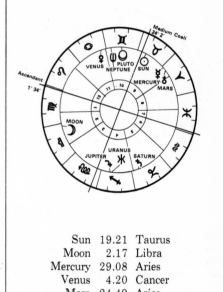

Sun	19.21	Taurus
Moon	2.17	Libra
Mercury	29.08	Aries
Venus	4.20	Cancer
Mars	24.49	Aries
Jupiter	8.08	Sagittarius
Saturn	4.30	Capricorn
Uranus	11.22	Sagittarius
Neptune	25.21	Gemini
Pluto	15.30	Gemini

It has already been mentioned that the division of the horoscope into 12 Houses has no strictly astronomical foundation. The Houses are numbered anti-clockwise from the Ascendant. The cusps (boundaries) of the 1st, 4th, 7th and 10th Houses are identical with the four angles (Asc, IC, Desc and MC) The boundaries of the remaining Houses will vary according to the mathematical system of House division employed.

As a result, one astrologer will show the Sun in, say, the 3rd House, while another working on an identical chart will have it in the 2nd. Most astrologers happily ignore this inconsistency. Furthermore, the mathematics of House division require a knowledge of spherical trigonometry. Hence the majority of astrologers are content to use Tables of Houses and are uninterested in the mathematical background.

Fig. 4 shows Krafft's horoscope with the

Those who excel at horoscope interpretation... can often deduce a few extremely salient facts of a purely psychological nature

twelve Houses calculated according to the Placidus system.

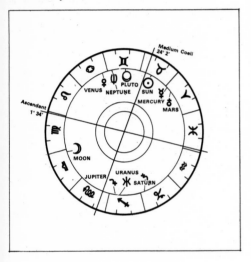

Finally there are the so-called 'aspects', which are certain angular distances, expressed in degrees, between any two or more planets. The aspects mainly considered are:

Conjunction	0°
Square	90°
Trine	120°
Sesqui-quadrate	145°
Opposition	180°
Semi-square	45°
Sextile	60°

Fig. 5 shows Krafft's horoscope with the addition of the more prominent aspects. For example, the Moon is square (90°) both Venus and Saturn and sextile (60°) Ascendant. Venus is in opposition to Saturn.

The Key to the Code

To sum up: a horoscope erected upon the basis of a known birth time and geographical co-ordinate contains the following factors: 12 30° zodiacal sectors (12 x 30 = 360°); 10 planets in their respective zodiacal positions; 12 Houses, the boundary of the first being the Ascendant; Four 'angles', Asc/Desc – MC/IC; the planetary aspects.

We have, then, a diagram that purports to record an 'astral' moment of time, but expressed in a symbolical code which must now be deciphered. This is the most difficult task of all. The astrologer works on the basis of a number of assumptions.

1. That each planet works or operates in a different and characteristic manner, hence the adjectives *martial* (Mars), *mercurial* (Mercury), *saturnine* (Saturn) and *jovial* (Jupiter). It is supposed that a planet's 'influence' will be particularly strong if it is close to an angle and, in particular, to the Ascendant and MC. In Krafft's case Neptune, Pluto and Sun are all 'dominant' because they are near to the MC. His Moon is possibly sufficiently near to the Ascendant also to be assessed as dominant.

2. That a planet reflects the qualities of the zodiacal sign in which it is placed. Hence Mars in Gemini will not have the same 'meaning' as Mars in Scorpio.

3. That a planet will operate according to its House position. Thus Venus in the 10th can suggest one thing and Venus in the 5th another.

4. That their angular relationships, or aspects will modify the influences of the planets concerned.

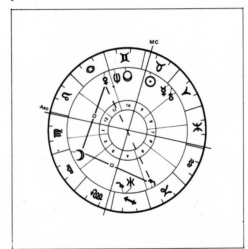

The art of interpretation involves the *combination* of all the available evidence and, as we have mentioned, this is where the difficulties begin. There are countless astrological manuals or 'cook books' which provide guidance of a kind for every conceivable factor. For instance, the novice scribbles: 'Sun in Taurus in the 9th House; Mars in Aquarius in the 6th House; Sun is square Mars.' According to the manual he uses he will now have to consider anything from a bald and very brief statement to an essay of up to 500 words. So he jots down his

interpretative material and is then uncertain how to combine it together. If he happens to be acquainted with the person whose chart he is studying, he will believe that this or that 'appears to fit' but will be left with a good deal of apparent nonsense. Most astrologers never get much beyond this 'cook book' method of interpretation.

Impressive Deductions

The few who seem to excel at horoscope interpretation, including the people who can often make quite impressive deductions on the basis of a 'blind diagnosis', meaning that they have no personal knowledge of the native (subject), do not have to depend on 'cook book' techniques. Nor do they necessarily try to find an interpretation for every factor in the chart. They appear to have an almost instinctive knowledge of astrological symbolism and at the same time a highly-developed intuition. The writer's own experience is that they can often deduce a few extremely salient facts of a purely psychological nature. The quality of their work is apt to become diluted when they attempt to wring the last shred of 'evidence' from a horoscope. It is a fallacy to expect that the chart itself will 'reveal all'; this does not appear to be the case. Nevertheless, when correctly interpreted, a horoscope will sometimes yield information of a surprisingly accurate nature.

There are, of course, a great many logical objections to astrology. For example, suppose you are confronted with two identical horoscopes: the first for a manual worker and the second for a surgeon. Their respective social and educational backgrounds will necessarily be different. Then how can one talk in terms of identical 'fates'? We are not so much concerned with fate, however, as with the possibility that each will react to life's psychological situations according to a common pattern, but always in relation to his social milieu and understanding. There will, for example, be a very large element of free will. To identify the common denominator is in any case extremely difficult. Thus in astrological interpretation very little is absolutely cut and dried.

It would be tempting to write astrology off as a waste of time were it not for case histories such as the one at the Institute for Border Areas of Psychology, at the University of Freiburg in Western Germany. A

team of qualified psychologists spent a fair number of hours interviewing a young juvenile delinquent who had been sent to them by the local police. Their extensive written reports were locked away in the Institute's safe. In the meantime Herr Walter Böer, a local schoolmaster who was not only an expert astrologer but had some psychological training, was invited to study the boy's horoscope.

Herr Böer did not know of the identities of either the young man or of the psychologists who had examined him. Nor had he any access to their reports. Herr Böer's findings were very much in line with those of the psychologists, meaning that he was able to identify a disturbed and erratic personality.

It is not that Herr Böer possessed some unknown astrological secret. One can only point to an unusually sound grasp of the principles of astrological interpretation allied to what were evidently highly-developed intuitive powers.

Here it is only possible to provide the briefest possible summary of some basic interpretative material: it is by no means definitive and gives only a fragmentary idea of astrological concepts.

The Planets

Sun: the living being, the physical body, psychic energy, the male principle.

Moon: the soul or psyche; fantasy and feeling, change and fluctuation (tides and months).

Mercury: intelligence, reason, movement, associative or connective function, communication (Mercury as the messenger of the Gods).

Venus: love, art, physical attraction, sentiment, sentimentality, sex.

Mars: action, energy, impulsion, aggressive function, libido (Mars, the god of war).

Jupiter: expansion, richness (material or metaphysical), health, humour, developing function.

Saturn: limitation, contraction, concentration, inhibition, separation, maturity, loss, parting (and death), saturnine temperament, restrictive function.

Uranus: suddenness, revolution, violence, transmutation (magic, alchemy, the occult arts), creative function.

Astrology is not only a western phenomenon: it has a long history in the East
Left A 13th century Persian astrological treatise showing Mars in the sign of the Ram in conjunction with Jupiter. The figures below represent the five planets: Jupiter, Mars, Venus, Mercury and Saturn
Right One of eight astrological pictures from an Indian temple, showing Saturn

R. K. Singh

Neptune: susceptibility, fantasy, romanticism, mysticism, deception and self-deception, psychic powers.

Pluto: power, demagoguery, dictators, the masses.

The Signs of the Zodiac

Aries: courage, impetuosity, energy.
Taurus: patience, persistence, obstinacy.
Gemini: progressiveness, cleverness, instability.
Cancer: inspiration, sensitivity, evasiveness.
Leo: dignity, breadth of mind, power, pretentiousness.
Virgo: reason, logic, exactitude, pedantry.
Libra: harmony, evaluation, trivialities.
Scorpio: profundity, insistence, roughness.
Sagittarius: justice, propriety, sophistry.
Capricorn: independence, abstraction, stubborness.
Aquarius: spirituality, conviction, illusion.
Pisces: compassion, tolerance, indolence.

The Twelve Houses

1. (Ascendant) development of personality, environment, childhood, physical body and constitution.
2. Material possessions and money.
3. Family relationships, communication.
4. Parental home, hereditary characteristics.
5. Procreation, sexuality, pleasure, risks, speculation.
6. Servants, health.
7. The community, partnership, marriage, open enemies.
8. Accidents, death, inheritances, the wife's or husband's money.
9. Spiritual life, philosophy, religion, travel.
10. Vocation, profession, public life.
11. Wishes and hopes, friendships.
12. Secret enemies, seclusion (hospitals, prisons), obscure difficulties.

The Aspects

Traditionally there are 'good' and 'bad' aspects (angular relationships between two or more planets). The conjunction (0°) and opposition (180°) can be either good or bad, according to the planets concerned. A conjunction would increase the mutual influence of the planets in question. Examples are, Sun conj. Saturn: difficulties in connection with the development of the personality, Moon conj. Venus: intense emotional life, artistic leanings, self-love, Mercury conj. Mars: quick mental reactions, aggressive instincts, Venus conj. Uranus: strong emotional tensions, unusual preoccupations.

The square (90°) and semi-square (45°) are supposed to be 'malefic', unfortunate or difficult aspects. The trine (120°) and sextile (60°) are said to be beneficent or fortunate aspects.

An Analysis

With hindsight, what can one make of Krafft's horoscope (see Fig. 5)? Here there is only room for an abbreviated analysis of a few of the factors.

One might begin by examining the Sun, which is in Taurus and in the 9th House, in relation to his Virgo Ascendant. At the same time, one would look for the 'dominant' planets, those close to the Midheaven and Ascendant. It is true that Krafft was a Taurean and his Sun, high in the Midheaven, is dominant. The same also applies to Neptune and Pluto. Furthermore, one must ask how his Virgo Ascendant affected his personality.

Sun (Krafft's living being, essence) in Taurus reflects patience, persistence and obstinacy. He had the patience to embark upon vast though fruitless astro-statistical projects, and as a young man persisted in this work in spite of his father's sometimes violent objections. He was a pig-headed person. In spite of all the negative evidence, he obstinately believed that he was destined to create a new kind of scientific astrology (Cosmobiology), and after 1937 that he could successfully exercise his strange gifts in Hitler's Germany.

Ascendant in Virgo: exactitude and pedantry. His temperament enabled him to attempt tasks that required these qualities. The dominant Neptune in Gemini in the 10th House (vocation, profession, public life) could reflect his markedly unstable character, as a result of Neptune's fantasy, romanticism, mysticism and self-deception. Pluto (power) is in a strong position. Krafft hoped for both power and influence. In a strictly limited sense he achieved both, but died in a German concentration camp after a lengthy imprisonment. Krafft, who for years studied his own horoscope so closely, obviously had no idea of his 'fate'!

Moon in Libra square Venus in Cancer, also square Saturn in Capricorn, and Venus opposition Saturn: all may reflect Krafft's sexual complexes and unfulfilment, also his inhibitions regarding sexuality and pleasure.

Sun in the 9th House: his preoccupation with a spiritual life. Neptune in the 10th House suggests Neptunian interests, including astrology and the prophecies of Nostradamus as a vocation or profession. During 1940–1 he worked on the Nostradamus texts for Goebbels' Propaganda Ministry. Moon in the 2nd House: his fluctuating attitude to money and material possessions.

From these snippets you can begin to understand that a full-scale interpretation must consist of an adequate synthesis of a great many fragmentary and hypothetical propositions. In the case of Krafft one can now see how this or that would probably apply to him. An accurate blind diagnosis is far more difficult to achieve. Experience suggests that about 60% of any interpretation will appear to be correct, but the validity of the remainder can seldom be easily evaluated.

New Systems in Germany

During the past half-century two completely non-traditional astrological systems have been developed in Germany. The first was Alfred Witte's 'Hamburg School' of astrology with its eight hypothetical Transneptunian planets, for which equally hypothetical ephemerides have been published. This system still has a number of devoted supporters. Latterly some of its textbooks have been available in English in the U.S.A.

An interesting by-product of the Hamburg School is the Ebertin system, developed by Reinhold Ebertin, who does not use the hypothetical planets. Herr Ebertin has jettisoned most of the medieval astrological tradition and you can operate his system without bothering about the Houses or, for that matter, the so-called zodiacal influences. A dial apparatus is used in conjunction with the horoscope chart to identify planets and their 'mid-points' on a common 90° axis. The only aspects considered are the conjunction, opposition, square, semi-square and sesqui-quadrate. The trines and sextiles are ignored. A fair amount of simple arithmetical work is required to establish a sequence of 'planetary equations' from which a synthesis can be made with the help of Herr Ebertin's excellent manual *Combinations of Stellar Influences*, which is available in English. It would appear that this heretical system works just as well as any traditional one, and at least a lot of old-fashioned and suspect ballast has been ruthlessly thrown overboard.

No Short Cut

There is no short cut to even a modest knowledge of the principles of natal astrology. Once the novice has learned the elements of the art, a lot of time and experience is required before he will be able to free himself from the 'cook book' method of interpretation. Furthermore, in the majority of cases what may be described as 'astrological insight' is never achieved. Nobody can teach this, and if it is not latent in an individual it never emerges.

It is almost always safe to ignore the pretensions of professional astrologers who

European interest in astrology is reflected in this 17th century French engraving showing an allegorical figure, combining the signs of the zodiac with the works of such astronomers as Tycho Brahe and Copernicus

publicize themselves energetically. The same applies to the pretensions of the more prominent members of the astrological Establishment. The interesting practitioners — they exist and include some professionals — mostly prefer comparative anonymity.

The professionals, in particular, are expected to provide accurate predictions, especially in relation to financial expectations, love affairs, marriage and death. There are comparatively few full-time professionals in Great Britain, but more in France and Germany and many more in the U.S.A. It is generally safe to disregard claims that this or that professional is the trusted adviser of financial magnates, captains of industry and statesmen.

Predicting Events

It is true that there are records of impressively accurate predictions, but astrology's predictive techniques simply do not respond to scientific investigation. Indeed, as far as

the latter is concerned it is extremely difficult to formulate satisfactory tests even for ordinary natal astrology. A proportion of any astrologer's predictions will appear to come true, if only on the law of averages. The astrologers are quicker to proclaim their apparent successes than their numerous failures but many of the more sensible amateurs do not bother to attempt predictive astrology and leave it to the professionals, for whom it represents a living.

Astrology, then, has a very lengthy and even fascinating past. At a time when man has already begun to travel in outer space and when it is likely that an attempt will be made to send a manned spaceship to Mars during the 1970s, it is reasonable to ask if astrology itself has any future. The chances of scientific recognition appear to be as remote now as they were half a century ago, when the Germans first began to investigate the territory with their traditional thoroughness. Today, at a guess, there may be up to 20,000 people in Western Europe and the U.S.A. who have a practical knowledge of astrological techniques, and even that figure may be too large. There is no evidence to suggest that the number of enthusiastic recruits is increasing.

Finally, one can only hazard a guess that astrological beliefs will not disappear in the immediate future. There is no reason to suppose that the popular press will cease to provide its usual astrological pabulum, and for a long time to come there will presumably be individuals who are attracted to the study of this elusive and, in spite of all its pitfalls, fascinating territory.
(See also articles on individual planets and zodiac signs.)

ELLIC HOWE

FURTHER READING: Many books by astrologers are available in public libraries and bookshops. A detailed guide is M. E. Hone, *The Modern Textbook of Astrology* (Weiser). For the zodiac signs and character analysis, see A. F. Seward, *Zodiac and Its Mysteries* (Wehman, 1967) and R. Gleadow, *The Origin of the Zodiac* (Atheneum, 1969). For help in reading an ephemeris, see J. Mayo, *How to Read the Ephemeris* (Llewellyn Pubns.). See also E. Howe, *Astrology: The Story of Its Role in World War II* (Walker & Co., 1968); C. McIntosh, *The Astrologers and Their Creed* (Praeger, 1969).